TALES FROM THE LONG TWELFTH CENTURY

TALES *from the* LONG TWELFTH CENTURY

The Rise and Fall of the Angevin Empire

RICHARD HUSCROFT

YALE UNIVERSITY PRESS
NEW HAVEN AND LONDON

For information about this and other Yale University Press publications, please contact:
U.S. Office: sales.press@yale.edu   www.yalebooks.com
Europe Office: sales@yaleup.co.uk   www.yalebooks.co.uk

Set in Adobe Caslon Pro by IDSUK (DataConnection) Ltd
Printed in Great Britain by Gomer Press, Llandysul, Ceredigion, Wales

Library of Congress Cataloging-in-Publication Data

Names: Huscroft, Richard, author.
  Title: Tales from the long twelfth century : the rise and fall of the Angevin
    Empire / Richard Huscroft.
New Haven : Yale University Press, [2016] | Includes
  bibliographical references.
LCCN 2015035080 | ISBN 9780300187250 (alk. paper)
LCSH: Great Britain—History—Angevin period, 1154-1216. | Anjou,
  House of. | Great Britain—History—12th century.
Classification: LCC DA205 .H87 2016 | DDC 942.03/1—dc23
LC record available at http://lccn.loc.gov/2015035080

A catalogue record for this book is available from the British Library.

10 9 8 7 6 5 4 3 2 1

Contents

Illustrations

Plates

1. King Henry I on the throne, mourning. Peter de Langtoft, *Chronicle of England* (*c*. 1307–27). © The British Library Board (Royal MS 20 A. II, f. 6ᵛ).
2. Aerial view of Framlingham Castle from the west. © Skyscan Balloon Photography. Source: Historic England.
3. Daniel Maclise, *The Marriage of Strongbow and Aoife* (*c*. 1854). © National Gallery of Ireland.
4. Coronation of Henry the Young King. From *La Vie de Seint Thomas de Cantorbéry* (*c*. 1220–40). British Library, Loan MS 88 f. 3ʳ.
5. The death of King William II of Sicily. From Peter of Eboli, *Liber ad honorem Augusti* (1196). Burgerbibliothek Bern, Cod. 120.II, f. 97ʳ.
6. Thomas Becket, mosaic in Monreale Cathedral, Palermo, Sicily. Courtesy of Louis Mendola.
7. Joan of Sicily and Richard I meeting Philip Augustus II of France. From William of Tyre, *Histoire d'outremer* (*c*. 1232–61). British Library, Yates Thompson MS 12, f. 188ᵛ.
8. Silver double seal of Joan (*c*. 1196–9). British Museum.
9. James Fittler, *Death of Arthur*, engraving after William Hamilton. From *Bowyer's History of England* (1793). © Trustees of the British Museum.

10. John George Murray, 'Archbishop Stephen Langton showing Magna Carta to the Barons', engraving (1833) after Arthur William Devis. © Trustees of the British Museum.
11. Seal of Archbishop Stephen Langton (1228). British Library.
12. The Battle of Lincoln, thirteenth century. From Matthew Paris, *Chronica Majora*. Parker Library – MS 16, f. 51ᵛ. Reproduced with permission of the Master and Fellows of Corpus Christi College, Cambridge.

Genealogies

Maps

Acknowledgements

It will be obvious to anyone reading this book how reliant I have been on the work of other historians. Anything remotely novel that I might say here is based in the end on what they have done. Others have helped more directly, of course. Louise Wilkinson read early drafts of two of the chapters, and her comments and encouragement were invaluable at a time when the book was a very long way from completion. The two anonymous readers who more recently pointed up mistakes and misconceptions in my manuscript were also a great help. The staff at Yale have worked tirelessly, too, to make this book better than it would otherwise have been. My editors, Heather McCallum and Candida Brazil, have been patient and tolerant, supportive of the idea behind this book from the start; they have seen it through to publication with great skill and authority. My copy-editor, Richard Mason, has been a model of professionalism; without his meticulous care and his sensitive way with a suggestion, the book would have contained many more errors of detail and infelicities of style. Needless to say, any of these that still remain are exclusively mine. Closer to home, Jo and Tilda have allowed me the time and space to get on with all the work. I could not have written this book without their loving support.

A Note on Money

During the period covered by this book there was only one coin in circulation in England, the silver penny. There were twelve pence in a shilling, 240 pence (twenty shillings) in a pound and 160 pence in a mark (two-thirds of a pound). However, shillings, pounds and marks were terms used for accounting purposes only, and there were no coins with those values. Throughout the book, and for the sake of simplicity and ready comparability, I have given large sums in pounds.

For comparative purposes, it is useful to remember that during the twelfth century a penny was the average daily wage for a labourer, whilst the average annual baronial income was about £200. The richest men in England below the king, the earls, probably had incomes of between £2,000 and £3,000 a year.

The Kings of France, 1060–1226

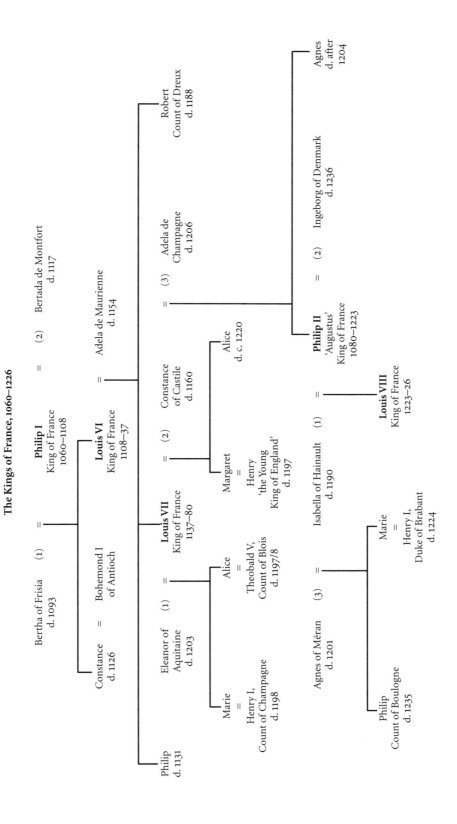

The Rulers of England, Normandy and the Angevin Empire, 1066–1272

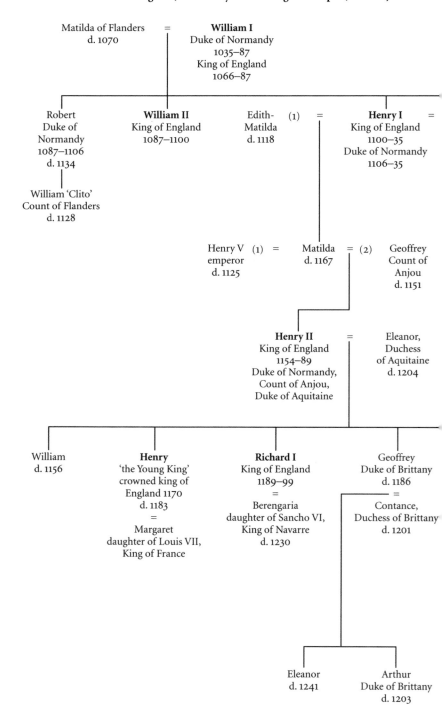

Matilda of Flanders = William I
d. 1070   Duke of Normandy
1035–87
King of England
1066–87

Robert
Duke of
Normandy
1087–1106
d. 1134

William II
King of England
1087–1100

Edith- (1) =
Matilda
d. 1118

Henry I =
King of England
1100–35
Duke of Normandy
1106–35

William 'Clito'
Count of Flanders
d. 1128

Henry V (1) = Matilda = (2) Geoffrey
emperor   d. 1167   Count of
d. 1125   Anjou
                  d. 1151

Henry II =
King of England
1154–89
Duke of Normandy,
Count of Anjou,
Duke of Aquitaine

Eleanor,
Duchess
of Aquitaine
d. 1204

William
d. 1156

Henry
'the Young King'
crowned king of
England 1170
d. 1183
=
Margaret
daughter of Louis VII,
King of France

Richard I
King of England
1189–99
=
Berengaria
daughter of Sancho VI,
King of Navarre
d. 1230

Geoffrey
Duke of Brittany
d. 1186
=
Contance,
Duchess of Brittany
d. 1201

Eleanor
d. 1241

Arthur
Duke of Brittany
d. 1203

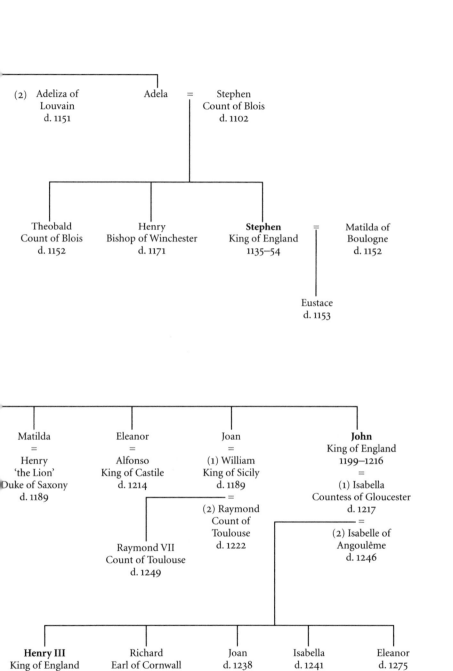

(2) Adeliza of
Louvain
d. 1151

Adela = Stephen
Count of Blois
d. 1102

Theobald
Count of Blois
d. 1152

Henry
Bishop of Winchester
d. 1171

Stephen
King of England
1135–54

= Matilda of
Boulogne
d. 1152

Eustace
d. 1153

Matilda
=
Henry
'the Lion'
Duke of Saxony
d. 1189

Eleanor
=
Alfonso
King of Castile
d. 1214

Joan
=
(1) William
King of Sicily
d. 1189
=
(2) Raymond
Count of
Toulouse
d. 1222

John
King of England
1199–1216
=
(1) Isabella
Countess of Gloucester
d. 1217
=
(2) Isabelle of
Angoulême
d. 1246

Raymond VII
Count of Toulouse
d. 1249

Henry III
King of England
1216–72

Richard
Earl of Cornwall
d. 1272

Joan
d. 1238

Isabella
d. 1241

Eleanor
d. 1275

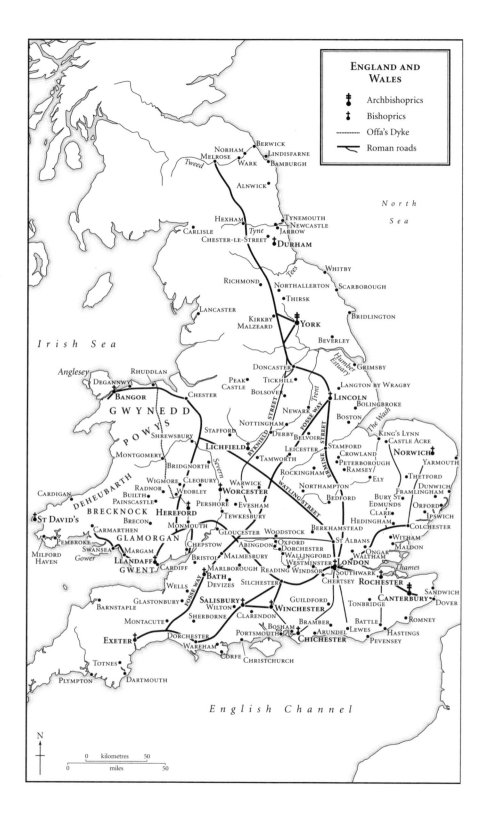

*North
Sea*

BERWICK
NORHAM   LINDISFARNE
MELROSE   WARK   BAMBURGH
Tweed

ALNWICK

HEXHAM   TYNEMOUTH
          NEWCASTLE
CARLISLE *Tyne* JARROW
CHESTER-LE-STREET **DURHAM**

WHITBY

RICHMOND NORTHALLERTON SCARBOROUGH
          THIRSK

LANCASTER

KIRKBY   **YORK**   BRIDLINGTON
MALZEARD

Irish Sea

BEVERLEY

Humber Estuary GRIMSBY

DONCASTER

ANGLESEY   RHUDDLAN   PEAK   TICKHILL
                          CASTLE   LANGTON BY WRAGBY
DEGANNWY   BOLSOVER **LINCOLN**
        BANGOR CHESTER   BOLINGBROKE
G W Y N E D D   NEWARK   BOSTON
        P O W Y S   NOTTINGHAM   *The Wash*
        SHREWSBURY STAFFORD   STAMFORD   KING'S LYNN
                          DERBY   CASTLE ACRE
MONTGOMERY   **LICHFIELD** BELVOIR CROWLAND **NORWICH** ✝
        BRIDGNORTH   TAMWORTH LEICESTER PETERBOROUGH YARMOUTH
                                          RAMSEY   THETFORD
        WIGMORE CLEOBURY WARWICK ROCKINGHAM ELY   DUNWICH
CARDIGAN RADNOR WEOBLEY **WORCESTER** NORTHAMPTON FRAMLINGHAM
D E H E U B A R T H BUILTH PERSHORE EVESHAM BEDFORD BURY ST ORFORD
        PAINSCASTLE **HEREFORD** TEWKESBURY   EDMUNDS CLARE IPSWICH
ST DAVID'S BRECKNOCK BRECON MONMOUTH   HEDINGHAM COLCHESTER
        CARMARTHEN   GLOUCESTER WOODSTOCK BERKHAMSTEAD
PEMBROKE GLAMORGAN CHEPSTOW ABINGDON OXFORD ST ALBANS WITHAM
MILFORD SWANSEA MARGAM   BRISTOL MALMESBURY DORCHESTER ONGAR MALDON
HAVEN *Gower* **LLANDAFF**   WALLINGFORD WESTMINSTER WALTHAM
        GWENT CARDIFF MARLBOROUGH READING WINDSOR **LONDON**
                          BATH   SOUTHWARK *Thames*
                  WELLS DEVIZES SILCHESTER CHERTSEY **ROCHESTER**
        GLASTONBURY   **SALISBURY**   SANDWICH
BARNSTAPLE   WILTON   GUILDFORD **CANTERBURY** ✝✝
        MONTACUTE SHERBORNE CLARENDON **WINCHESTER** TONBRIDGE DOVER
                                  BRAMBER BATTLE ROMNEY
EXETER DORCHESTER PORTSMOUTH BOSHAM ARUNDEL LEWES HASTINGS
        WAREHAM   **CHICHESTER** PEVENSEY
TOTNES CORFE CHRISTCHURCH

PLYMPTON DARTMOUTH

English Channel

N

0 kilometres 50
0 miles 50

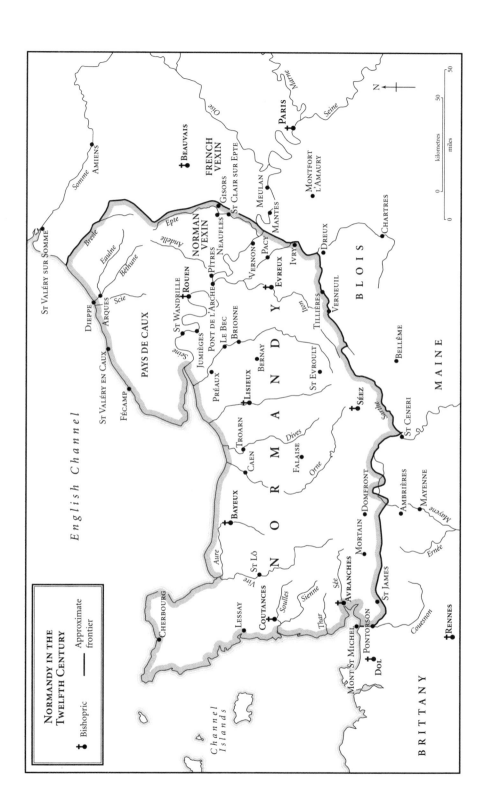

NORMANDY IN THE
TWELFTH CENTURY

✝ Bishopric

—— Approximate
frontier

N

50
50
kilometres
miles
0
0

English Channel

St Valéry sur Somme

Somme

AMIENS

Bresle

Eaulne

Béthune

DIEPPE

ARQUES

Scie

St Valéry en Caux

FÉCAMP

PAYS DE CAUX

Seine

JUMIÈGES

St Wandrille

ROUEN

Epte

Andelle

NORMAN
VEXIN

Ptres

Pont de l'Arche

Le Bec

BRIONNE

Préaux

LISIEUX

BERNAY

St Evroult

GISORS

St Clair sur Epte

NEAUFLES

VERNON

PACY

EVREUX

Eure

Iton

TILLIÈRES

VERNEUIL

FRENCH
VEXIN

✝ BEAUVAIS

MEULAN

MANTES

DREUX

IVRY

Oise

PARIS

Seine

Marne

MONTFORT
L'AMAURY

CHARTRES

B L O I S

BELLÊME

M A I N E

N O R M A N D Y

TROARN

CAEN

Dives

FALAISE

Orne

SÉEZ

Sarthe

St Ceneri

BAYEUX

Aure

St Lô

Vire

Vire

COUTANCES

Soulles

Sienne

Thar

Sée

AVRANCHES

MORTAIN

DOMFRONT

AMBRIÈRES

MAYENNE

Mayenne

Ernée

St James

Couesnon

✝ RENNES

LESSAY

CHERBOURG

Channel
Islands

Mont St Michel

PONTORSON

✝ DOL

B R I T T A N Y

WALES

Thames

LONDON

E N G L A N D

CALAIS

FLANDERS

Bouvines, 1214 ✕

ARRAS

English Channel

PÉRONNE
AMIENS

ARQUES
DRINCOURT

LAON

CHERBOURG

ROUEN
ANDELI

VALOGNES

GISORS

BAYEUX
CAEN

VAUDREUIL
EVREUX

MEULAN
PARIS

COUTANCES

N O R M A N D Y

MANTES
POISSY

VIRE
FALAISE
CONDÉ
EXMES

AVRANCHES
MORTAIN
ARGENTAN

NONANCOURT
VERNEUIL

ST MALO
DOL

DOMFRONT

ALENÇON

ÉTAMPES

SENS

B R I T T A N Y

RENNES

M A I N E

LE MANS

B L O I S

ORLÉANS

GIEN

CHÂTEAUNEUF-
SUR-SARTHE

LA FLÈCHE

ABIGNY

Loire

ANGERS

BAUGÉ
BEAUFORT

NANTES
SAUMUR
LANGEAIS

TOURS
MONTBAZON

BOURGES

A N J O U
THOUARS
LOUDUN
CHINON
LOCHES

T O U R A I N E
ISSOUDUN

MIREBEAU

POITIERS

TALMONT

NIORT
LUSIGNAN

LA ROCHELLE
BENON

P O I T O U

Bay of

ST JEAN
D'ANGÉLY

SAINTES

Biscay

COGNAC

A
Q
U
I
T
A
I
N
E

LIMOGES

L I M O U S I N

A N G O U L Ê M E

BOURG

BORDEAUX

Dordogne

THE CONTINENTAL
POSSESSIONS OF THE
ENGLISH KINGS, c. 1200

At his accession in 1199,
King John exercised direct
rule or overlordship of
the areas west of this line

Lands over which
Philip II exercised direct
rule, c. 1200

Centres of Capetian
power

LA RÉOLE
BAZAS

A G E N A I S

Q U E R C Y

N

G A S C O N Y

DAX

Garonne

BAYONNE

TOULOUSE

Garonne

kilometres 100

miles 100

B É A R N

IRELAND, *c.* 1200

English expansion to
c. 1200

Areas reserved for
Henry II and his barons
under the Treaty of
Windsor, 1175

ULSTER

Foyle

*Lough
Neagh*

B R É I F N E

KINGDOM

OF

CONNACHT

KINGDOM OF MEATH

Boyne

*Irish
Sea*

Liffey

•DUBLIN

Shannon

•LIMERICK

KINGDOM

OF

LEINSTER

Barrow

CASHEL
•

WEXFORD
•

WATERFORD
•

KINGDOM OF

MUNSTER

CORK
•

Atlantic Ocean

0   kilometres   50

0   miles   50

N

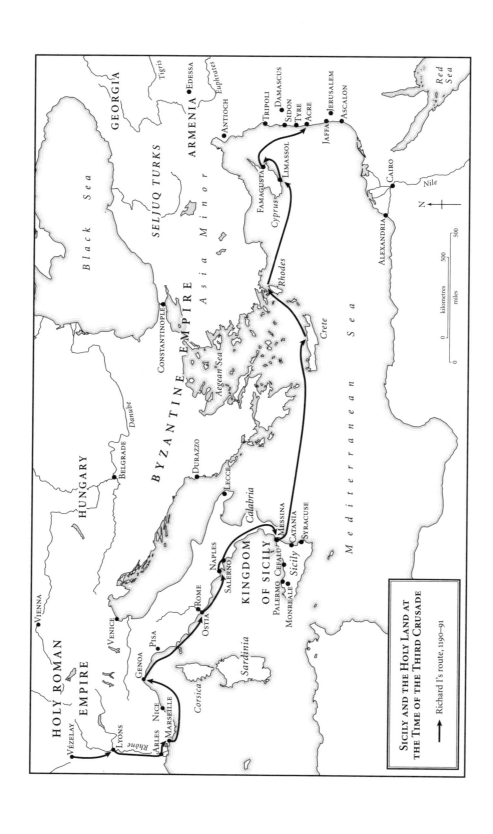

SICILY AND THE HOLY LAND AT
THE TIME OF THE THIRD CRUSADE

→ Richard I's route, 1190–91

A Diabolical Dynasty

THERE WAS ONCE a beautiful countess with a beautiful name –
Mélusine. Her husband, who ruled the county of Anjou in northern
France, had good reason to be happy. His lovely wife had given him four
fine sons and he was the envy of all his friends and enemies. But he was
not completely content for all that. For one thing, nobody knew where
the countess had come from. This had not mattered to the count when
he had met her in a land far away and married her – it was enough that
she was the most beautiful woman he had ever seen, and he had not
troubled to enquire further about her past or her background. Now,
though, he was starting to wonder, because the countess had one very
odd habit that was making her husband increasingly uneasy. She only
came rarely to church, and, when she did attend, she showed little sign
of devotion and always left in a hurry straight after the Gospel reading.
She was never there for the mass itself. People were starting to notice
this and whisper about the countess's behaviour, so the count decided to
find out what was going on. The next time the countess was in church,
she got up to leave as usual after the Gospel, but four of her husband's
men took hold of her and tried to force her down into her seat. The
countess struggled and threw off the robe that the soldiers were grasping
tightly. Then she picked up two of her four sons and in full view of the
startled congregation she flew up into the air and out of the church
through its highest window. She and her boys were never seen again.
Mélusine, of course, was no mortal woman. She was the daughter of

Satan himself, and she could not bear to look upon the consecrated host. As for her children, they were of the Devil's stock, and from the two she left behind were descended the Angevin kings of England – Henry II, Richard I and John.

So legend had it, at least. And it was a useful story.[1] Contemporaries relied on it when they tried to explain the ferocious tempers and the tyrannical leanings common to all of these kings. Gerald of Wales, who told this tale and knew these men personally, confidently saw the moral of it: 'Since the root was so completely corrupt,' he asked, 'how can fruitful or virtuous offspring come from it?' Henry II's father, Count Geoffrey of Anjou, had committed sexual crimes, Gerard alleged, whilst Henry's mother, the Empress Matilda, was guilty of bigamy. And when Henry himself had married Eleanor of Aquitaine, things only got worse. Eleanor was the product of an immoral union, and before marrying Henry and whilst still married to the French king Louis VII, she had had an affair with Henry's father. Such bad blood could only lead to violence and further wickedness.

Such violence took many forms and was directed towards opposing armies as well as individuals. But it was so pervasive and so inescapable that it must surely have had diabolical origins. The Angevin kings themselves were notorious sinners – avaricious and lustful, proud and angry, all died miserably, surely a sign of divine punishment for their carnal and worldly behaviour. Nonetheless, this was a legend that the kings themselves were also pleased to remember. Richard I is said to have joked about it often. He used it to explain why his family was so notoriously volatile, why he and his brothers quarrelled and fought so often with each other, with their father and with their mother. How could they be virtuous when their origins were so tainted, he asked? They had all come from the Devil, he said, and to the Devil they would all return.[2]

And in a sense Richard's prediction was correct. The story of the Angevin kings is very much one of 'rise and fall'. Henry II came to the English throne in 1154 after fifteen destructive years of civil war. However, when his son John died in 1216, England was once again being convulsed by internal conflict and foreign invasion. And between those dates, scandal and controversy were never far away. Thomas Becket's murder in 1170 usually claims the headlines, but there were other murders, too, as well as disastrous foreign wars and large-scale rebellions. Nevertheless, out of all this turmoil sprang some remarkable achievements. Henry II reconstructed a broken kingdom and has gained a reputation as 'the founder of the English common law'; Richard I was arguably England's most glamorous and impressive warrior-king; and, of course, there was Magna Carta, the product of rebellion to be sure, but above all the totemic foundation stone of the English constitution.

This story has been told many times before. Nevertheless, the period remains relatively unknown and unappreciated by a wider public. Most people have heard of Becket and Magna Carta, but beyond that there tends to be at best only a limited understanding of why the twelfth and early thirteenth centuries were formative times in the histories of England, the British Isles and Europe. Henry II, Richard and John were not just rulers of a single kingdom. They had aspirations to rule over the whole of Britain and Ireland, and at times they came close to doing so. But they were also rulers across the English Channel too. The county of Anjou in central France was their ancestral homeland (hence the 'Angevin' kings), and their duchies of Normandy and Aquitaine between them made up the greater part of northern and southern France. They were perhaps the richest and most powerful rulers of their day and, given the choice, they spent far more time in France than anywhere else. They were international figures, whose connections extended across Europe and the Mediterranean to the Middle East and beyond. So, at a time when the United Kingdom's own future is as uncertain as its relationship with the European mainland, it is important to remember that the twelfth and early thirteenth centuries constituted an era like no other. This was a period when England was as integrated as it has ever been into the wider international landscape, and when the kingdom was simply one part of a much greater political entity known to historians as the Angevin Empire.

Individual biographies of these kings abound, as do general histories of their reigns. This is the conventional way of writing about these events, through the lives of the rulers; inevitably so, given the nature of the source material that survives. The chroniclers focused their attention on the exploits of the leading figures, and the administrative records come almost exclusively from the royal archives. But this story is about more than the kings and queens, for other remarkable individuals also played a significant role. It is those stories which I have tried to uncover here and it is through the careers of these important but less well-known men and women that I have tried to describe what happened during this crucial time. This has been problematic for various reasons. Most obviously, the choice of subjects is severely limited by the available evidence and it has only been possible to write about people who moved in the upper levels of society – the children of the rulers or leading nobles and clerics who regularly, if not always frequently, caught the attention of contemporary writers or featured in the records of government. Even then, the evidence is patchy and inconsistent; there are large gaps and many uncertainties. And, more frustratingly still, the fish in this already small pool are overwhelmingly male. Unless she was a queen or a saint, it is very difficult indeed to reconstruct the life of a woman from this period to any telling degree, especially if the purpose of the exercise is to consider wider political developments through her experiences. The lives of the two women featured here – Princess Joan (sister of Richard I) and Nicola de la Haye – are indeed remarkable in allowing this to be done.

But why 'the long twelfth century'? It would have been possible to start this book with Henry II, with his rise to power, perhaps, or even his accession to the English throne in 1154. However, none of those developments or events is really understandable without a longer, deeper focus. Historians are tyrannised by dates, and by the attractions of neatly book-ended time periods. However, there is some sense in viewing the period 1066 to 1216, from an English point of view at least, as relatively self-contained. Whatever arguments still rage about the significance of the Norman Conquest, 1066 was an important year: it is meaningful to say that one era in English history ended then and that another one began. The same goes, albeit less decisively perhaps, for 1216. There was no change in dynasty or in the nationality of England's rulers (although these things nearly did happen), but the appearance of Magna Carta on the political scene and the death of John did in some fundamental ways mark the end of one kind of ruling system and the beginnings of another. Having said all this, I have given much greater weight here to the second half of this period. The years up to 1100 are dealt with only in passing, and the first half of my long century is covered by just the first two of my ten chapters. By contrast, the final four chapters cover the last seventeen years, the reign of King John. With the eighth centenaries of Magna Carta (2015) and of John's death (2016) in mind, and with so many good tales to tell, this emphasis felt justified.

So, despite some considerable difficulties, it has been possible to put the men and women who feature in these tales at the centre of the broader narrative in what I hope is a fresh and unusual way. Each chapter begins with a more or less contemporary anecdote about the individual concerned. Some of these anecdotes are based on verifiable evidence, whilst others read more like yarns or fables than credible accounts of actual events. But even if, to a modern reader, a few of these stories appear 'more true' than the rest, they all evoke and reveal important things about the characters they describe, the preoccupations of their authors and the times in which they all lived. Each anecdote is followed by a short explanation of the relevant wider context within which the main events of the chapter take place and an account of the issues that emerge, before the main character takes centre stage again for the rest of his or her tale. Their stories are truly gripping in their own right, and without exception these were extraordinary men and women. They are revealed here as recognisable human beings, noble and brave, flawed and fallible, trying to exercise control whilst subject to forces over which they held no sway. All of them were at the centre of momentous events, and the rise and fall of the Angevin Empire can be seen through their eyes.

PART ONE

The Birth of an Empire

CHAPTER ONE

THE PRINCE'S TALE
William Atheling and the *White Ship* Disaster

THOMAS FITZSTEPHEN WAS proud of his new vessel. Any captain would have been – the *White Ship* was splendid, fast and sleek, fit for a king as great as Henry I. King Henry was leaving Normandy for England that night, so Thomas had to move quickly. As soon as the royal party arrived at the quayside of Barfleur, he forced his way through the bustling crowd, presented himself to the king and offered him his ship. He was quick to remind Henry of the link between their two families: Thomas's father, Stephen, had captained the ship that had taken the king's father, William I, to conquer England in 1066. The king listened to Thomas politely and thanked him for his offer, before telling him that he had already arranged passage in another vessel. Thomas was disappointed, but Henry consoled him with the privilege of ferrying William, the king's heir and only legitimate son, instead, along with Richard, one of his many illegitimate children.

As high water in Barfleur harbour approached at about ten o'clock that night, 25 November 1120, Prince William and the members of his young, glamorous entourage crowded on board the *White Ship*, jostling each other in the torch light, shouting and joking. Rowdy and boisterous, they had been drinking for much of the day, and the contents of the casks of wine on board had been shared with the crew, too. Amongst the three hundred or so men and women waiting to embark with the prince, the atmosphere was carefree and reckless. At this point, some of the more sober passengers thought better of travelling on the *White Ship* and disembarked. Another, Stephen, the second son of the count of Blois, was feeling too ill to go anywhere. His upset stomach meant that he would still be alive the next morning and that he would eventually become king. Meanwhile, Thomas was challenged by those remaining on board to put his ship and its crew to the test. The crossing to England would normally take about twelve hours. Why not make some of that time more interesting with a race? King Henry had only just reached open water on his own voyage to England. If Thomas's boasts about the fabulous *White Ship* were to be believed, surely it could easily catch and overtake him?

There was no wind and the sea was calm. But the new moon made for a dark night, and the tides and rocks on the approach made Barfleur's harbour notoriously difficult to navigate at the best of times. Nevertheless, undeterred by the familiar hazards and heedless of the need for caution, the *White Ship*'s fifty oarsmen saw this as a chance to show off their skill and their strength. They had no time for the priests who arrived to bless their efforts, and laughed them scornfully, drunkenly away. By eleven o'clock the ship had pulled out from the dock and the oars had found their rhythm. As the goading from the inebriated passengers grew louder, the ship quickly picked up speed, travelling 'swifter than a feathered arrow', according to one contemporary.[1] After about twenty minutes, though, a mile and a half from shore, the vessel came to a jolting stop. The ship had hit a great rock on its port side; concealed beneath the waves at high tide, and unseen by the helmsman in the dark, the rock had breached the hull and the vessel had begun to take on water. A momentary silence on board was followed by anxious cries and shouts; alarm quickly turned to fear and the passengers began to panic. Then, as the drunken crew took up their oars and began straining to prise the ship free from its rocky hold, they only succeeded in destabilising it even more. Already listing and taking on water, with frantic passengers only adding to the confusion, the *White Ship* capsized. Few if any of the passengers or crew could swim, and many drowned quickly; but a lucky handful managed to find a place in a small boat. One of these was Prince William himself, but, realising his half-sister Matilda had been left stranded on the sinking ship, he turned the boat around and headed back to try and rescue her. His bravery and devotion counted for nothing: as the prince came alongside the upturned ship, his boat was overwhelmed by those desperate to escape, and it sank under their weight. Some people managed to cling for a while to a broken mast floating in the cold water. One of these was the captain, Thomas. He asked what had become of the king's son and was told that he had drowned. 'It is vain for me to go on living,' he declared in desperation, and rather than face the wrath of Henry I he released his grip on the wooden spar and sank beneath the waves.[2]

As the prince's boat went down so did the *White Ship* itself. Back on shore, the cries of the dying could be heard by the priests whose attempts to bless the voyage had earlier been ridiculed. They were audible further out to sea on the king's own vessel, too, but nobody who heard the screams knew their cause. They found out what had happened later from the only man who survived the disaster. He was a butcher from Rouen named Berold, the humblest and lowliest man aboard. By midnight on 25 November everyone else who had clambered aboard the *White Ship* a couple of hours earlier was dead.

After news of the disaster off Barfleur reached England, a whole day and night passed before anyone dared tell the king. In the end, Henry's repeated demands for news of his children could not be ignored any longer and his advisers, terrified of telling him themselves, chose a boy to deliver the blow. Weeping and terrified, he threw himself at the king's feet, and, on hearing what had happened, Henry collapsed to the ground. Overwhelmed and unable to speak, the king had to be helped away. Henry had not just lost two of his sons. His illegitimate daughter Matilda, countess of Perche, had also been drowned along with his niece, also called Matilda, and her husband Richard, earl of Chester. The king was by no means alone in his grief either. Few prominent aristocratic families were left untouched by the shipwreck. Perhaps as many as sixteen noblewomen had been drowned in addition to the king's own female relatives. Noblemen were lost, too; indeed, so many as to devastate the ruling class of England and Normandy. And trusted royal servants had perished alongside eminent churchmen, the king's chamberlain and chaplain amongst them. As poignant as any other loss was that of Othuer, the half-brother of Earl Richard of Chester. He was Prince William's devoted tutor and he sank to his death in the English Channel with his arms reportedly wrapped around his dear pupil.

In the days that followed the disaster, the French coastline was scoured for wreckage, treasure and bodies. The wealthy paid 'experienced swimmers and famous divers' to search for their dead, so that they could be properly buried.[3] In the end, only a few bodies were recovered and identified by their clothing. Prince William was never found.

* * * *

Prince William's tale provides one of the great 'What ifs?' of European history. Had he survived to succeed Henry I, the argument runs, there would have been no civil war under King Stephen, no Angevin Empire, no Richard the Lionheart, no King John, no Magna Carta; and so it goes on. But such speculation, whilst seductive and entertaining, is distracting. For one thing, it minimises the role played by any number of other chance occurrences in major events. If William had landed safely in England on 26 November 1120, he might have fallen off his horse and broken his neck on the way to see his father. Had he survived, his marriage to Matilda of Anjou might have produced a dozen sons, and there is no telling what might have followed from that. It is simply impossible to know what would have happened if William had not drowned, and the kind of guesswork that these dramatic events prompt is nothing like as important or as revealing as attempts to understand why his death was significant and what actually did happen as a result of it.

The sinking of the *White Ship* was a tragedy for Henry I and for his surviving family, friends and associates. It was also of enormous political significance. Most immediately, it left Henry without an obvious heir. But there was more to it than this. After a series of striking diplomatic successes, the king had planned to return in triumph to England in November 1120, with his position as the dominant ruler in western Europe confirmed and the future of his dynasty assured. Early that summer, after years of intermittent and often perilous warfare, he had finally made peace with King Louis VI of France, and Louis had also accepted Prince William's right to succeed Henry as duke of Normandy. What is more, Henry's relationship with another of his rivals in northern France, Count Fulk of Anjou, had just been stabilised by Prince William's marriage to Fulk's daughter, Matilda, in 1119. The death of the prince left her a widow, but it also ruined the arrangements Henry had made with her father. And taken together with the collapse of the English king's deal with King Louis, William's death utterly destroyed the political and diplomatic structure which Henry had struggled so hard and so long to build.

Born in 1103, William had been central to Henry I's plans long before the prince was old enough to play an active role in events, and his tale provides an object lesson in the perils of dynastic politics. That so much hung on the life of one young man may seem incredible now, and for Henry I to have made his son the indispensable centrepiece of such a complex and fragile diplomatic strategy may look foolhardy and imprudent. However, Henry's approach made for typical twelfth-century politics, where the roles and contributions of individuals really mattered and where, consequently, the line between triumphant success and disastrous failure was treacherously thin. Effective rulers were invariably able, assertive and masterful in a range of different ways: Henry I was a canny politician and a good general, he was rich and, when necessary, brutal. All these qualities contributed to his achievements. However, a ruler had to be lucky at the right time, too, particularly as far as his family was concerned. It is hard to overstate the importance of this to the world in which Henry I operated, where the production of legitimate children, boys and girls, was an essential part of statecraft. The girls could be used to make alliances through marriage. So could the boys, but they, or the eldest one or two at least, would serve to take on and ideally extend a ruler's power into the next generation. The problem was that once a suitable wife had been found, there was no guarantee that children would follow or, if they did, that they would survive for long. If there were no offspring, the only option was to take another wife and try again. And what today would be considered eminently treatable illnesses or injuries could prove quickly fatal for even the highest-status husband, wife, son or daughter. Henry I only had one legitimate son and one legitimate daughter, so inevitably all his hopes were invested in them. They both survived to adulthood, but in late November 1120, with William's death, Henry's luck ran out. Once he had recovered from the emotional shock of these events the king had to stir himself to revive his fortunes and build his power once again. The decisions he made and the options he pursued over the next decade and a half set the histories of England and France on a new and, as it turned out, frequently hazardous course.

* * * *

Henry I was not born to be king. He was the fourth and youngest son of William the Conqueror, and he had become king of England, aged about thirty-two, after the sudden death in August 1100 of his elder brother, William II (Rufus). However, Henry's hold on power was initially weak. As he was being crowned, his eldest brother, Robert, who had fought gloriously on the First Crusade and helped take Jerusalem from its Muslim occupiers in 1099, was returning to Europe to reclaim the duchy of Normandy, which, as the first son, he had inherited on his father's death in 1087. Robert and his supporters almost certainly had their eyes on the kingdom of England, too, therefore quick, decisive action was essential if Henry was to consolidate his authority there before his brother could challenge it. One way of doing this was through marriage, and Henry's choice as wife was the twenty-year-old Edith (or Matilda, as contemporaries knew her), the daughter of the Scottish king, Malcolm III, and his revered, saintly, English queen, Margaret. Malcolm and Margaret had both died in 1093, and in 1100 the Scottish king was their son, and Matilda's brother, Edgar. He would be an important ally for Henry in the north as the new king of England strained to establish his rule over the whole of his kingdom. More importantly, though, through her parents, Henry's bride was descended from two separate royal lines. Matilda's English relatives had ruled England until 1066, and she was, in the words of the *Anglo-Saxon Chronicle*, 'of the true royal family of England'.[4] By connecting himself to her and her illustrious ancestry, Henry was hoping to give further legitimacy to his own kingship. Moreover, any children born to Henry and Matilda would have Norman and English blood in their veins. With hereditary connections to both the dukes of Normandy and the kings of England, their succession credentials would be impeccable.

Nevertheless matters were not as straightforward as they might have been for Prince William's future parents. Matilda had spent most of her early life in an English convent. Her education had been entrusted to her aunt, herself a nun, and because Matilda had dressed as a nun whilst growing up, some contemporaries assumed that she had pledged herself to the celibate life of the cloister and was therefore not free to marry anyone, even a king. One person who did not share this view, however, was her father. In 1093, when she was still only about thirteen, King Malcolm had been so angry when he saw his daughter wearing a veil that he had snatched it from her head and taken her back to Scotland. Despite this, doubts still persisted about her suitability as a bride when Henry I proposed to marry Matilda in 1100. The Archbishop of Canterbury, Anselm, certainly needed to be convinced that Matilda was no fugitive nun, and she put her case to him herself. She denied adamantly that she had ever been a nun and claimed that she had been forced against her will to wear a hood in the convent. The archbishop and a group of bishops, nobles and clergy eventually decided that Matilda had never become a nun and was therefore free to marry. She was pleased with their verdict (it seems clear that she wanted to marry Henry), and on 11 November 1100 Anselm performed the wedding ceremony and crowned her queen at Westminster Abbey.

Matilda's principal duty as queen was to provide a male heir to stabilise the dynasty. But a daughter came first, also called Matilda, in February 1102. When a son was born, late in 1103, there was celebration but also relief. Named William, after his Norman grandfather, his birth was more than timely, as Henry's position was still far from secure. In July 1101, his brother Duke Robert had landed in England at the head of a large army, intending to topple Henry and replace him as king of England. Only a handful of magnates gave Henry their full support; others sided with Robert or held off whilst waiting to see what happened. The two armies eventually confronted each other at Alton in Hampshire, not far from Winchester, where the barons on both sides helped negotiate a peace. Robert gave up his claim to the English throne, in return for the custody of some Norman lands which Henry had held and an annual payment of £2,000. Even at this point, however, Henry could not relax. The deal made at Alton was supposed to settle things between the two brothers for good, but Henry could not be sure Robert would stick to it, or that Robert's followers would allow him to. The situation across the Channel grew more problematic still for Henry in 1102 when Robert had a son of his own, also called William.

Contemporaries called Robert's son William 'Clito', a Latin term that translates roughly as 'prince', but which really signified the boy's status as a legitimate heir to a kingdom or principality. Its application to William underlines the fact that, as the only son of William the Conqueror's eldest son, his right to succeed as king of England as well as duke of Normandy posed a grave danger to Henry I's regime. The Old English equivalent of the Latin word 'Clito' was 'Atheling' and this word was used several times by Orderic Vitalis in the twelfth-century in relation to Henry I's son, William. This suggests that Orderic saw this William as Henry's rightful heir, and he says others did too.[5] But, of course, the issue was not as straightforward as this. Henry I certainly wanted his son to succeed him, but, even after the agreement of 1101, it was far from certain that he would. It was clear to Henry that, if he wanted to eliminate the threat from Normandy entirely, he would have to take the duchy for himself.

The king and queen may have had other children, but Matilda and William were the only ones to survive. Henry I, though, was famously productive outside his marriage. The names of several of his mistresses are known, and there were almost certainly others whose identities are lost. Henry produced a large number of children by these women: the precise number is unknown, but the king publicly acknowledged nine illegitimate sons and thirteen illegitimate daughters. The girls were regularly married to important men as a way of sealing a deal or establishing a political relationship – one married the count of Brittany and another married the king of Scots, for example. Some of the boys, most notably Robert and Reginald, who became earls of Gloucester and Cornwall respectively, were to play significant political and military roles in years to come. Another, Richard, a renowned soldier, died with his half-brother on the *White Ship* in 1120. These children were useful to the king, but there is no reason to think that Henry was not fond of them too. The apple of his paternal eye, however, was his only legitimate son, William. He was groomed for the succession with love and care. Othuer was appointed tutor to William and his half-brothers, and he was also made castellan of the Tower of London. It is easy to imagine the young William playing with his friends and servants in and around the great keep which, in the early 1100s, had only just been completed.

The man who had baptised Prince William, and who became his godfather, Gundulf, bishop of Rochester, had also been instrumental in the design and construction of the White Tower, the single greatest monument to the Norman Conquest.

There are no details to reveal what William's upbringing and education were really like. It was later alleged that he was spoilt and over-indulged by his father, but it is hard to accept this charge at face value. It may in fact have derived from a desire to put William's ultimate fate into some kind of moral context. The shipwreck of 1120 was divine punishment for a sinful life of luxury, after all. According to Henry of Huntingdon, nearly all of those who died 'were said to be tainted with sodomy and they were snared and caught'. And he adds almost gleefully: 'Behold the glittering vengeance of God!'[6] But attacks like this on the lifestyles of William and his friends cannot be substantiated. However, like the eldest son of any twelfth-century aristocratic family, William would have been taught to ride, hunt and fight. As a future king, he would also have learnt about his family's history and ancestry, and what was expected of a grandson of William the Conqueror. He would have heard tales of the heroes of classical and biblical literature. The prince's father could probably read Latin (as the fourth son of the Conqueror, Henry may originally have been destined for a career in the Church), and there is no reason to think that William was not taught to do the same, at least to a basic standard. His first language, though, despite his status as the English king's heir, would have been French, which remained the vernacular tongue of England's ruling aristocracy into the thirteenth century. It is tempting to think that William's mother may have taught him some English, as she herself may have learnt it from her mother, Margaret, and perhaps even some Scots. But this is impossible to know.

For the first ten years of his life William remains in the historical shadows, and the great events of the early 1100s, which would make his future, were shaped by others. He was still a baby as the struggle over Normandy between his father and his uncle reached its climax. Since Duke Robert had left England in 1101, Henry had been preparing the ground for his own attempt to seize power in Normandy. He had lacked support in 1101 and arguably held onto England then only because his brother had had no stomach for a fight. Henry was not prepared to find himself in that position again and systematically set about building up his alliances inside Robert's duchy. By making generous promises of lands and arranging prestigious marriages to noble women, Henry constructed a formidable network of supporters there. Breteuil, one of the wealthiest lordships in Normandy, was especially important. It had been left without an undisputed heir when its lord, William de Breteuil, died in 1102. After a struggle between rival claimants, Henry's supporters eventually engineered the transfer of the lands to William's illegitimate son Eustace, who had married Henry's own illegitimate daughter, Juliana. Such an approach brought its rewards. By the time Henry travelled to Normandy in 1104, he was influential in the duchy and he was received enthusiastically by many magnates. And when he met his brother, Henry charged Robert with failure to protect Normandy from thieves and robbers. In reality, of course, any recent disorder in Normandy had been provoked by Henry's destabilising interventions. It was not Henry's plan to try and take power at this point, though. The trip served its purpose in sowing doubt amongst the wavering Norman nobility about their duke's fitness to rule.

Henry returned to Normandy in force early in 1105, but his campaign was a failure and showed how far he still was from achieving his aims. The biggest obstacle in his way was neither his brother nor the Norman nobles. It was the Church, represented by the archbishop of Canterbury, Anselm. Anselm had become the leader of the English Church in 1093, but he had fallen out with Henry's predecessor, William II, and was still in exile when Henry seized the English throne in 1100. Henry's political weakness at the start of his reign led him immediately to recall Anselm to England in 1100. During his absence, however, Anselm had absorbed the latest papal ideas about the relationship between lay rulers and the Church, in particular the renewed stress on the unacceptability of what historians refer to as 'lay investiture'. In other words, the reformers in Rome wanted to eradicate the practice of lay rulers giving the emblems of their office, the ring and the staff, to new bishops at their consecration. The symbolism of this practice, which seemed to imply that a bishop was dependent on a secular ruler for his spiritual power, was intolerable, and so lay investiture was condemned at papal councils in 1098 and 1099, as was the performance of homage by a churchman to a layman.

Such ideas, if put into effect, would have impinged seriously on the king's authority over his ecclesiastical subjects and their lands, and Henry I was determined to retain what he saw as his traditional rights. For his part, Anselm was determined loyally to enforce the pope's reforming decrees, and on his return he refused investiture at the king's hands and would not perform homage to him. Anselm was thus forced into exile again in 1103, and was in France when Henry landed there in 1105. Henry had justified his return to Normandy in part by arguing that his purpose was to rescue the Norman Church from the anarchy caused by his brother's incompetent rule. These claims looked thin, however, in the face of Anselm's opposition and his threats to excommunicate Henry, and it soon became clear that Henry would not be able to gather enough support in Normandy to take on his brother unless he settled with the archbishop first. Henry's sister Adela, countess of Blois, arranged a meeting between the king and archbishop, and Anselm and Henry negotiated a compromise. The king could continue to take homage from his bishops and abbots, but Henry gave up the practice of investiture with ring and staff. With these terms agreed, Henry sailed back to England in August 1105.

Henry returned once more to Normandy in the early summer of 1106, but apart from meeting Anselm in August to confirm the agreement on investitures, little happened and the situation there became increasingly tense. Finally, events began to gather pace. Henry left his men to besiege the castle of Tinchebrai in south-western Normandy, which was held by one of Duke Robert's leading supporters, William, count of Mortain. The siege was a failure and Henry, disappointed by the ineffectual efforts of his troops, decided to take matters into his own hands and go there himself. This prompted Count William to call on the duke for help and Robert demanded his brother's withdrawal, threatening war if he failed to comply. Henry refused to move and battle was inevitable. It was more in Henry's interest to provoke a decisive contest whilst Robert might have preferred to avoid one. But both probably thought they could win. When battle began at about nine one morning some time in the last week of September, a hard-fought encounter between foot soldiers on both sides was turned in Henry's favour by the intervention of a cavalry force led by Count Helias of Maine, which had been kept in reserve. Duke Robert's troops proved no match for these mounted knights and over two hundred of his men were killed in the first attack. Others turned and fled, leaving Robert and his remaining followers at the mercy of the victors. The duke was imprisoned by his brother Henry, albeit comfortably, for the rest of his life. He died in 1134.

Forty years after his father had sailed from Normandy to conquer England in 1066, Henry I had travelled the other way and reunited the two territories under his sole authority. However, if the battle of Tinchebray was decisive, its effects were not necessarily bound to be permanent. Henry's success in 1106 had come as a result of his determined and relentless approach to the challenge presented by his brother's power in Normandy. He had first undermined that power through clever diplomacy and judicious patronage, and he had finally smashed it on the battlefield. Such skills would be required even more in the years to come, and everything Henry did from this point on would be geared towards keeping England and Normandy together, for himself and his son William. But Henry's triumph had also been made possible by the temporary weakness or goodwill of neighbouring rulers. It was not long before these favourable conditions began to change and Henry was threatened once more.

In 1108 the old, corpulent King Philip I of France died and was succeeded by his son, Louis VI, who was a much more vigorous and resolute opponent for Henry. In the following year Count Fulk IV of Anjou also died and his son, Fulk V, proved even more hostile to Henry than his father had been. Then, in 1111, Henry's ally Count Robert of Flanders died and was succeeded by his son, Baldwin VII. All three of these French princes viewed Henry I's growing power as a threat to their own security, and all three were prepared to work together to attack it. The ace up their sleeve, moreover, was William Clito. Unlike his father Robert, Clito had not been imprisoned after Tinchebray, but had been given into the care of a guardian, Hélias de St Saëns, count of Arques, whom Henry thought he could trust. Henry came bitterly to regret this magnanimous act, for his French neighbours were able to

justify their opposition to him as a defence of Clito's legitimate claims
to rule in England and Normandy.

With the coalition against him growing stronger and more determined, Henry knew he needed allies. With this in mind, in 1109 his
first legitimate child, his daughter Matilda, was betrothed to the German
king, Henry V. Negotiations for the marriage had been going on
for several years by the time Matilda left England early in 1110. She was
no more than eight years old, whilst her husband to be was about
twenty-four. The marriage itself eventually took place in 1114. The
prospect of his grandchild inheriting the imperial throne (Henry V
was crowned emperor by the pope in 1111, and Matilda became an
empress) must have added to the attraction of this union for Henry, but
it was the emperor's political and military muscle that really mattered to
the English king as events continued to conspire against him in France.
For generations the dukes of Normandy and the counts of Anjou had
competed for control over the county of Maine, which lay enticingly
between their two principalities. In 1110, Count Helias of Maine, a
long-standing ally of Henry I, died, leaving only a daughter, who was
married to none other than Count Fulk of Anjou. Through his wife,
Maine therefore passed to the counts of Anjou, significantly altering
the balance of power in northern France. In the same year, William
Clito was taken into hiding by his supporters. Henry's enemies were
gathering to confront him and in 1111 open war broke out and
continued inconclusively for two years. In the end, Prince William was
central to the ending of hostilities. In February 1113, Fulk of Anjou met
Henry and performed homage to him for the county of Maine. In this
way, Fulk kept possession of the county he already held through his
wife, but in accepting Henry as his overlord, he was also signalling the
end of his alliance with King Louis of France, who in turn came to
terms with Henry shortly afterwards. To give a degree of permanence to
the new relationship established between Henry and Fulk, Prince
William was betrothed to Fulk's daughter, Matilda. He was ten, and she
was probably much younger than that.

From this point on, William becomes more prominent as a player on
the stage of Anglo-Norman politics. His growing involvement in affairs
is shown by his increasingly frequent appearance as a witness to his

father's charters from at least 1113, and regularly from 1115; he attended a royal council in September 1115 and was present with his parents at the dedication of St Alban's Abbey three months later. Then, in March 1116, the English nobles gathered at Salisbury, swore oaths of loyalty to the prince and acknowledged him as their next king. The archbishop of Canterbury and the other English bishops swore to transfer the kingdom and the crown to him on Henry's death. Something similar had already happened in Normandy. At the start of 1115, at Rouen during his Christmas court, Henry had arranged for all the leading Norman magnates to perform homage and swear allegiance to William, accepting him as the heir to the duchy. There was a sticking point, however. King Louis stubbornly refused to accept William's offer to perform homage to him as the heir to Normandy. The French king continued to support William Clito's claim to the duchy, and there was no reason why Louis should abandon him as long as his publicly principled, but privately mischievous, stance continued to frustrate Henry I's plans.

Permanent security as the ruler of England and Normandy continued to elude Henry I, and Prince William's future remained uncertain. He stayed single, too, as the prospect of him ever marrying Matilda of Anjou became increasingly remote. Warfare in France dominated the concerns of the king; Henry was there permanently from Easter 1116 until his fateful return to England in November 1120. The climactic year was 1118, when mounting political tensions within Normandy shook and almost broke Henry's grip on his duchy. William, count of Evreux, died that year without a son and heir, and his lands were claimed by his nephew, Amaury de Montfort, who had fought against Henry in the war of 1111–13. Henry, who as duke was entitled to determine the succession to the county in circumstances such as these, refused to accept Amaury's claim. Amaury therefore began to make trouble for Henry from his base at Montfort l'Amaury just beyond the southern border of Normandy. Other Norman lords now also began to take their chances against Henry and disorder spread quickly. Soon it was hard for Henry to know whom he could trust: 'men who ate with him favoured the cause of his nephew', Orderic Vitalis alleged, and even Henry's own daughter, Juliana, turned against him with her husband. Orderic describes a farcical attempt by Juliana to kill her father with a crossbow. When she misfired, she attempted to escape from the castle she was in by leaping from its walls, but she 'fell shamefully, with bare buttocks, into the depths of the moat'.[7] Orderic uses this story to make a point about the fickleness of women generally, and it is probably far-fetched. Nevertheless, Henry was under pressure. A plot to assassinate the king was indeed uncovered within his own household at about this time. The conspirators may have been led by Henry's chamberlain, Herbert. The identity of the architect of the scheme was never revealed, but he was caught, blinded and castrated. From that point on, it was said, Henry never slept easily again: he rarely spent more than a few nights in the same bed and wherever he slept he kept a sword and a shield within reach.[8]

Henry's difficulties in Normandy were seized on by his opponents elsewhere. Once again he found himself confronted by the king of France, the count of Flanders and the count of Anjou, all fighting for William Clito's cause. Towards the end of 1118, Count Fulk of Anjou entered Normandy and laid siege to the castle at Alençon. When Henry tried to relieve the siege he was defeated in battle by Fulk's army. This brought a terrible year to a disastrous end, and as Henry retired to lick his wounds and consider his response, he had to do so without the support of his queen. Matilda had died at Westminster in May 1118. She had been a model consort in many ways: she had given the king the son he needed, and, having performed that duty, Matilda had developed a reputation for piety and good works. On one occasion she had been scolded by her brother David, the future king of Scots, when he saw her washing and kissing the feet of lepers. When he suggested that her husband would never kiss her again if he found out what she had done, Matilda replied that the feet of the eternal king were preferable to the lips of a mortal one. She had also been a politician in her own right, regularly acting on Henry's behalf in England when he was in France, listening to petitions, presiding over legal disputes, and issuing writs authorised by her own seal. In the unruly, turbulent and overwhelmingly masculine world of early twelfth-century politics, Matilda had given Henry assertive, loyal support; and when she died the tributes to her were many. 'From the time England first became subject to kings,' one monastic historian wrote, 'out of all the queens none was found to be comparable to her, and none will be found in the time to come, whose memory will be praised and whose name shall be blessed through the ages.'[9] What Henry made of her death is unclear. He did not attend her funeral at Westminster Abbey, but after his return to England in 1120 the king ordered that a halfpenny should be paid every day to keep a light burning before her last resting place. And as late as 1130 there is a payment of three shillings recorded in the royal accounts for the purchase of a cloth to cover the queen's tomb.[10] As for Prince William, we can only guess at how he reacted to the loss of his mother and how her death might have affected what was left of his own life. There is evidence to suggest that he was acting alongside his mother in government towards the end of her life, and he seems to have taken over from her as regent in England just before she died or immediately on her death. In a charter that appears to date from around the middle of the following year, 1119, when William left England for Normandy, never to return, he was referred to as 'rex designatus', a description which made clear his status as Henry's heir to the kingdom.[11]

If England was relatively stable, well governed and untroubled at the start of 1119, things looked bleak for Henry and William in Normandy. However, by the end of that year their fortunes in France had been transformed. In May, Henry persuaded Fulk of Anjou to break his alliance with King Louis and make peace. The marriage alliance of 1113 was revived and in June 1119 Prince William finally married Matilda of Anjou at Lisieux. In this way, Fulk was offered the prospect of his grandson succeeding to England and Normandy, and also to Maine, which Matilda brought to the marriage as her dowry. The reconciliation with Fulk relieved the pressure on Henry in southern Normandy. He was helped by events in the north too, when Count Baldwin of Flanders died, also in June. Only King Louis was left to continue the fight, but on 20 August 1119 Henry and his army decisively defeated Louis's troops at Brémule in eastern Normandy. The battle was well described by several contemporaries. Their versions of events differ in detail, but in general they agree about what happened.[12] The French, with William Clito leading the front line of cavalry and King Louis commanding the next, attacked first and scattered the Anglo-Norman troops. This plan was criticised later as poorly conceived and rashly executed; Louis lacked the patience to prepare carefully, it was said.[13] And, to be sure, if the opening French move went reasonably well, Clito and Louis soon found themselves in trouble. After breaking through the Anglo-Norman front line, the French were confronted by King Henry himself, fighting on foot whilst commanding his own second line of infantry, made up of a large number of dismounted knights. Henry was struck heavily on the head, but he and his men fought back fiercely and turned the French attackers. The regrouped Anglo-Norman cavalry, including Henry's sons William, Richard and Robert, then routed them. Over a hundred French knights were captured, but of the nine hundred or so who fought on both sides in the battle, only three were killed.

The defeat at Brémule was a humiliating one for the French king. Henry bought Louis' standard for twenty silver marks from the man who had captured it, and kept it as a souvenir. But Henry was gracious enough to return Louis' horse to him, with its harness and saddle, on the day after the battle. Prince William, it was said, did the same with William Clito's horse; they were cousins, after all.[14] These gestures must have been accepted by Louis and Clito through clenched teeth, pointed as they were. More broadly, after coming close to catastrophe in Normandy less than a year before, Henry's victory at Brémule had turned the military and political tide decisively in his favour; and in the months that followed the war with Louis petered out and the groundwork for a permanent settlement between the kings was laid. Rebels came to terms, as a result of force, persuasion or both, and finally in mid-1120, with the help of papal mediation, Henry and Louis agreed the terms of a definitive peace. A part of this may have been Prince William's performance of homage for Normandy to Louis. However, this is not certain. Even at this stage, the French king may not have been prepared to lose face by completely abandoning Clito, and, whilst it seems certain that Prince William did perform homage of some kind, he may have done so before Louis' son, Philip, not Louis himself. The symbolism of such an event would have allowed both Henry and Louis to claim something of what they each had wanted: the French king's support for Clito remained notionally uncompromised and Prince William was confirmed as Henry's heir. In any event, whatever uncertainty surrounds William's homage, there is no lack of clarity about what happened next, when the Norman magnates renewed the oaths they had first sworn to William in 1115. They were signalling their acceptance of Henry I's son as the next duke of Normandy, while William Clito's claims now counted for nothing.

Henry and William must have set off on their journeys back to England feeling relieved and satisfied. There was plenty to celebrate in the deal with Louis and the defeat of William Clito. After twenty years of uncertainty and, latterly, four years of intense fighting and diplomatic activity, Henry had got the better of his French enemies and secured the succession to England and Normandy for his cherished son. Now married and with children of his own sure to come soon, the prince's own future, as well as his family's, could not have looked brighter or more secure. It is hardly surprising that the drink continued to flow after William and his friends arrived at Barfleur on 25 November 1120.

When he died at sea, a general sense of shock was mixed with no little ambivalence about the sort of ruler William would have made. Some commentators thought that the prince and his companions were too proud and distracted by lust and a love of luxury. But these allegations were not written down until later, and this kind of moralising may tell us more about its authors than the prince himself. More convincing is the opinion of William of Malmesbury. He had met Queen Matilda and perhaps even the prince himself. In his view:

> Many provinces looked to the boy's lightest wish, and in him it was supposed King Edward [the Confessor's] prophecy was to be fulfilled: the hope of England, it was thought, once cut down like a tree, was in the person of that young prince again to blossom and bear fruit, so that one might hope the evil times were coming to an end. But God had other plans; these expectations went down with the wind, for the day was already at hand when he must fulfil his fate.[15]

The prince had certainly spent the second half of his short life training to be a ruler. What is more, his involvement in English government after 1116 and his conduct on the battlefield at Brémule suggest that he had learnt his lessons well. The hopes of many were invested in him and 'lifted as to a tower's top', in William of Malmesbury's words.[16] The prince's death was a careless accident, not a punishment from God for a loose, immoral life. He left a widow (Matilda had crossed to England on Henry I's ship, not her husband's) who returned to her family and became a nun, and a distraught father. In the course of one dark night, Henry's heart was broken and twenty years of political planning and military endeavour had come to nothing. What would happen to England and Normandy now?

CHAPTER TWO

THE EARL'S TALE

Hugh Bigod, Civil War and Royal Recovery

B Y THE TIME he died on Sunday, 1 December 1135, King Henry I
had been ill for nearly a week. On the previous Monday he had
been hunting in the forest of Lyons, about twenty miles east of Rouen.
Some time in the afternoon, after giving his huntsmen their orders to be
ready for him again on the following day, Henry had returned to his
hunting lodge at Lyons la Forêt and fallen ravenously on a meal of
lampreys. These fish look like small eels and, like eels, have no scales.
They are also jawless but with teeth in their funnel-like sucking mouths.
They are not pretty, but they were a delicacy that Henry loved. This was
unfortunate: lampreys always disagreed with the king, and Henry's
doctors had told him to avoid them. But the king couldn't resist and he
ignored their advice. During the night his sickness began. First he was
gripped by a deadly chill; this was followed by violent convulsions, a
fever and heavy sweating. As the days passed, the king's condition worsened and it became clear to everyone, including Henry himself, that he
was not going to recover. He called his chaplains to him so that he could
make confession and he summoned his friend and counsellor, the archbishop of Rouen. On the archbishop's advice the king proceeded to
make his peace with the world: he revoked all the sentences of forfeiture
he had pronounced on guilty men, and he allowed exiles to return and
the disinherited to recover their ancestral inheritances. Then he ordered
his illegitimate son Robert, the earl of Gloucester, who was in charge of
the king's treasure at the great Norman castle of Falaise, to take £60,000

and pay out wages and gifts to the members of his household and his mercenaries. The king then gave instructions that his dead body was to be taken to England for burial at Reading, where he had established an abbey about ten years before. Henry implored all to devote themselves to the preservation of peace and the protection of the poor; he made his confession, received penance and was absolved by his priests. Finally, having been anointed with holy oil and given Holy Communion, he commended himself to God and, as darkness descended on that Sunday, Henry I, king of England and duke of Normandy, died. He was sixty-seven or sixty-eight years old.

Henry I's death was sudden and unexpected. He had been healthy and strong enough to go hunting in the bracing late-November air, and his final illness had struck without warning. What was to happen to his lands? Who would succeed him in England and Normandy? Henry's only legitimate son, William, had drowned in 1120, and since then Henry had tried to have his first-born and legitimate daughter, Matilda, acknowledged by the English and Norman barons as his heir. But with the old king now dead, anything could happen. According to some, as he lay dying, Henry had once again repeated his wish that Matilda should succeed him in England and Normandy. Others, conversely, claimed that the king had changed his mind at the last minute, that he had turned against Matilda and her husband Geoffrey of Anjou and nominated as his heir his nephew, Stephen of Blois.[1] There is even an account of what Henry had actually said at this moment, as his magnates crowded round him, desperate to hear what the dying king wanted. "You!' he said. 'Great men and wise! I present to you as king my comrade-in-arms Stephen, an earl of mine, my most beloved kinsman, noble in his valour, but exceedingly devout in his trust to God; I lay down that you should accept him in place of me and by right of inheritance, and I solemnly affirm that this is, in all respects, how things are.' Having said this, the report continues, the king immediately died.[2] What is more, one man was prepared to swear an oath on the Gospels that this was exactly what had happened. He was the royal steward, Hugh Bigod. Having rushed across the Channel to England straight after the king's death, Hugh presented himself before Archbishop William of Canterbury and the other English bishops, and his testimony about

Henry's last wishes was instrumental in persuading the hesitant arch-bishop to crown Stephen king on 22 December 1135.[3]

Meanwhile, King Henry's corpse remained unburied. The day after his death the body, accompanied by 20,000 men according to one esti-mate, had been taken to the cathedral at Rouen. There, 'in the corner of the cathedral' William of Malmesbury evocatively remarked, the corpu-lent body was opened by a skilled embalmer, disembowelled and filled, Orderic Vitalis said, with 'fragrant balsam'. It was then cut all over with knives, sprinkled with large quantities of salt and wrapped in ox hides to stop what Henry of Huntingdon described as 'the strong, pervasive stench'. So powerful was the smell, in fact, according to Henry, that it was said to have killed the man who had been hired to cut off the king's head with an axe and take out his 'stinking brain'. In the chronicler's morbid view, this unfortunate unnamed man 'was the last of many whom King Henry put to death'. The rest of the king's insides were taken to the nearby town of Émendreville in an urn and buried in the church of Notre Dame du Pré, which had been begun by Henry's mother, Matilda, and completed by Henry himself. The funeral cortège was then accompanied to the abbey of St Stephen at Caen, where the body lay for a month alongside the tomb of Henry's great father, William the Conqueror, waiting for a suitable wind to carry it across to England.[4] As the corpse rested in the church, though, its wrappings failed to prevent 'a fearful black fluid' seeping out, which had to be collected in bowls and disposed of by terrified attendants.[5]

On 4 January 1136, over a month after his death, King Henry was finally buried at his abbey of Reading. In attendance at his funeral was the new king, Stephen, the nephew whom Henry may or may not have nominated as his successor with his last breath. Almost certainly, too, the new king's steward would not have been far away. Hugh Bigod's efforts on Stephen's behalf had paid off: the new king was in his debt and Hugh had kept his position at the heart of royal affairs. But if Hugh had helped himself by helping Stephen, others felt less confident about their future under the new regime and were less convinced by Stephen's claim to be Henry I's legitimate successor. Hugh's oath may have resolved matters in the short term, but it had also prepared the ground for nearly two decades of civil war.

* * * *

Hugh Bigod's story is remarkable partly because he lasted so long. He was over eighty years old when he died in 1177, and by then he had lived through the reigns of four different kings. Hugh was a major figure on the national stage for most of the twelfth century, and he had taken part in events that shaped and then reshaped the political map of England and the kingdom's relationship with Europe. At Henry I's court he had been at the centre of the continent's richest and most powerful regime. He had then experienced the collapse of royal authority during fifteen years of civil war under King Stephen, and he had joined in the reconstruction of the English kingdom under Henry II. Hugh witnessed the rise, fall and recovery of England's fortunes and, astonishingly, he survived it all. He held high office and became an earl; he dominated whole swathes of eastern England for over fifty years. Whether Hugh supported the king or, as he regularly did, opposed him, he could not be ignored.

Hugh's resilience, his stamina and his unfailing energy over such a long period are striking, but his reputation is not good. Conventionally he has been seen as a selfish man who held only lightly to his allegiances. He was fickle and untrustworthy, and he would shift frequently and without scruple from one side to another in any kind of quarrel whenever it suited him to do so – in other words, the only cause Hugh Bigod was ever interested in was that of Hugh Bigod. He was seen for a long time as a typical English baron of the twelfth century – narrowly self-seeking, predatory and eager to seize whatever resources he could lay his hands on in order to increase his personal power and wealth; heedless and scornful of loyalty for loyalty's sake and, of course, violent and brutal into the bargain. This made him representative of a class of men who could only be kept in check by the kind of strong, masterful royal authority (or tyranny, some of them would have thought) exercised by Henry I and Henry II. Freed from such restraints, for example when a weak king like Stephen came to the throne, powerful men would reveal their true characters and instincts, turn into rampaging robber barons, and plunge the kingdom into civil war and anarchy.

Such views, of course, have served to underpin the popular stereotype of the irredeemably turbulent marauder on the fierce black horse as well as its necessary opposite, the generous and brave knight on his noble white steed. No serious historian, though, would suggest that such characterisations fit any kind of meaningful reality. This was much more complex. Hugh Bigod and his contemporaries lived in difficult times. Their priorities were the security of their families' fortunes and the stability of their local power. Everything they did, from arranging their children's marriages, to building their castles and strongholds, to fighting for one side or another in a civil war, was geared towards achieving these goals. Families competed and collaborated with each other for local standing and influence; in turn, if successful, they might acquire national power too. Yet, inevitably, if one family prospered, another lost out, and rivalries developed as those with disappointed claims over lands, titles, rights and inheritances nurtured grievances and feelings of injustice. It was ultimately the king's job to manage these tensions and handle the relationships between his leading subjects. There were any number of ways of doing this – subtly, through tactful diplomacy and negotiation, or decisively through forceful leadership. But whichever way he chose, it was almost certain that someone would be unhappy with the result. And if what the loser wanted could not be obtained from one source of patronage, he would look for another. This is what happened after the death of Henry I in 1135, when the emergence of rival claimants to the throne, each urgently in need of support, provided an environment in which everyone with a competing claim to the same estate, heiress or position had somewhere to go to pursue it. And because there were so many of these claims, an explosive situation was inevitable, as for the next twenty years private and local disputes between individuals and families were played out on a public and national stage.

In such circumstances consistent loyalty to one side or another, whilst admirable, was difficult to sustain. Hugh Bigod, like many others, did change sides more than once. He was fiercely loyal to Henry I until the latter's death, but he abandoned Henry's chosen heir and gave his backing to King Stephen at the start of his reign and for several years thereafter. Nonetheless, and notwithstanding his key role in Stephen's accession, Hugh was never comfortable on his side. Stephen's humiliating defeat by an army loyal to the Empress Matilda at the Battle of Lincoln in 1141 and the king's capture there by Robert, earl of

Gloucester, gave Hugh the excuse he had probably been seeking to give his backing once again to the direct line of Henry I's descendants. Thereafter for the rest of the civil war he was notably faithful to Matilda and her son, the future Henry II. So Hugh was not as unpredictable with his support as may at first sight appear. What is more, in some areas he was completely consistent. Like every other magnate, his efforts were directed towards protecting his local power. In East Anglia, Hugh was challenged by other local families and later by the royal family itself. His fixity of purpose and his determination to defend what was his proved to be his defining characteristics.

So Hugh Bigod is important, first because his career provides an entry point into an extraordinary series of turbulent events that defined England's future. But over and above this, he is notable not because he represents the innately vicious and irrepressibly aggressive traits of the twelfth-century English aristocracy, but because he represents that group's conservatism and its instinct for self-preservation at a time of national crisis. To be sure, these men were not innocent victims of royal failure, and if they sometimes took advantage of events to further their own interests, that is hardly surprising. In the end, however, they were doing what they had to do in order to survive. Hugh Bigod did that as well as anyone, although not without great difficulty and great determination.

* * * *

His enemies and rivals later claimed that Hugh Bigod had not been at Henry I's bedside before the king died, so he could have had no idea what might have been said about the succession.[6] In other words, when Hugh gave his evidence to the archbishop of Canterbury on oath, he was making it all up. Now it is impossible to know for sure whether Hugh was at Lyons la Forêt on 1 December 1135; and, even if he was, he may have lied about what was said. Either way, whether he was telling the truth about what happened or not, Hugh Bigod made a deliberate choice when he backed Stephen's claim to succeed Henry I. For him, as for all the other English and Norman magnates, there was an enormous amount at stake as one reign ended and the next one began. Hugh would have known from his family's experiences how important it was to be on the winning side in a dispute over the claim to the throne. His father, Roger Bigod, had profited hugely from the Norman seizure of England. An impoverished Norman knight in the 1050s, Roger had become the sheriff of Suffolk and Norfolk by 1086, and probably earlier than that. As a result, responsible as he was for the management of the king's estates in those counties, Roger Bigod had become one of the richest men in England. On William I's death in 1087, however, Roger and the rest of the Anglo-Norman aristocracy faced a choice between the claims of two of the late king's sons, Robert Curthose and William Rufus, to the English throne. The Conqueror seems to have wanted to divide his territories between them: Robert, the eldest, would keep the family lands (the patrimony) and become duke of Normandy, whilst William Rufus, the second son, would take the lands his father had won by force, the kingdom of England. But, despite their father's intentions, both brothers wanted to rule both territories, and men like Roger were compelled to take sides. Roger made the wrong choice: he backed Robert, who kept Normandy but failed to take England. Roger consequently lost his place as sheriff, and it is not clear whether William II ever gave it back to him. Then, in 1101, after the death of William II, another succession crisis developed as Robert Curthose and his younger brother Henry locked horns over England and Normandy. This time, Roger decided not to support Robert, and he was amongst the handful of barons in England who backed the new king. When Henry's grip on England was assured, he rewarded Roger by appointing him sheriff of Norfolk and Suffolk, and he held on to these positions until his death in 1107.

By this time the Bigods were firmly entrenched in East Anglia, and their great castle at Framlingham had been built to tower over the Suffolk countryside. Hugh Bigod may have been born there some time in the 1090s, but his date and place of birth are unknown. We do know, nevertheless, that Hugh's mother was Roger Bigod's second wife, Alice de Tosny, and that Hugh was not his father's intended heir. It was Hugh's elder half-brother, William, the son of Roger and his first wife, who was supposed to take up where Roger had left off. William, though, may also have been no more than a boy when his father died. This made the Bigods' position at court and in their east Anglian heartland vulnerable and precarious. A minority like this exposed a family to covetous rivals and neighbours, and it was vital that William regained the king's favour as quickly as he could once he was old enough to do so. In 1114/15 the signs were promising as he received the offices his father had held and became sheriff of Norfolk and Suffolk, and he was appointed a steward of the royal household too. But he had soon been replaced as sheriff and he was clearly struggling to re-establish his family's position. To make matters worse, by 1115 both of William's sisters had been married off by the king to powerful lords, and had taken large chunks of Bigod territory with them as their dowries. Henry I seems to have shown little interest in William's position, and as a result William may have felt he had to look elsewhere for potential patronage. Between 1115 and 1120 his failure to appear as a witness to any of Henry I's charters suggests strongly that William was more or less permanently absent from court. It is not clear what happened to him during these years, but he may have thought that if the current king would not help him, maybe in time the next one would. This would account for his presence on board the doomed *White Ship* in 1120, as a member of Prince William's entourage.

William Bigod's death at sea brought his half-brother Hugh out of the shadows. Like William and Roger before him, Hugh was made royal steward by the king. Then again, other positions, most notably the sheriffdoms of Norfolk and Suffolk, remained in other hands. Undeterred, Hugh was keen to remain in the king's line of sight so as to be in the right place at the right time if prizes were being given out. Unlike his half-brother, Hugh was frequently in attendance at the royal court after 1120: his appearance as a witness to forty-five of Henry I's charters between then and 1135 shows this. And, unlike his father, he was also prepared to travel: the sixty or so charters that Roger Bigod had witnessed were all issued in England, whereas a third of those witnessed by Hugh were given in Normandy. Hugh was particularly keen to attend the king in the last two or three years of the reign. A third of the charters he witnessed date from the last three years of Henry's life and several were issued at important centres of ducal power in Normandy such as Rouen or Falaise in 1134 and 1135. Such evidence is difficult to interpret conclusively, but it does suggest that Hugh was determined to make every effort to appear loyal and ingratiate himself with the king as the reign drew towards its end. It also lends credibility to the idea that Hugh was with the king until the last.

By then, however, Hugh had witnessed fifteen years of uncertainty about the royal succession. After Prince William's death in 1120, Henry I remarried in 1121. (His first wife, Matilda of Scotland, had died in 1118.) His new wife, Adeliza of Louvain, was said to have had the necessary beauty, morals and character to become queen of England. The marriage also strengthened England's existing diplomatic alliances within the German Empire: Adeliza was the daughter of Godfrey, count of Lower Lorraine and duke of Brabant. But her qualities would have mattered less to Henry than Adeliza's ability to bear a desperately needed son and heir. There was every chance this would happen. The new queen was young (about eighteen in 1120) and Henry was famously productive. Yet, mysteriously, no child was born to the couple. Adeliza was not responsible for this: after Henry died she remarried and had seven children by her second husband. So the problem must have been Henry's, and perhaps his age and lifestyle had finally caught up with him.

Failing the arrival of a new son, there was of course at least one obvious potential heir: William Clito, Henry's nephew and the son of his elder brother, Robert. But the king's determination to prevent Clito succeeding to the throne remained as strong as ever, even as the old coalition began to regroup around him. By 1123, King Louis VI and Count Fulk of Anjou had resumed their support for Clito. Fulk even arranged for Clito to marry his second daughter, Sibylla, and gave her the county of Maine for her dowry. A rebellion on Clito's behalf then broke out in Normandy, and Henry, with his steward Hugh Bigod amongst the members of his entourage, crossed from Portsmouth to Normandy in June 1123. Despite having French and Angevin support, the opposition behind Clito collapsed the following spring when, on 26 March 1124, a troop of Henry's household knights defeated and captured almost the entire rebel force near the town of Bourgthéroulde, about a dozen miles south-west of Rouen. Meanwhile, Henry managed to keep French forces out of Normandy by persuading his son-in-law and Matilda's husband, the emperor Henry V, to invade France from the east. The German invasion was hardly a triumph, but it probably did enough to prevent King Louis intervening directly in the Norman rebellion. Henry also dealt a further blow to Clito's hopes when he persuaded the pope to annul his marriage to Sibylla of Anjou on the grounds of consanguinity.

Despite such military and diplomatic successes, Clito would remain a problem unless Henry could resolve the succession issue once and for all. By 1125, Henry's hopes of fathering a new heir were fading. So, it was said, 'in grief that [Queen Adeliza] did not conceive, and fearing that she would always be barren', the king turned to his daughter, Empress Matilda.[7] The timing of events helped Henry here. Matilda had just been widowed, Henry V having died in May 1125. This meant that there was nothing to keep her in Germany, and as a result various new possibilities opened up. One option was to position Matilda to succeed Henry and rule England and Normandy in her own right. Women rulers were not unheard of in twelfth-century Europe. For example, Queen Urraca had ruled the Spanish kingdoms of León and Castile since 1109. Another option was to marry Matilda to a powerful man so that she could bear a son, and then she and her husband could act as regents or guardians until the boy was old enough to rule himself. King Henry's own sister, Matilda's aunt, Adela, had been left in charge of the county of Blois whilst her husband, Count Stephen, had been on crusade, and after his death she had acted as regent for their son, Theobald, until he came of age. And the widow of Count Roger the Great of Sicily, Adelasia, had ruled the island until her son Roger II assumed power in 1112. These precedents were problematic, however. Queen Urraca had come to the throne as the undisputed heir of her father, Alfonso VI of León, and she was unquestionably able. But her reign had been plagued by struggles between her supporters, those of her son by her first husband and those of her estranged second husband, King Alfonso I of Aragon. And in Blois and Sicily, it had at least been clear what was supposed to happen: the regencies were temporary and the successions of Theobald and Roger were never in doubt. Things were nowhere near as clear-cut in England and Normandy in the mid-1120s. Henry wanted Matilda to succeed him, but on what basis? Moreover, she was now unmarried and it was assumed that, if she was to make anything of her claims, she would need the support of a strong second husband. At the same time, Queen Urraca's experiences showed that the choice of husband in such a situation was a highly charged political matter. What role would he expect to play? And, more importantly, where would he come from?

Such questions must have been asked increasingly often by members of the English and Norman nobility during the mid-1120s. Hugh Bigod would not have been alone in wondering what the king's plans were and how they might affect him. As royal steward in regular attendance on the king, he was better placed than most to judge the course of events and, like Henry, assess Matilda's qualities as a potential heir. And Hugh would have observed them getting to know each other again (father and daughter had not met since Matilda had left for Germany in 1110). So for much of 1125 and 1126 Hugh was with the king and the empress in Normandy. He was at Rouen in October 1125, for example, and was amongst those who witnessed a grant by the king to his new abbey at Reading.[8] Lavishly endowed with lands and privileges since it had been founded in the early 1120s, the importance of the abbey to the king, particularly in the aftermath of William Atheling's death and Henry's own remarriage, was already well established. This grant served to reinforce that, as did the length of the witness list and the status of those on it. In addition to Hugh Bigod, the document was witnessed by the queen, a papal legate, three archbishops, eight bishops, five abbots, three earls and one count. This was a major gathering of the Anglo-Norman elite and Hugh was an established member of that select community. In September 1126, Hugh returned across the Channel with the rest of the royal party and landed at Portsmouth. There he witnessed another document that concerned Reading Abbey.[9] In it the king notified the monks that, at the request of Empress Matilda, who had brought with her from Germany the hand of St James the Apostle, he was sending them this precious and famous relic. This surely suggests that the relationship between Henry and his daughter had been successfully re-established: by allowing her to patronise his own abbey so publicly, the king was in some way associating Matilda with his rule. Once in England, negotiations and consultations about the succession continued with the leading churchmen and nobles, and after holding his Christmas court at Windsor, Henry moved his entourage to London for the start of the New Year.

By now, at least parts of the king's plan must have been known to his leading subjects, for on 1 January 1127 a great ceremony was held in which those present, of whom Hugh Bigod was almost certainly one, swore an oath of loyalty to Matilda. The oath-taking itself was supervised by the king's chief minister Roger, bishop of Salisbury. The first to take the oaths were the archbishops of Canterbury and York, followed by the other bishops present. David, king of Scots (the empress's uncle), was next to swear, then Queen Adeliza. An argument about who was to swear next then broke out. Should it be Robert, earl of Gloucester, King Henry's eldest illegitimate son, or Count Stephen of Boulogne, the king's nephew? In one account, each claimed precedence over the other. In another, Bishop Roger called on Earl Robert to take the oath first: 'Get up, get up and swear the oath as the king wants', the bishop demanded. But Earl Robert deferred to his cousin. Stephen was older and therefore senior in rank, the earl argued.[10] Such set pieces were used by the writers who described them to presage the quarrels that erupted after King Henry's death, when Robert and Stephen became implacable enemies. But on this occasion it seems that Stephen did swear next, followed by Earl Robert, the rest of the lay magnates, and only then (in an outrageous breach of protocol, according to some monastic writers) the abbots. When the abbot of Bury St Edmund's complained about the lack of respect shown to him and his fellow abbots, the king told him bluntly to shut up and get on with it.[11]

It is impossible to know for sure precisely what Hugh Bigod and his companions swore to do in January 1127. The *Anglo-Saxon Chronicle*'s version of events is brief and to the point: the magnates swore 'to give England and Normandy after [Henry's] death into the hands of his daughter'.[12] But other accounts only blur the issues. According to John of Worcester, if Henry died without an heir and Matilda had an heir herself, she would receive England with her lawful husband. So Matilda needed to marry and have a son before this scenario played itself out, and even then the oath made no mention of Normandy. William of Malmesbury's account is slightly different: in his view the nobles swore that 'they would immediately accept ... Matilda, formerly empress, as their lady' if King Henry died without a male heir. But this oath referred only to England, too, and also left Matilda's future status unclear: what did it mean to be 'lady' (*domina*) rather than queen? Yet another account describes how the kingdom's chief men promised 'to defend the English realm on her behalf against all' if King Henry died without a legitimate male heir and that Henry had 'transferred the rights to the crown to his daughter' on this basis.[13] That no clear, definitive version of what was sworn in January 1127 survives is suggestive, on the one hand, of promises made provisionally and conditionally, of men hedging their bets and looking to avoid any kind of firm commitment; or, on the other, of writers later aiming to dilute the categorical nature of the oath sworn so as to justify its eventual abandonment by so many of those who took it.

Following hard upon the oath-taking came the start of negotiations for Matilda's marriage. Indeed, the formalisation of Matilda's position may have been an essential precondition demanded by her intended husband, Geoffrey, the son of Count Fulk V of Anjou. Just as he had done more than once in the previous decades, Henry was trying to solve his political and dynastic problems by means of a marriage (William Atheling's marriage to Matilda of Anjou had been the cornerstone of Henry's plans in both 1113 and 1119) with the rulers of Anjou. Some of his magnates certainly felt uneasy at the prospect of an Angevin prince marrying the king's heir and then fathering the heirs to England and Normandy. And yet for Henry the match continued to make sense. In the longer term the expectation was that Matilda and Geoffrey would produce a grandson to replace the lost William Atheling and guarantee the succession in England and Normandy to Henry's direct heir. But more immediately, of course, the marriage was designed to separate Anjou from France and reduce wider support for William Clito. This was no trifling concern in 1127, as King Louis' support for Clito grew ever stronger. Already by February of that year, Clito had married into the French royal family. His new wife, Jeanne de Montferrat, was the half-sister of Louis' wife. Louis had also made Clito lord of the French Vexin, the strategically crucial territory bordering Normandy's eastern frontier. Shortly afterwards Clito led an armed force to Henry's castle of Gisors, where he issued a formal claim to the duchy of Normandy. Then fortune smiled on Clito once more when, on 2 March 1127, the childless Count Charles the Good of Flanders was murdered whilst at mass in Bruges. Louis VI intervened immediately (as French king, he was overlord of Flanders), and on his orders the Flemings chose Clito as their new count. He had a hereditary claim as the grandson of Matilda of Flanders, the daughter of Count Baldwin V and wife of William the Conqueror; but others, not least Henry I (the son of Matilda of Flanders) had better claims. Nevertheless, Clito now had the resources of a great French principality to draw on, and there was no reason why he should not continue to covet Normandy.

Henry I responded to these ominous developments by secretly giving financial support to the several unsuccessful claimants to Flanders, placing himself nominally at their head by asserting his own claim to the county, and encouraging them all until it became clear which one might win enough support to unseat Clito. By 1128, as a result of Henry's manoeuvring and Clito's inept handling of his new Flemish subjects, Flanders was in uproar. Out of this chaos emerged Thierry, count of Alsace, as Clito's chief rival to the Flemish countship. Hostilities continued in Flanders until late in July 1128, when Clito was mortally wounded in an assault on Thierry's castle of Aalst. Clito's death brought the crisis, and Henry's troubles, to an abrupt end only a month after the marriage of Geoffrey of Anjou and Empress Matilda had taken place at Le Mans in the presence of King Henry and Count Fulk.

The death of his nephew and the marriage of his daughter should have combined to give Henry I's reign a peaceful and trouble-free end. By 1130 he had defeated or made peace with all his enemies, and when he landed in Normandy, accompanied by Hugh Bigod amongst others, in September of that year, there were no wars for Henry to fight. In January 1131 he and his courtiers could even afford to travel to Chartres, the chief city of the county of Blois, where Henry's nephew, Stephen's elder brother Theobald, was ruler. There the king made a grant, witnessed by Bigod, to the great abbey of Fontevraud in Anjou.[14] The apparent stability and the public-relations successes could not fully mask the problems developing behind the scenes, however; and, once again, it was the succession that returned to plague the ageing king. When Hugh Bigod crossed the Channel back to England with Henry and Adeliza in August 1131, the voyage was rough and almost a disaster.

So close did the king come to being shipwrecked that, when he landed in England, he promised not to collect geld for seven years and to go on a pilgrimage to the shrine of St Edmund at Bury.[15] The stormy weather could nonetheless have been construed as an omen of the troubling times to come. Also on board during that voyage was Empress Matilda, unaccompanied by her husband. By this time she had not seen Geoffrey for the best part of two years and Henry's dynastic plans were once again under threat.

When they had married in 1128, Matilda was a widow of twenty-five and her husband a boy of fourteen. She, moreover, was the widow of an emperor, whilst Geoffrey was to be a mere count. These differences in age and status must have contributed to what was certainly a bumpy first few years of marriage. By the summer of 1129, husband and wife were separated. The reasons for the estrangement are unclear (one chronicler claimed that Geoffrey had thrown Matilda out), but there was probably too much at stake for it to be just a clash of personalities.[16] Aristocratic marriages did not work this way in the twelfth century, and it is much more likely that Geoffrey's expectations about the role he was to play did not match those of his wife or father-in-law. The circumstances of their reunion, which did not take place until late 1131, support the idea that there were political issues at stake in the quarrel between Matilda and Geoffrey. It was Geoffrey who eventually suggested a reconciliation, but before it happened, Henry summoned 'all the leading men of England' to discuss his daughter's marriage. The king clearly thought he needed to involve his most important subjects in what happened next. This group of leading councillors was remarkably large (another indication of the importance of this issue): it included one cardinal, two archbishops, ten bishops, seven abbots, five earls and twenty-two others, one of whom was Hugh Bigod. They gathered at Northampton early in September 1131, and between them it was formally decided that Matilda should return to her husband 'who was asking for her'. Those present then swore an oath of loyalty to the empress, whether they had done so before or not.[17] Once again, it is not clear from the chronicler's account of this episode precisely what the terms of this oath were. Yet it must be the case that Hugh Bigod took the oath like everyone else. Whatever he actually swore to do, on some level it would have involved supporting Matilda on her father's death, whether as his direct heir or as regent for any son she might yet produce with Geoffrey. It must have been clear to those leaving Northampton in the second week of 1131 that the old king was determined that his daughter should succeed him in one capacity or another. And by their oaths they had bound themselves to this plan.

Once back together, things were clearly better between Matilda and Geoffrey second time around. In March 1133 at Le Mans their first child, a son, was born. He was named Henry, after his grandfather, who must have been mightily relieved by the news. When the king left England for Normandy in August 1133, accompanied once again by Hugh Bigod, he intended to visit his new grandson and his daughter. Matilda may already have been pregnant again by then: she gave birth to a second son, named Geoffrey after his father, at Rouen in May 1134. This voyage was given a different significance in the end, however. Accompanied as it was by an eclipse and earthquakes, it turned out to be the king's last trip across the English Channel, a fact not lost on the chroniclers who wrote about it later.[18] That it took place on the anniversary of Henry's consecration in 1100 added to its ominous significance, and this only became more obvious to contemporaries as the final troubled phase of Henry's reign played itself out.

Whilst the birth of two grandsons secured Henry's dynastic plans in many ways, there was still a great deal of uncertainty about Count Geoffrey's present and future role. This issue was made more acute for a time immediately after Matilda had her second son: she fell gravely ill and her eventual recovery surprised everyone. Henry's long stay at Rouen over the summer of 1134 suggests a desire to be near to his daughter and his grandsons at this difficult time, and the fact that 'Matilda the Empress' features as the first witness to a charter given by Henry in that year at Rouen (Hugh Bigod was another witness) suggests that they were still reasonably close.[19] Nevertheless, as Matilda recovered and returned to her husband's care, so her relations with Henry began to deteriorate. For the old king, the most important person was his eldest grandson and his position needed to be safeguarded. Henry may have wanted to live long enough for the boy to succeed him immediately. But this was unlikely to happen, and the question arose of what the status of Geoffrey and Matilda would be when the old king was dead and their son a minor. There are indications that Matilda expected to succeed Henry as ruler of England and Normandy – what were all those oaths for if not for that? But if this happened, then contemporary practice would dictate that her husband ought to rule by right of his wife. In other words, when Henry died, Geoffrey was expecting to become the ruler of England and Normandy.

The argument turned in practice on the control of castles in strategically important locations. Geoffrey and Matilda demanded that Henry surrender control of certain fortified sites to them before he died, in particular those frontier castles promised as part of Matilda's dowry, so that they could put some military muscle behind their theoretical claims when the time came to take control. However, Henry refused to hand over any power at all, and his obduracy provoked Geoffrey into taking aggressive action of his own. He even went so far as to besiege and then burn down the castle of another of Henry's sons-in-law, Roscelin of Beaumont-sur-Sarthe. Tension was highest along the southern frontier of Normandy. There, Norman and Angevin lords with lands close to the border felt the pull of both sides. Between August and November 1135, Henry, in the words of one chronicler, 'prowled' this area, seizing the possessions of lords he suspected and shoring up the defences of his own castles.[20] His personal presence probably stopped matters getting completely out of hand, but this was no kind of permanent solution and Henry must have known it. So when he arrived at Lyons la Forêt at the end of November 1135, he would have been looking forward to forgetting his problems for a while and to getting on with some hunting. These problems were nonetheless considerable and growing. The king, of course, would never see them resolved.

It is clear from everything that is known about his career up to this point that Hugh Bigod was scrupulously loyal to Henry I. But despite the support he gave the new king in 1135, his relationship with Stephen would always be uneasy at best. It did not start well. After the king's Easter court at London in 1136, rumours quickly spread that Stephen was dead. They were not true, of course, but in this atmosphere of continuing political uncertainty Hugh Bigod seized Norwich Castle in an attempt to extend his influence out of Suffolk and into Norfolk.

Hugh refused to surrender the castle to anyone but the king himself and he eventually did so only when Stephen arrived outside the walls. This could be construed as a sign of Hugh's loyalty towards the king, but he relinquished control 'with great reluctance' according to Henry of Huntingdon, and the same chronicler saw this ominous sign as the start of all the 'faithlessness and treachery' that were to follow.[21] For, only two years after these events the internal peace England had enjoyed for over three decades was shattered.

In May 1138, Earl Robert of Gloucester, Henry I's illegitimate son and the empress's half-brother, declared his support for Matilda's claim to the throne. By the summer there were risings against Stephen in all parts of his kingdom. But the crucial event came a year or so later, on 30 September 1139, when Matilda and Robert landed on the south coast near Arundel. Civil war had begun and during 1140, as support for the empress became more widespread and public, the powerful men of the kingdom had to decide where their loyalties lay. One of these, of course, was Hugh Bigod. His influence in eastern England would have been an asset to king or empress, but Hugh's first concern was with his own best interests. After the events at Norwich in 1136 and until the end of 1137, Hugh maintained some kind of working relationship with the king and attended court. But from 1138 onwards there is less evidence of his being in the king's company and it may be that Stephen's handling of local politics in East Anglia was beginning to drive a wedge between them. It must have been galling for Hugh when he failed to become sheriff of Suffolk on the death of the incumbent in March 1138. And as the political scene became more unstable nationally from around that time, Hugh must have been waiting for his chance to make a point. So, twice in 1140 the king had to march into Suffolk to keep Hugh in line. On the first of these occasions, in January, he took Bigod's castle at Bungay into royal custody, but after the second occasion, in August, the two men came to terms. One chronicler says that their agreement did not last long, and this is true. But there was time enough for Hugh to be created earl of Norfolk, a title he held when he took part in the climactic battle of the civil war, at Lincoln, in early 1141.[22]

It is reasonable to see the award of the earldom as the price Stephen was prepared to pay for Hugh's support against Empress Matilda. And that support was soon needed more than ever before as the crisis of Stephen's reign approached. Some time before Christmas 1140, the castle of Lincoln had been seized by Ranulf, earl of Chester. Ranulf's power lay in northern England and the north Midlands, but he also had a long-standing claim to the castle. Stephen marched to Lincoln and made a deal with Ranulf, presumably feeling that the earl was too important a man to alienate. But their agreement allowed Ranulf to keep the castle and much else besides, and at his Christmas court Stephen probably encountered a storm of protest from other magnates about his generosity. Thinking better of what he had done, the king returned to Lincoln in January 1141 and laid siege to the castle. Ranulf managed to escape and looked for support to his father-in-law, none other than Robert of Gloucester. Ranulf and Robert then led a large army to Lincoln at the beginning of February. On the morning of 2 February battle was joined. In the front line of Stephen's army were six earls, including Hugh of Norfolk, but this did nothing to prevent the battle turning into a disaster for the royalists. All of the contemporary accounts stress the king's personal bravery and impressive martial skill, but his forces were outnumbered and after a brief and bitter struggle he was felled by a rock thrown at his helmet and captured. As for Hugh Bigod, like the others alongside him that morning in the king's front line who had not been either captured or killed, he had fled at the first charge of the empress's army. Orderic Vitalis later said that they panicked. But he also alleged that 'treachery ran wild' during the battle. Some of the magnates (he gives no names, unfortunately, and we will never know whether Hugh Bigod was one of them) betrayed Stephen when they 'joined the king with a handful of their men and sent the main body of their retainers to secure victory for their adversaries'.[23]

Defeat at Lincoln was a humiliating disaster for Stephen. Suddenly, it seemed inevitable that Matilda would become queen. However, supporters did not flock to the empress's banner immediately after the battle and her position remained precarious. Across the kingdom her support was patchy, strongest in the west but weak elsewhere. The archbishop of Canterbury, Theobald of Bec, refused to abandon Stephen unless the king stood down voluntarily; and this despite Stephen's own brother, Bishop Henry of Winchester, siding with Matilda in his capacity as papal legate in England and acknowledging her with the title 'Lady of England and Normandy'.[24] The support of the English nobility was not guaranteed either. Unnerved by the prospect of being ruled by a woman, many hesitated over their next step. But not Hugh Bigod. The empress refused to recognise the titles Stephen had bestowed since 1135, but at Oxford in April 1141 she granted the earldom of Norfolk to Hugh as a reward for his defection from the king's side after the battle of Lincoln and in the hope that he could bolster her cause in eastern England.

A more immediate priority, and one vital to any chance the empress had of retaining power, was control of London and Winchester, the homes of the royal administration and the royal treasury respectively. Her progress was slow. She eventually entered London in the summer of 1141 after she confirmed the Keeper of the Tower, Geoffrey de Mandeville, in the earldom of Essex, which Stephen had granted to him a year before. But she soon started to give offence. Contemporary observers remarked on her self-important and haughty manner – most unbecoming in a potential queen, they thought, although they would probably have seen such qualities in a man as admirable determination and resolve. The author of the *Gesta Stephani* was appalled when, as soon as Stephen was in captivity, Matilda 'put on an extremely arrogant demeanour instead of the modest gait and bearing proper to the gentle sex'.[25] Probably more importantly, she alienated London's merchant leaders by refusing to confirm their commercial privileges and by making extortionate financial demands of her own. They sent messages to Stephen's queen, also called Matilda, who had refused to give up the fight and was encamped with an army on the southern bank of the Thames, and on 24 June the Londoners drove the empress and her supporters out of the city.

Within a couple of months the empress had regrouped. By then, too, the game of political musical chairs had gone through a few more rounds. Bishop Henry of Winchester had abandoned the empress, partly because the pope had told him to do so, and he was attacked at Winchester by Matilda in August 1141. Her forces in turn were hemmed in by the queen's, and a double siege ensued from which the empress and her uncle King David of Scotland just managed to escape.

Many of her followers were seized, including Earl Robert of Gloucester. A deal was then struck by the two sides whereby, at the start of November 1141, Stephen was freed in return for Robert's release. It was probably clear by this time to all the leading participants in the war that the empress had lost any chance she had ever had of becoming queen. Partly because she was a woman, and partly because she had managed her campaign poorly since landing in England, her supporters now began to focus their energies on the cause of her young son, Henry. He was only eight years old at the end of 1141, but from this point onwards the empress's efforts were devoted to securing her son's inheritance rather than obtaining the Crown for herself.

For the next six years or so, the civil war was at its most intense and inconclusive. Looking back on this time over two decades later, the *Anglo-Saxon Chronicle* was sure that feeble kingship lay at the heart of the problem:

> When the traitors understood that [Stephen] was a mild man, and gentle and good, and did not exact the full penalties of the law, they perpetrated every enormity. They had done him homage, and sworn oaths, but they kept no pledge; all of them were perjured and their pledges nullified, for every powerful man built his castles and held them against him and they filled the country full of castles.[26]

It also painted a famously graphic picture of the horrors the defenceless English people experienced at the hands of the marauding armies. They plundered their resources, burnt their villages and destroyed their crops, and then, 'both by night and day they took those people that they thought had any goods – men and women – and put them in prison and tortured them with indescribable torture to extort gold and silver – for no martyrs were ever so tortured as they were'. All the same, these tortures were not so 'indescribable' as to go undescribed by the chronicler: the lucky ones were starved to death; whilst others were hanged by their thumbs, feet or neck; some had ropes tied tightly round their heads and the ropes were then 'twisted till they penetrated to the brains'; or they were pressed to death in a narrow chest full of sharp stones.[27] It was imagery like this that led historians in the nineteenth century to characterise Stephen's reign as 'the Anarchy' – a period when the king had lost control and his barons were able to do as they pleased at the expense of the innocent and the weak. More recent assessments have been less dramatic and more cautious about taking the chroniclers lurid opinions at face value. The consensus now is along the lines that, whilst there was violence in England during this period, there was no consistent pattern to it. It was patchy and intermittent. Some people suffered, to be sure, but the fighting was concentrated in certain areas, whilst others were largely unaffected. Views of the English aristocracy have developed and evolved too. The stereotypical image is of the turbulent, self-seeking nobleman with a passion for violence taking advantage of the power vacuum at the centre of politics and law to seize whatever he could get his hands on. Of course there were unscrupulous chancers amongst them, but, as a group, such men are more likely to be seen now as pragmatic and necessarily self-reliant, doing whatever they could to protect their own lands and rights and pass them on intact to their successors. For them the disappearance of a single, dominant, kingdom-wide authority presented many more problems than opportunities, and they simply had to make the best of things until normality was restored.

Hugh Bigod was no different from many in this respect. His power base was Suffolk, and the centre of that was his great castle at Framlingham. The indications are that, for the first half of the 1140s, Hugh ran the county much as he pleased. Now it would be easy to characterise his conduct during the 1140s as purely self-seeking, and of course to an extent it was. But his opposition to Stephen was steady and consistent after 1141. Nor were Hugh's actions just mindlessly brutal, and he had to work hard to maintain his position in East Anglia as his local rivals sensed an opportunity to undermine his influence there. As Hugh dominated Suffolk, the neighbouring county of Norfolk was controlled by two other families, the Warennes and the d'Aubignys. William de Warenne and William d'Aubigny had both been made earls (of Surrey and Arundel respectively) by Stephen, and they remained loyal to him throughout the civil war. They were vital to the royalist cause in providing a counter-weight to Earl Hugh's power in Suffolk. There was more to their rivalry than this, however, and here long-standing family grievances had a significant impact on political allegiances. The Bigods and the Warennes had vied for dominance in eastern England since the reign of William I, and as a result they had found themselves on opposite sides in succession disputes more than once before Stephen's reign. In 1088 the Warennes had supported William II whilst the Bigods backed Robert Curthose. By contrast, in 1101, Henry I had Roger Bigod on his side and William de Warenne had opted for Robert. But Hugh's antipathy towards the Warennes can only have intensified in about 1148 when William de Warenne's daughter and only surviving heir, Isabel, married the king's younger son, William of Blois. This move, at a crucial point in the civil war and in the same year as William de Warenne's death on crusade, gave Prince William control over the extensive Warenne estates and resources in Norfolk. It was made even more threatening to Hugh either then or shortly afterwards when the prince was also granted all the king's rights within Norfolk – this gave William control over the royal estates, income, tenants, castles and much more. His sudden entry into East Anglian politics and society was clearly designed to intimidate and pressurise the Bigods.

As for the Bigods and the d'Aubignys, even more pressing issues were at stake. When Roger Bigod died in 1107, his son William was a minor and so the family estates had passed into royal custody. During the minority, Henry I had given Roger's daughter Matilda to William d'Aubigny in marriage along with a significant slice of the Bigod estates as her dowry. Therefore their son, also called William as well as being Hugh Bigod's local rival in the 1140s, was also related to him (William's mother was Hugh's half-sister). But there was little family affection here. There can be no doubt that this loss of land and resources to William's father still rankled with Hugh Bigod in the 1140s.

But family ties could motivate men to fight alongside each other during the civil war as well as against one another. Hugh Bigod was married to a sister of Aubrey de Vere, as was another leading baron, Geoffrey de Mandeville. These three brothers-in-law all defected to the empress's side in 1141, and all three were made or confirmed as earls by her. Geoffrey soon returned to the royalist camp, but in 1143 the king arrested him on dubious grounds and at the prompting of Geoffrey's jealous rivals at court, and only freed him after he had surrendered all his castles and lands. On his release, Geoffrey vented his fury at the way he had been treated and, according to the anonymous author of the *Gesta Stephani* ('The Deeds of Stephen'), he 'raged everywhere with fire and sword', pillaging and plundering livestock and crops, and terrorising old and young. He seized Cambridge and drove the monks of Ramsey out of the abbey.[28] The king tried to respond by leading an army into Cambridgeshire, but Geoffrey retreated into the Fens where he was joined by many of the king's enemies, including his brother-in-law, Hugh Bigod, 'a man of distinction with influence in those parts, because he too, as has already been said, most vehemently troubled the king's peace and the king's forces, he set the whole country in a turmoil, showing cruelty everywhere and sparing nether sex nor rank'.[29] It was probably not a coincidence either that Geoffrey de Mandeville had an axe of his own to grind with William d'Aubigny over parts of the dower of the latter's second wife, which Geoffrey claimed were rightfully his. This alone can hardly have prompted Hugh Bigod to join forces in rebellion with Geoffrey on such a scale, but their common sense of injustice can only have heightened the hostility they felt towards the royalist side.

However, in 1145, Hugh went too far when he set about plundering the king's lands in Suffolk. His target may have been the royal castle of Eye, a few miles south of the Norfolk border. Stephen responded quickly by marching on Hugh's forces. He took Hugh (described in the *Gesta Stephani* at this point as 'the most restless opponent of his sovereignty') by surprise, captured some of his knights and ravaged his lands. The king then 'built three castles in that region, just where Hugh was most in the habit of raiding, [and] he remained there for a very long period'.[30] This incident was recounted in the *Gesta Stephani*, and it is fair to say that the author's sympathies remained very much with the king throughout his account of the civil war. Nevertheless, other evidence in the form of coins and royal writs does support the idea that the king tried to reassert royal control over Suffolk after the mid-1140s. The sheriffs of Norfolk and Suffolk for much of the 1140s and the early 1150s were Stephen's own tenants, and the king's installation of his son in Norfolk after 1148 must have been part of a wider plan to curb Bigod's power. Whether he was successful or not is another matter. In 1147, when the archbishop of Canterbury and several other bishops were received at Framlingham Castle, parts of Suffolk were still referred to by another chronicler as 'the land of Hugh Bigod'. And, certainly, the consistency of Hugh's opposition to Stephen after 1141 is striking. In 1149 he was still fighting and was described in the *Gesta Stephani* as 'an inveterate enemy of the king's cause'.[31]

By this time, though, the civil war was entering its final phase. Stephen had campaigned with great vigour during the 1140s. He had also been helped by the deaths of some of Matilda's most influential supporters (most notably Robert of Gloucester in October 1147), and by the empress's own departure from England in the spring of 1148. Nevertheless, Stephen's meaningful authority did not really stretch far beyond southern England and parts of the south-east, so the king lacked the resources and the support required to inflict the final blow on his enemies and England remained divided. Events outside the kingdom also conspired against Stephen and his cause. Across the Channel, large parts of Normandy had submitted to Geoffrey of Anjou, the empress's husband, in the early 1140s, and in 1143/4, after finally overrunning the rest of the duchy, he had become duke of Normandy as well as count of Anjou. Although Geoffrey never came to England himself, and never gave his wife the military or financial support that might have sustained her own cause there, they had the interests and claims of their eldest son, Henry, in common. Henry visited England several times, in 1142, 1147 and 1149. On those occasions he was a relatively powerless and impoverished boy. He had enough support to enable him to elude capture by Stephen in 1149; nonetheless his claim to the throne remained highly theoretical. But by the time Henry arrived in England for the fourth time, in 1153, the situation had been transformed. He was now nearly twenty years old. Moreover, since his last visit he had become one of the most powerful princes in Europe. Henry had been made duke of Normandy by his father in 1149 and he had become count of Anjou on Geoffrey's death in 1151. In the following year he had also become duke of Aquitaine by marrying the duchess, Eleanor. (This marriage took place only six weeks after Eleanor had been divorced by King Louis VII.) All of a sudden, Henry was in control of most of France and the rapid growth of his power shifted the momentum in England dramatically.

In January 1153, Henry landed in England to make his bid for the throne. The two sides manoeuvred inconclusively for much of the year. At one point, Henry successfully besieged Stamford in Lincolnshire and Stephen was unable to come to its relief because Hugh Bigod 'was attacking him very heavily at that time'.[32] Stephen gained some sort of victory over Hugh when he forced the earl to surrender Ipswich Castle to him. But this must have been a small consolation for the increasingly beleaguered king, and the stuffing was finally knocked out of the royalist cause when Stephen's eldest son Eustace died in August 1153. This ruined the king's plans for the succession (the English bishops had already refused to confirm Eustace as heir to the kingdom in 1152) and almost certainly added to his personal woes after the death of his wife in May 1152. So, although he had another son (Hugh Bigod's East Anglian rival, William), there was little enthusiasm on the part of the king or his supporters to carry on the struggle. In fact, there was no willingness on the part of the English barons to carry on fighting for either side. So, by the Treaty of Winchester of November 1153, both sides agreed to lay down their arms, and Stephen recognised Henry as his heir in return for lifelong possession of the throne.[33] Stephen's surviving son, William of Blois, also had to abandon his claim to the throne. In return he was allowed to keep his lands in England and Normandy. These included his assets in Norfolk, those he had acquired by marriage and from his father in the late 1140s. But the treaty made it clear that Hugh Bigod was still an earl. Little more than a year later, Stephen was dead and Henry II had become king. The civil war was over and Hugh Bigod had emerged from more than a decade of opposition to the Crown on the winning side. So, when the new king confirmed Bigod's status as earl of Norfolk right at the start of the reign, Hugh may well have expected to play a prominent role in the events to come.

The early years of Henry II's rule in England were dominated by his efforts to restore royal authority after twenty years of civil war. When Henry became king, the English kingdom had been reduced in size through the incursion of the king of Scots in the north, and elsewhere the king's power was patchy and intermittent. Royal lands had been given away, royal rights surrendered, and royal revenue was down by two-thirds from the level of the 1130s. Henry II's intention was to change all this and to recover everything that had been lost or given up. His model was Henry I and his plan was expressed in the charter he issued at the time of his coronation in December 1154:

> Know that for the honour of God and holy Church, and for the common restoration of my whole realm, I have granted and restored, and by this present charter confirmed, to God and holy Church, and to all my earls, barons and vassals all concessions, gifts, liberties and free customs, which King Henry, my grandfather, granted and conceded to them.[34]

Expressed as an act of royal generosity, this was in fact a clear warning to the English barons that the reign of Stephen now counted for nothing. Anything they had acquired after 1135, whether lands, titles, offices or rights, might now be taken away by the new king, whose objective was to master his whole kingdom, and all his subjects, as Henry I had done.

Henry II began by ordering the expulsion from England of Stephen's foreign mercenaries, the demolition of castles that had been built without royal permission, and the return of those strongholds which rightfully belonged to the Crown. Some barons resisted and defied the king, but soon enough Henry had intimidated and bullied them into submission. One who lost out was William of Blois, King Stephen's son, who had been made perhaps the most powerful magnate in England by the Treaty of Winchester. In clear contravention of the treaty's terms, Henry forced him to give up his castles at Pevensey, Eye, Lancaster and Norwich in 1157. But Hugh Bigod suffered as well. In the same year he handed over his castles in East Anglia to the king. These events have been variously interpreted and their precise significance, and relationship with each other, remain unclear. Some historians have argued that Henry confiscated William's castles and Hugh's together, as part of an attempt to neutralise their local rivalry, pre-empt the possibility of conflict between them and keep the peace. On this reading, William and Hugh gave up their castles grudgingly and resentfully and their sense of injustice lingered for the rest of their lives. On the other hand, it has also been argued that the king's actions were not aimed at William and Hugh personally. Rather this was all part of a strategy on Henry's part to place East Anglia under something like a state of emergency in anticipation of a French invasion that never materialised. Viewed in this light, Hugh and William complied with the king's demands more freely and perhaps even voluntarily. But Henry had probably been impatient to overturn the terms of the Treaty of Winchester since they had been agreed in 1153 – he can never have been happy with the lavishness of the concessions Stephen extracted for his son William and may have viewed William's extensive landholdings as an ongoing challenge to the new regime. William's death without heirs in 1159 was more than convenient for the king.

As for Earl Hugh, the evidence of his relationship with King Henry is ambivalent at best. Some survives to suggest that he was on cordial terms with the new king. Hugh was regularly at the royal court at the start of the reign, and after he lost his castles too. He acted as sheriff of Norfolk and Suffolk in 1154–5, and in 1157–8 – hardly the sort of job for a man who had lost royal favour. And in 1155, of course, Henry had confirmed Hugh as earl of Norfolk. Yet beyond this, the king's approach to Hugh during the first decade and a half of his reign was predominantly cautious and controlling. Hugh did not recover his most important castle, Framlingham, until 1165, and it is hard to think that the king's treatment of him in 1156–7 was not bruising at the very least. In 1163 Hugh was named as one of the hostages used by the king to guarantee the terms of a treaty with the count of Flanders, and in 1165 the royal records show that he owed the king nearly seventy pounds.[35] This may have been the amount that Hugh offered for royal permission to recover Framlingham and build his great new stone castle at Bungay. He paid half of this sum in the end, before the balance was waived by the king. But this act of royal munificence only happened in 1175/6, ten years after the original debt was incurred. What is more, it is likely that the huge amount Hugh had by then already paid had been used by the king over the same period to build his own castle on the Suffolk coast at Orford. With Orford fifteen miles from Framlingham and thirty from Bungay, it is possible that these three castles were designed as separate parts of an integrated system of coastal defence. But Orford must also have served as a reminder to Hugh about where power in

Norfolk ultimately lay. Scattered oddments of information like this are impossible to interpret coherently, but they hardly testify to a comfortable relationship between king and earl. And what is certain, as chapter 5 will show, is that Hugh still had one last act of rebellion in him. Maybe the sum of all these accumulated grievances was what propelled him into it.

It is also hard to know how to read the king's intervention on Hugh's behalf after the latter fell foul of Thomas Becket. Hugh had become involved in a dispute with the priory of Pentney, between King's Lynn and Swaffham in Norfolk, and he was excommunicated by the archbishop in 1166. Three years later, a royal council quashed the excommunication on the grounds that it contravened the Constitutions of Clarendon. Whatever the legal merits of this, the king had clearly taken Hugh's side. Yet he probably did this to get at the archbishop more than to support the earl of Norfolk, because by this time Henry II's quarrel with Thomas Becket was at its height and its most notorious phase was about to begin.

PART TWO

The Growth of an Empire

CHAPTER THREE

THE DISCIPLE'S TALE

Herbert of Bosham and the Becket Dispute

THE KING KNEW what to expect as he waited for the next man to enter the room. 'See, here comes a proud one,' Henry II remarked to his companions.[1] And he was right. Herbert of Bosham was tall, handsome and stylishly dressed. His splendid tunic and his cloak, which hung from his shoulders to his ankles (in the German style, it was said), were both made from the expensive green cloth of Auxerre. Herbert was also confident and poised in his conversation with the king – anything but intimidated, it seems, by Henry's fearsome reputation. They knew each other, of course. Herbert had once been a clerk in the royal chancery and the king had once been happy to entrust him with important missions abroad. But things were different now. The two men were on opposite sides of a bitter quarrel, at the centre of which was Herbert's master and Henry's former friend, Thomas Becket.

The meeting between Herbert and the king took place at Angers in the Loire valley on 1 May 1166. Henry had been celebrating Easter in the chief city of his ancestral duchy of Anjou when a group of visitors had arrived. No ordinary visitors either: at their head was Henry II's overlord, King Louis VII of France, whom Henry had arranged to meet. But accompanying Louis was the archbishop of Canterbury, Thomas Becket, and a group of the archbishop's clerks, including Herbert of Bosham. Becket had been in exile in France since he had fled from England in October 1164, and King Louis was keen to try and negotiate some sort of reconciliation between him and Henry. However,

Henry would not even meet Becket, and Louis was left to intercede on behalf of the archbishop's clerks on the grounds that they were innocent parties in the quarrel between the king and Becket. John of Salisbury was the first of the clerks to put his case to an impatient king. He did not fare well. He asked Henry to restore him to favour and return to him the ecclesiastical benefices he had lost through his support for Becket. John pleaded that he had committed no offence against the king and that he remained a loyal and devoted subject. Henry was firm, however: John would have to swear his fealty to the king against all men and promise to abide by what Henry claimed to be his own customary rights over the Church. But John had also sworn oaths of loyalty to the pope and to Becket. John was prepared to accept what the king did only if it was acceptable to them. Henry could not tolerate such dilution of his authority and John was dismissed from his presence. His journey had proved to be an expensive waste of time – £13 and two horses it had cost him, and all for nothing, John later complained.[2]

Herbert of Bosham was next into the room and he soon found himself in the same position as John of Salisbury. As he tried to reason with the king, he could not reconcile his desire to regain Henry's favour with the unconditional support he had sworn to give to his archbishop. Herbert was not going to miss his chance to tell the king what he thought, however, and there was no question of him meekly giving up. He told Henry how honest and loyal Becket was and that the king should value a servant who spoke his mind much more than any obsequious flatterer. And as for the so-called 'customs' that the king set so much store by, Herbert criticised Henry's attempt to have them set down in writing. There were many evil customs relating to the Church in France and in the lands of the king of the Germans, Herbert said, but they were not written down and therefore could more easily be abolished. Henry took offence at Herbert's reference to his fellow monarch, Frederick I. 'Why do you slight him by not calling him emperor?' he demanded to know. Herbert replied, 'He is the king of the Germans, but when he writes he writes "Emperor of the Romans forever triumphant".' Herbert's tone was now making Henry increasingly angry and the king's famous temper was starting to show. 'For shame!' he exclaimed, 'Does this son of a priest trouble my kingdom and disturb my peace?'

But Herbert refused to be cowed and went further still. 'Not I indeed,' he answered back, 'nor am I the son of a priest, since I was not conceived in the priesthood, for my father became a priest afterwards; nor is he the son of a king unless his father was king when he was born.' This was pointedly a reference to the fact that King Henry's father, Geoffrey of Anjou, had never been more than a mere count. To say the least, Herbert was being provocative, and after a speechless moment a furious Henry ordered Herbert to leave and out the proud fellow went. One of Henry's barons was left to comment admiringly on Herbert's performance: 'Well whoever's son he is, I would give half my land for him to be mine!'[3]

This tale is important because it displays the dogged and unflinching way in which Herbert of Bosham confronted authority of any kind. He could not be easily intimidated or bullied. He was a man of strict, stern and unbending opinions, and he was also Thomas Becket's closest friend and most tenacious supporter. Herbert wrote one of the dozen or so accounts of Becket's life that were composed soon after the archbishop's murder to support his claims to sainthood. Many of these other writers had known Becket personally, but none had known him as well as Herbert and none had stood so loyally alongside the archbishop throughout the traumas of the 1160s or influenced his conduct so much. This makes Herbert's account of the dispute invaluable, but it also makes it challenging. Of course Herbert was convinced of the justice of Becket's cause and of his sanctity, and he was sure that his enemies had conspired to destroy him. So Herbert's is not an impartial account of what happened. Nevertheless, it is an insider's account and all the more remarkable for that.

* * * *

The quarrel between Henry II and Thomas Becket is one of the most famous episodes of the Middle Ages. It is dramatic and ultimately tragic, conventionally told as a story of two friends forced apart by their stubborn bloody-mindedness, and ultimately culminating in Becket's savage murder at Canterbury Cathedral on 29 December 1170. The killing of an archbishop in his own church, with the king himself deeply implicated in what happened, was the great scandal of its time. Becket was immediately seen as a martyr; within a few years he had been canonised and his shrine would be one of Europe's most popular pilgrimage destinations for centuries to come. But there was more to this controversy than the larger-than-life personalities involved, because the Becket dispute was about political and spiritual power: who had it and by what right? At stake, as far as Henry II was concerned, was control over an English kingdom so recently torn apart by civil war. For him, this meant not just control over the political systems and leading laymen of England, but control over the Church and clergy within the kingdom too. For Becket, however, Church and clergy were independent and autonomous, not subject to any kind of secular authority. These two points of view, when taken to their extremes, were irreconcilable. And when they were firmly held in opposition by two powerful men, conflict was inevitable.

But if this quarrel was not just about individuals, nor was it just about England. In a sense the king and the archbishop were merely the representatives of a much wider struggle that was being played out across Europe during the twelfth century. Only a hundred years before, it had been largely taken for granted that secular rulers should exercise enormous amounts of power over the administration and personnel of the Church within their kingdom, duchy or county. They cherished in particular their power to select new archbishops, bishops and abbots – and with good reason. The Church controlled vast resources. Therefore influence over its lands, the money they produced and the people who lived on them were vital to a lay ruler's political power. Meanwhile the pope in Rome remained a distant celebrity, with little practical control outside central Italy. Unable significantly to influence the clergy of England, France, Germany or Spain, he remained a figurehead at best. From the 1050s onwards, however, this started to change as the principles of the so-called 'Gregorian Reform' movement began to spread. Named after Pope Gregory VII (r.1073–85), the ideas central to his reforming agenda were actually first enunciated by one of his predecessors, Pope Leo IX (r.1049–54). Leo's aim had been to purify the clergy and separate it from worldly affairs: his main targets were the two abuses of simony (the buying and selling of positions within the Church) and clerical marriage, which was widespread. With their emphasis on money on the one hand and sex on the other, these practices represented the wider entanglement of the Church in materialistic, sinful lifestyles. Gregory VII took this agenda further. Of course the clergy should renounce greed and live chaste lives, but the hold of secular rulers over the Church should be broken too. They had no right to appoint bishops, Gregory argued, and certainly no right to conduct the ceremony, known as 'investiture', in which they handed the new bishop the symbols of his office, his episcopal ring and staff. For Gregory, the investiture of a bishop by a secular ruler suggested that the former owed his power to the latter (in other words, that the Church was subordinate to the State), when, in fact, it was the secular ruler who owed his position to the Church. What Gregory was outlining amounted to a revolution in the relationship between the priestly order, the *sacerdotium*, and the lay power, the *regnum*. He aimed to free the Church entirely from the dominance of secular rulers and, even more radically, to place the papacy firmly at the head of the Church with a real, meaningful say over how the Church within a particular kingdom, duchy or county should be run.

Unsurprisingly, not everyone who learnt of Gregory's ideas approved of them or of the way he went about voicing them. However, responses differed. Emperor Henry IV (r.1056–1106), for example, became involved in a bitter and sometimes violent struggle with Gregory, going so far as to declare him deposed and appoint his own pope. William I of England (r.1066–87), by contrast, more or less ignored what Gregory was trying to do and carried on as normal. However, whilst Gregory's confrontational stance led eventually to his own failure (he died in exile from Rome, with the imperial pope inserted there in his place), his ideas did not die with him. By the 1120s, rulers across Europe had given up the practice of lay investiture, and the power of the papacy was spreading steadily through other channels: the use of Church councils and synods which bishops from across Europe attended, papal legates who visited individual territories and pressed papal claims to supremacy, and, perhaps most importantly, through the spread of canon law.

Canon law, in the most general sense, is the law of the Church. It has been derived over the centuries from a wide range of authorities, most notably the Bible and the writings of the Church Fathers (men like St Augustine and St Jerome). However, canon law was never static and has always continued to evolve. The decisions (known as 'canons') against abuses such as simony and clerical marriage made at papal synods and reforming councils during this period had the status of law, for example, as did many of the pronouncements (known as 'decretals') in papal letters. By the eleventh century, however, there was no universally agreed or codified body of canon law, and the vast pile of conciliar and synodal decisions, papal decretals and the rest, which all counted as law, were not systematically organised or arranged. Different canons made at different times might conflict with one another, and there was no way of deciding which was to be preferred in a particular set of circumstances. However, as ideas on papal authority developed from the 1050s, the reforming popes began to appreciate the importance of canon law in reinforcing their claims to superiority and jurisdiction over the whole of Christendom. Thus, collections of canon law were produced by the supporters of Gregorian reform, and they were designed to support the papacy's arguments. Undoubtedly the most important of these was Gratian's *Decretum*. Gratian was a canon lawyer in Bologna, the European centre of legal studies, in the first half of the twelfth century. The *Decretum*, which was first published in the early 1140s, is a collection of nearly 3,800 canonical texts touching on all areas of Church discipline and regulation. The work is not just a collection of texts, however, but also a treatise attempting to resolve the apparent contradictions and discordances in the rules accumulated from different sources.

Once progress had been made towards agreeing the substance of canon law, institutional structures had to be put in place to make sure that those laws were enforced strictly. This gave the papacy its chance. The papal curia in Rome had always, in theory, been the final court of appeal in spiritual matters. Whilst the papacy was weak and lacking in influence, however, litigants rarely used this option. Even under Gregory VII, relatively few cases ever reached Rome. However, the sudden availability of a reinvigorated papal curia stimulated an enthusiasm for papal justice, which soon spread. One single dispute, for example, the contest for spiritual supremacy in England between the archbishops of Canterbury and York, was referred to Rome no fewer than six times between 1102 and 1126. Much smaller disputes, about the payment of tithes or the location of parish boundaries, could just as easily be adjudicated in Rome too. And it was not only the clergy who were

affected by this. The lives of ordinary laymen and women were dominated by the rules of the Church. Church courts had authority over all
sorts of personal matters: marriage, the legitimacy of children, rape,
bigamy, incest and other family relationships; wills and testaments too.

By the 1160s, therefore, when Henry II was king of England and
Thomas Becket archbishop of Canterbury, these developments were
already well under way and the Church, under increasingly assertive
papal leadership, had gone a long way to asserting its independence of
lay control and its power over the lives of all Christians across Europe.
Popes were making law, interpreting it and enforcing it, either in person
or through representatives directly answerable to Rome. The system
was not yet fully formed and it did not always work as well in practice
as it did in theory. But the development of canon law, and of the structures and mechanisms that enabled it to function in a practical way, was
one of the great achievements of the papacy in the century and a half
after 1050. By 1200 the pope in Rome was at the heart of a centralised
system of ecclesiastical government and justice. It was a truly international system too, which cut across national and local law and helped to
make the presence of the papacy felt at all levels of society throughout
western Christendom. The popularity of papal justice, moreover, showed
that people had faith in the effectiveness of this new regime. The power
that had always existed in theory could now be backed up by clear and
well-defined rules and by meaningful coercive authority. It was in this
context that the Becket Dispute took place.

* * * *

Little is known about the early life of Herbert of Bosham. Bosham
itself, almost certainly where Herbert was born, is in Sussex, about six
miles west of Chichester. It was memorialised forever in the Bayeux
Tapestry as the place where Earl Harold Godwineson of Wessex prayed
and feasted before his fateful trip to Normandy in 1064 or 1065. Bosham
was one of Harold's most important and richest manors (it had an
annual value of £40 in 1086, according to Domesday Book), and it was
the only estate in Sussex retained in his own hands by William the
Conqueror after 1066. It is intriguing to wonder whether the connections between Herbert's family and the manor of Bosham stretched

back that far, and whether Herbert had heard stories from his grand-
parents about the great Earl Harold, and about the upheavals that
affected the Sussex coastline and its hinterland before and after the
Battle of Hastings. We can be fairly sure, though, that Herbert's father
became a priest after his son was born (Herbert told Henry II as much
himself during their meeting at Angers in 1166) – one of the ministers
of the royal chapel at Bosham perhaps – and that Herbert was destined
for a religious life of some kind from a young age.

Herbert must have had a good early education, probably learning the
Psalms from a local priest or other clergyman to ground him in the
basics of Latin, and he eventually crossed the English Channel to
further his studies in Paris. During the first half of the twelfth century,
Paris and Bologna became established as the two most important
centres of learning in western Europe. In the Paris schools, ambitious
young men could learn the more advanced and sophisticated Latin
required to take up service in the household of a high-status lay lord or
a bishop. Beyond that, they could also study theology, canon law or
Roman law, which still formed the basis of legal systems across Europe.
This was a time when great teachers like Peter Abelard and Hugh of St
Victor attracted students to Paris from all corners of the Christian West.
And it was another of these eminent scholars, Peter Lombard, who
taught Herbert of Bosham. Peter had arrived in Paris in the mid-1130s
and he taught there into the 1150s (he became bishop of Paris in 1159),
so Herbert must have been there sometime between these dates. In this
environment he became an excellent Latinist and rhetorician, skilled in
the arts of letter-writing and diplomacy. He also acquired a good knowledge of Hebrew. By the end of his studies Herbert was entitled, like all
the graduates of the Paris schools, to use the title 'Master'.

In the middle of the twelfth century there may have been around
three thousand students in Paris, about 10 per cent of the city's total
population. The schools were concentrated on the Île de la Cité, and
around, even on, the Petit Pont that joined the Île to the Left Bank of
the river Seine. Herbert was only one of a number of Englishmen who
studied in Paris during the 1130s and 1140s. John of Salisbury, who was
to plead his case so unsuccessfully before Henry II at Angers in 1166,
arrived there in 1136, stayed for the next twelve years, and made a

reputation for himself as a great scholar. And Thomas Becket himself studied in Paris for a couple of years from about 1138. Becket was probably born late in 1120, and so he was maybe eighteen when he went to Paris. It is quite possible that Herbert was roughly the same age as his future master, and that it was in Paris that he met Becket, and indeed John of Salisbury, for the first time.

At this point, however, the careers of the three men started to take their own shapes. John of Salisbury prospered in Paris, whilst Becket gave up his studies there and, on returning to England, took a job handling the accounts of one of his relatives, a financier in the City of London. This did not last long, though, and he was soon presented to the archbishop of Canterbury, Theobald. Theobald must have liked what he saw in Becket because he immediately recruited him into his household. Here Becket joined a group of men whose main task was to serve Theobald's administrative and legal needs; Becket and his colleagues were the archbishop's secretaries and messengers. However, there was much more to this particular household. Its members were remarkably able and talented. Amongst them were three future archbishops and six bishops. And it was in this energising but undoubtedly competitive environment that Becket met for the first time some of the men who would play leading roles in the controversy to come, notably Roger de Pont l'Évêque, the future archbishop of York, and Bartholomew, later bishop of Exeter. No less a figure than John of Salisbury had also joined the household by 1147–8 and he remained in the archbishop's service for the next twelve years.

Becket now found himself involved in the affairs of Church and State at the highest levels. He was sent for a year to study law at Bologna and Auxerre, and went on several missions to the papal court where he probably met at least one pope, Eugenius III, and several cardinals, at least two of whom later became popes themselves. These connections would be important in the later crises of Becket's life. Meanwhile, in England, the high point of this phase of Becket's career came in 1154. When Archbishop Theobald secured the archbishopric of York for one of his former clerks, Roger de Pont l'Évêque, he gave the archdeaconry of York, which Roger had held until then, to Becket. The archdeaconry was the centrepiece of an assortment of benefices which

Becket gradually acquired during his time on the archbishop's staff, including St Mary-le-Strand in London, Otford in Kent, Bramfield in Hertfordshire, the provostship of Beverley in Yorkshire, and prebends in London and Lincoln cathedrals.

Becket was prospering (the archdeaconry of York alone gave him a substantial income of £100 per year), but he was also on the fast track to even higher office. In the same year that he became archdeacon of York, 1154, Henry II succeeded to the English throne. He wanted a new chancellor and Archbishop Theobald's recommendation of Becket for the post was accepted by the king. The chancellor supervised the king's chancery, or writing office, where royal charters granting lands, offices and privileges were written and royal orders and letters were drafted. All of these documents were authenticated with an impression of the king's seal, which was in the chancellor's custody. According to one contemporary, William Fitz Stephen, who worked in Becket's chancery, the chancellor had no fewer than fifty-two clerks working under him there.[4] They carried out the routine, day-to-day business of government, at a time when the king's administration was becoming more bureaucratic and professionalised than ever before. However, there was more to the chancellor's duties than the production of documents. Fitz Stephen described the chancellor as 'second to the king in the realm', implying a general all-round authority. He was in charge of the royal chapel, and thus intimately involved in the king's spiritual provision; he supervised the administration of lay and ecclesiastical estates in the interval between the death of one lord and the installation of another; and, perhaps most importantly, the chancellor 'attends all the king's councils to which he does not even require a summons'.[5] In other words, the chancellor was entitled and expected to advise the king on all matters of policy and planning. And in Becket's case, the role was augmented further still. He and King Henry became great friends very quickly. 'Never in Christian times were there two greater friends, more of one mind,' claimed Fitz Stephen.[6] The king and his chancellor travelled together regularly in England and France. Henry also entrusted Becket with missions abroad. In 1158 the chancellor negotiated a marriage between Henry's infant son and the even younger daughter of King Louis of France, and in 1161 the six-year-old prince was placed in Becket's care. The chancellor was also involved in the king's military campaigns in France in 1159 and 1161. He was at the heart of everything Henry II did to restore royal power at the start of his reign.

Herbert of Bosham probably assisted Becket on many of these occasions, because by 1157 he had joined the chancery staff. Whether he was already a chancery clerk in 1154, or was recruited when Becket became chancellor, is unclear. However, by the end of the 1150s Herbert had begun to contribute in his own way towards the implementation of Henry II's plans. Henry's overriding aim on becoming king was to re-establish royal power after the chaos of Stephen's reign. This meant restoring it geographically and politically so that the king's authority covered the whole of his kingdom meaningfully once again. But it also meant restoring the status quo in the king's dealings with the English Church. Henry II wanted to exercise power over the Church in England in the same way he thought his Norman predecessors had done. That is to say, he expected to control it personally to a significant degree and get his way over such things as the appointment of bishops and the resolution of disputes. The king was also determined to restrict the opportunities for external powers, principally the papacy, to influence ecclesiastical affairs within England, and he was prepared to intervene aggressively in the Church's business if he thought his royal rights were in any way at stake or, indeed, just flex his royal muscles and remind everyone of who was in charge. Henry got a chance to do this in 1157, when he became involved in a long-standing dispute between the bishop of Chichester and the abbot of Battle. The abbey of St Martin's, Battle, was in the diocese of Chichester, but it claimed to be exempt from the authority of the bishop. The abbey had never received a papal exemption, but relied instead on its special relationship with the English kings; it had been founded by William the Conqueror as an expression of gratitude and act of penance after the Battle of Hastings. Under King Stephen it had retained its autonomy, but after Stephen's death Bishop Hilary of Chichester had excommunicated the abbot, who had in turn appealed to the papacy. The appeal backfired, however, as Hilary obtained from both popes Eugenius III and Adrian IV orders for the abbot to obey the bishop. In May 1157 the then abbot of Battle, Walter de Luci, brother of Richard de Luci, the king's chief justiciar, took the case before Henry II, at a council held at Colchester. At the council Abbot Walter produced William I's foundation charter and its confirmation by Henry I, Henry II's grandfather. In 1155, Henry II had confirmed the validity of both these documents, putting himself directly at odds with the papal position. At the 1157 council, though, Bishop Hilary was bold enough to argue that no king could grant such an exemption, unless he had a licence from the papacy. Henry was unimpressed by this idea, as it implied that there were limits to his power over the Church and that the pope's authority in such matters was superior to the king's. To reinforce his points, the king ordered Becket to defend the abbot's case; the chancellor enthusiastically complied and the bishop was eventually forced to back down and accept the king's decision.

It is now accepted by modern scholars, and it was probably known to many of the participants in the dispute, that the documents relied on by Abbot Walter were at best of doubtful authenticity and at worst forged. This is not the point, however. Henry II intervened in the Battle Abbey case not because of its intrinsic merits one way or the other, but so that he could show to everyone the kind of dominance he expected to have over the English Church. The plain fact of the matter is that the abbot won his case not because right was on his side, but because the king decided that he should; and the most enthusiastic supporter of the king's position seems to have been Thomas Becket.

As a Sussex man, born and brought up so close to Chichester, Herbert of Bosham would have taken a keen interest in the outcome of this case. Was he as ardent an advocate of royal power over the Church at this stage as his master the chancellor? Or did he feel squeamish about the way the king had bullied the parties into making the decision he wanted them to reach? If Herbert had any misgivings, he must have kept them to himself, because he was soon being entrusted with the conduct of important royal business. In July 1157, shortly after the resolution of the Battle case, the king sent Herbert from his great council at Northampton on an embassy to Emperor Frederick I. At Würzburg on 28 September 1157, Herbert presented Henry's letter, which had been witnessed by Becket, to the emperor. It explained why Henry could not return an important holy relic, the hand of St James, which his mother, the Empress Matilda, had brought to England when widowed in 1125, and which in 1133 her father, Henry I, had transferred to his abbey at Reading.

This is a good example of Becket and Herbert working together for the king. This, after all, was their job as royal servants. Another of Becket's clerks, William Fitz Stephen, later commented how 'the noble realm of England was renewed, as if it were a new spring' by the efforts of Henry's earls and barons, but principally 'through the industry and counsel of the chancellor'.[7] Fitz Stephen, indeed, paints a remarkably colourful picture of the condition of England at this time: 'The realm . . . was enriched, the horn of plenty was filled to the brim. The hills were cultivated, the valleys abounded in corn, the pastures with cattle and the folds with sheep.' And at the heart of all this prosperity was Chancellor Thomas Becket. He was popular with everyone, generous and affable. His house and table 'were open to the needs of any visitors to the king's court of whatever rank . . . Hardly a day did he dine without earls and barons as guests.' There are hints here of the enjoyment Becket took in sumptuous living: 'His house glistened with gold and silver vases, and abounded in precious food and drink.'[8] These appetites were most clearly revealed when Becket went to France in 1158 to negotiate the marriage between Henry II's son and Louis VII's daughter. The chancellor's entourage was extraordinary: about two hundred men on horseback travelled with him, all dressed in magnificent new clothes. Becket himself, Fitz Stephen said, took twenty-four changes of clothing with him.[9] There were hunting dogs and birds, all kinds of food and drink, and the chancellor's own furnishings ('gold and silver, vessels, cups, bowls, goblets, casks, jugs, basins, salt cellars, spoons, dishes and fruit-bowls') were carried in eight cases by twelve carthorses.[10] The procession also contained singers and exotic animals. Becket clearly revelled in his status and used his closeness to the king to indulge in this kind of conspicuous display. But for men like William Fitz Stephen and Herbert of Bosham, who later wrote about their master's life in order to bolster his claims to sanctity, such luxurious and earthly pursuits presented a problem and had to be explained away, not as evidence of Becket's worldly shallowness, but of his generosity and, overwhelmingly, of his devotion to the king. He gave great banquets and entertained lavishly, not for his own sake, but as selfless acts of open-handedness towards his guests. And when he paraded in pomp through a French village, he was not showing off but honouring his royal master. Fitz Stephen records how this affected the French: 'If this is how the chancellor proceeds,' they argued, 'how great the king must be!'[11] In any event, his supporters argued, this was not the real Becket: his true character remained quietly hidden away beneath the layers of worldly display. He gave alms to the poor and gifts to his friends; he would visit churches at night and in disguise to pray, and he was whipped in secret so as to mortify his sinful flesh and suppress any impure urges. According to Fitz Stephen, Becket remained celibate after becoming chancellor 'and kept his loins girded'.[12]

When Archbishop Theobald of Canterbury died in April 1161, Henry II was determined that Thomas Becket should succeed him. Henry wanted Becket to be as reliable and effective a leader of the English Church as he had been of the king's government. Indeed, the king seems to have foreseen no difficulty about Becket performing both roles at once: he could continue to help Henry rebuild his political power whilst doing the same with the king's authority over the Church. Henry thought Becket would, in the words of one contemporary, 'follow his desire in all things'.[13] The chancellor, however, was uncertain: surely his loyalties would now be divided? How could he serve both king and Church equally well? And, what is more, Becket had serious doubts about his own qualifications for the job: he was no great scholar, he had never been a monk, and he knew there were those among the English bishops who thought they would make a much better archbishop. Herbert of Bosham later described how Becket responded when the king told him of his plan. As he looked down at his fancy clothes, the chancellor remarked with heavy irony, 'How religious, how saintly a man you wish to appoint to such a holy see and above such a renowned and holy community of monks.' More telling still, however, was Becket's prediction about how such an appointment would expose him to attack from all sides and lead only to strife. He warned the king, 'I know indeed that you would demand much, and even now you presume a great deal in ecclesiastical matters, which I would not be able to tolerate with equanimity.'[14] Henry was untroubled by any such misgivings and went ahead with the required formalities.

The new archbishop of Canterbury could not simply be appointed by the king. First, he had to be elected by the appropriate body and then consecrated. There were two sets of electors in this case: the monks of Christ Church, Canterbury, and the bishops of the Canterbury province. Most of these men were almost certainly unhappy at the prospect of Becket's promotion, and in theory they could elect another candidate entirely. However, they were well aware that, if they did, they would provoke the king and that could have any number of dangerous consequences. To make sure that the first 'free' election, by the monks, went in Becket's favour, the king sent his chief justiciar, Richard de Luci, Richard's brother, Abbot Walter of Battle and three bishops to remind them what the king expected. Richard de Luci reassured the monks that the king wanted them to have a free election, but made it clear that the person elected should be 'equal to such a burden, worthy of the honour and pleasing to the king'.[15] Herbert of Bosham described later how some monks tried to resist this royal pressure: Becket was the king's man, they argued, the Church would be vulnerable in his hands, and anyway it was wrong 'for a man chained by the military belt rather than the monastic office, a follower and pastor of hounds and hawks, to be established as pastor of the sheep'.[16] Such anxieties were put to one side, however; the monks had got the king's message and they proceeded to elect Thomas Becket as their new archbishop. The bishops followed suit, probably no more than a few days later, on 23 May 1162 at the end of a meeting in the refectory of Westminster Abbey. Some disquiet was voiced; the bishop of Hereford, Gilbert Foliot, who probably wanted the archbishopric for himself, objected to Becket's appointment.[17] But the appearance of unanimity was eventually preserved and Becket's promotion was approved.

Many of those involved in Becket's election would have been deeply troubled by his appointment. Perhaps they remembered the dinners and parties they had attended at his house, or the reports of how he had behaved on his embassy to France. Some of them would have looked down their noses at him as the son of a London merchant, a man whose spiritual qualities seemed obviously lacking. But perhaps most alarming was Becket's reputation as the king's right-hand man. How could he square his new responsibilities to the Church with his old relationship with Henry? Becket certainly knew the vultures would soon be circling. As he travelled from London to Canterbury for his consecration, he took Herbert of Bosham aside and spoke to him in private. 'This I desire, this I instruct you,' he said to Herbert, 'that whatever men say about me, you tell me boldly and in private. And if I fail in any of my work, as I say, I enjoin you to tell me freely and confidently, but secretly. For many things may be said about me from now on which are not said to me ... Likewise, also point out any transgressions that you see and judge to be so.' He concluded, 'Certainly four eyes see more circumspectly and clearly than two.' As he was ordained a priest on 2 June 1162, and as he was consecrated archbishop by the bishop of Winchester in Canterbury Cathedral the following day, the merchant's son from the rough streets of London must have wondered how on earth things had come to this. Meanwhile Herbert, now the new archbishop's most intimate and trusted adviser and his self-styled 'disciple', was already measuring the responses to these remarkable events.[18]

Herbert remained at the archbishop's side for most of the next seven and a half years. He went with Becket to Pope Alexander III's general council at Tours in May 1163. Herbert's own description of the event emphasises how much Becket was feted and honoured by the great and the good at the council. But 1163 and 1164 were dominated by the collapse of Becket's relationship with Henry II. This was a personal quarrel, of course, made much worse because the leading players were close former friends as well as men of extraordinary pertinacity. But there were also major issues of principle at stake, most importantly those concerning the limits of royal and ecclesiastical jurisdiction in England. During King Stephen's reign, it is probably fair to say that the autonomy of the English Church had developed at the expense of the king. In the thirty years after the death of Henry I, ecclesiastical affairs had been managed relatively free, albeit not completely, of royal interference. Papal influence over English ecclesiastical affairs had increased, too, particularly through the growing number of appeals on matters of canon law sent to Rome by the English Church courts. These changes were not unique to England. Across western Europe since the middle of the eleventh century, papal power had been expanding and ideas about the independence of the clergy had been gaining ground. Nevertheless,

Henry II viewed such trends as threats to his control over his kingdom and he was determined to slow them down and, in due course, reverse them. However, the king's hope that Becket would support his plans to reassert royal authority over the English Church was immediately dealt a blow when his new archbishop resigned the royal chancellorship straight after his election. He could not serve two masters, Becket said, and his first duty was now to God, not the king. And these were not just words. Becket's biographers were later keen to stress how much he changed after becoming archbishop. He was like 'a man awaking from a deep sleep', according to Herbert of Bosham. And William of Canterbury, who became a monk at Canterbury during Becket's exile, wrote of how Becket was transformed from the worldly courtier into 'another man ... more restrained, more watchful, more frequent in prayer, more attentive in preaching'. And it was at this time, too, that Becket secretly started wearing a hair shirt under his clerical vestments. This 'breastplate of faith', as William called it, was a means of constant bodily mortification and ongoing penance.[19]

Becket also had points to prove to his critics within the Church itself. The monks of Canterbury expected him to protect their estates and defend their rights, whilst the bishops waited for him to give them a lead. Inevitably, if he was to satisfy these two groups Becket would make enemies elsewhere and, sooner or later, he would have to challenge the king's view of his own royal rights. He did so over some specific issues at first. The king was outraged when Becket excommunicated one of Henry's tenants in chief without royal permission, and at the Council of Woodstock in July 1163, Becket refused Henry's order to make the traditional payment from the Canterbury estates (the so-called 'sheriffs' aid') directly into the royal treasury rather than to the sheriffs themselves. Henry's fury at Becket's intransigence (as he saw it) quickly grew. Becket, for his part, and no doubt with Herbert of Bosham confirming his suspicions, was increasingly convinced that the king was moving towards an all-out assault on the powers of the Church. The quarrel soon crystallised around a single issue, the status of clergymen who committed serious crimes (so-called 'criminous clerks'). To Becket, principle and practice were both clear. The clergy formed a separate order within the kingdom, and the Church had its own courts for trying them and its own punishments if they were found guilty. However, King Henry saw the issues very differently. He was the keeper of the royal peace and the guarantor of law and order in his kingdom. He could not tolerate the notion that large numbers of his subjects (there were thousands of men in religious orders of some kind in twelfth-century England) were automatically beyond the reach of his justice. Criminals should be dealt with in his courts and punished there for their crimes. And, in any event, the worst punishment an ecclesiastical court could impose was to remove a man's clerical status. What sort of deterrent was this, Henry argued, to the determined criminal? So, in October 1163 at the Council of Westminster, the king demanded that clerks accused of serious crimes, once they had been tried and convicted in an ecclesiastical court, should be handed over to his officials for trial and punishment (most likely mutilation or execution) in a secular court. This was probably not as challenging a notion in practice as it sounded in theory, as clerks convicted in a church court were not actually retried in a lay court; rather, they were sentenced there to an appropriate secular punishment. Nevertheless, Becket and his supporters interpreted the king's demand in the most threatening way possible and held firm to the idea that it was wrong in principle for a man to be tried and punished twice for the same offence. More broadly, the royal directive struck at the heart of the idea that the clergy was a separate group which regulated its own affairs. Not surprisingly, the king's orders were rejected.

The increasingly indignant king responded to this rebuff by making another, much bigger demand, this time that the bishops should give their consent to what he described as his 'royal customs'. When they met Henry at Clarendon in January 1164, it immediately became clear what this meant. The king's scribes had been busy and a document had been drawn up which claimed to list the customs and practices that had regulated the English Church during the reign of Henry I. His grandson simply wanted the English bishops to acknowledge that these customs were still in force. However, in their scope and detail they went far beyond anything Becket and his followers had already rejected. And they were also novel and dangerous simply because they were written down. This gave them a definitive sense of finality which, as Herbert of Bosham perceptively remarked to the king at Angers in 1166, made them much less easy to abolish. According to the king's document, which became known as the Constitutions of Clarendon, bishops could not leave the kingdom and tenants in chief could not be excommunicated without royal permission; appeals from Church courts in England could not be taken to Rome unless the king allowed it; and elections of bishops and abbots were to take place in the king's chapel. And as for 'criminous clerks', they were to be dealt with as the king had stipulated at Westminster in the previous year.[20]

Together the Constitutions amounted to a wholesale reassertion of royal control over the English Church, as if the developments of the previous century had never happened. But to the amazement of his bishops, and after initially condemning the Constitutions, Becket agreed to accept them. The archbishop immediately regretted this and Herbert of Bosham was left to console him in his distress at what he had done. St Peter himself had denied Christ three times, but from these depths he had risen to even greater righteousness; Becket would recover too, Herbert argued.[21] But if this reassured the archbishop to any degree, the king only saw Becket's capitulation at Clarendon as a sign of weakness and as an invitation to go further still. With Becket isolated and the bishops bewildered, in October 1164 Henry summoned Becket to Northampton and charged him with corruption during his time as chancellor. The king wanted to use these vindictively trumped-up charges to force Becket to resign as archbishop, and several bishops, most vociferously Becket's old rival Gilbert Foliot, now bishop of London, also tried to persuade him to stand down. Instead, before sentence could be passed against him, the archbishop fled in disguise from the court with a handful of followers and went into hiding. As they escaped from Northampton Castle, Herbert of Bosham was unable to mount his horse and Becket had to carry him away on his. Herbert was then sent to Canterbury to collect as much money as he could before meeting up with Becket once again at the abbey of St Bertin in Flanders. From this point on, to his friends Becket was the persecuted defender of the liberties of the Church; to his enemies, he was a cowardly traitor on the run from royal justice.

By the time Herbert reached St Bertin early in November 1164 he had managed to collect only a few silver vases and less than £70 in cash.

Then, after Becket's arrival there soon after his, Herbert was sent on a mission to the courts of Louis VII of France and Pope Alexander III. His task was to mitigate the harm that might be caused by the envoys Henry II was also sending in the same direction. Henry wanted Louis to refuse Becket's requests for protection, and he wanted the pope to take his side against the archbishop. However, Henry's criticisms of Becket failed to convince either Louis or Alexander, and, if Herbert's own account of what happened is to be believed, this was in no small way down to him. His 'tearful story' affected the king of France greatly and he was persuaded to give Becket a refuge within his lands. Moving on to Sens, where the pope was then staying, Herbert managed to move him to tears as well.[22] In reality, of course, both king and pope were assessing the situation to see where their own best interests might lie. Louis was keen to help Becket, not because he felt sorry for him, but because he might prove useful as a weapon in his ongoing quest to undermine the power of Henry II. Pope Alexander, meanwhile, had his own problems. He had become pope in 1159, but the election had been disputed and another pope, Victor IV, had been elected with the support of the emperor, Frederick Barbarossa. Alexander had been forced to flee to France and, in dire need of influential international support, he was desperate not to alienate either Henry II or Louis VII. So, whilst he was a natural ally of the exiled archbishop, Alexander found himself in a difficult position when Herbert appeared before him. For all the spin in Herbert's account of what happened, Alexander took care to give Becket moral support and sympathy only at that stage. A few days later, however, the stakes were raised when Becket himself travelled to Sens and put his case to the pope. More tears were shed when Becket showed Alexander a copy of the Constitutions of Clarendon, and yet more the next day when a remorseful Becket dramatically resigned his office before the pope. Alexander was quick to reappoint him, but he also sent Becket to the Cistercian abbey of Pontigny. Officially this was to allow Becket time and space for contemplation and prayer. More pragmatically, Alexander was keen to take some of the heat out of the controversy by getting the archbishop out of the way for a while.

Herbert accompanied his master into exile at Pontigny. Later he tried hard to paint a positive picture of their early experiences there. Becket was received enthusiastically by the monks; he and Herbert were even allowed to eat meat, although the monks did not join them, and they were given neighbouring rooms within the precincts of the monastery. There they set to work. According to Herbert, the archbishop eagerly seized this chance to devote himself to reading, prayer and meditation. Pontigny, Herbert claimed, 'was to us like a training school for combat, in which we were exercised together, a school of virtue in which we were educated together'.[23] At Becket's request, Herbert started his edition of Peter Lombard's 'great gloss' on the Psalms and St Paul's epistles, but he seems also to have been responsible for masterminding the strategy and tactics designed to publicise Becket's cause. Together for the best part of two years behind Pontigny's walls, master and servant prepared for the battles to come. But it was also a hard life. As his sense of grievance and injustice deepened, the archbishop adopted an ever more stringently ascetic lifestyle. Becket often prayed through the night, he fasted and punished himself further by plunging into the freezing waters of the stream that ran through the monastic grounds. He developed a painful ulcer in his throat that could only be relieved by the removal of two bones from his jaw. The archbishop was suffering and it seems likely that Herbert was suffering with him. He came to dislike his Cistercian hosts intensely (they ate like horses, Herbert thought), but the enforced inactivity at Pontigny must have been a torture in its own right.[24] Herbert's support for his master was always uncompromising and aggressive. He wanted to fight their opponents not hide from them, and, as the months went by, it must have felt more and more as if the archbishop's plight and the righteousness of his cause were being forgotten.

And, to be sure, for the first year and a half of Becket's exile, Henry II had the better of the quarrel. Having failed to convince Pope Alexander and King Louis to side with him against Becket, Henry took his frustrations out on the archbishop's friends and family. At Christmas 1164 he ordered the confiscation of Canterbury's estates and revenues and banished from England all Becket's relations and members of his household. The archbishop was powerless to help them or to resist the king's heavy-handed bullying. Indeed, 1165 was a particularly grim year for Becket and his allies. He was finding it impossible to recruit any influential new supporters, and he failed to persuade Henry's mother, the Empress Matilda, to mediate. The pope's attitude towards Becket also became more cautious than ever as Henry II came close to making an alliance with Frederick Barbarossa and recognising the new pope backed by the emperor, Paschal III. In the summer Alexander wrote to Becket urging him to be patient and not to take any steps against the king at least until the following Easter when the circumstances, he hoped, would be different again.[25] And different they were. By the end of 1165, Pope Alexander had taken advantage of the lack of support Paschal III had inside Rome to return to the city and begin the process of building his own power base there. By Easter 1166, Alexander felt able to flex his muscles to the extent of appointing Becket his legate within the province of Canterbury. This did not mean that Becket would be returning from exile any time soon, but it was a demonstration of Alexander's support for his cause, and it did give Becket the power to impose papal sanctions on England, albeit from a distance. The pace of the dispute now picked up once again. Becket, no doubt with Herbert's advice and assistance, wrote a series of increasingly belligerent letters to the king and then in June he excommunicated several royal officials and suspended the bishop of Salisbury. Meanwhile, the meeting at Angers between Henry II and the archbishop's clerks had taken place at the start of May. Both John of Salisbury and that 'proud one', Herbert, refused to desert Becket and the chances of any kind of reconciliation between king and archbishop seemed as remote as ever.

Over the summer and autumn of 1166 the tone of the quarrel became more bitter still. Becket wrote a series of letters that criticised the English clergy and some of its leading bishops in increasingly self-righteous and hostile terms for what he saw as their lack of support and loss of resolve during his exile. By this time, the opposition to Becket in England was being orchestrated by the archbishop of York (Roger de Pont l'Évêque, his old colleague from Theobald's household) and the bishop of London (Gilbert Foliot, his rival for the archbishopric of Canterbury in 1162). At the same time, Henry II was threatening the Cistercians with expulsion from his lands if they continued to shelter and protect the archbishop. In the end Herbert was able to secure from Louis VII a new refuge at St Columba's Abbey outside Sens, and Becket's small entourage moved there in November 1166. Pope

Alexander now shifted to centre stage as the attempts to negotiate a settlement between Henry and Becket began increasingly to focus on him. He was certainly keen to bring it to an end and in November 1167 the first of a series of papal missions arrived in France. The two cardinals who led it met the archbishop and his followers between the castles of Gisors and Trie on 18 November. They assured Becket that King Henry, who was not present, would allow him to return to England as long as he did not insist on a formal withdrawal of the Constitutions of Clarendon. The offending customs, they said, would effectively be abandoned. Herbert of Bosham for one, however, was not satisfied with this: only an explicit and public renunciation of the Constitutions would do and, in Herbert's view, the cardinals were not to be trusted. Their words were 'mollifying and honeyed, but dangerous,' he said.[26] Becket agreed and the envoys were forced to return disappointed to Rome.

The next papal attempt to intervene finally brought Becket and Henry II face to face with each other once again. Their meeting took place at Montmirail in north-eastern France in January 1169 and King Louis was in attendance too. The archbishop was put under enormous pressure by all sides to make an unqualified submission to Henry in return for royal permission to take up his position in England once more. The early signs were that Becket was prepared to do this, and when he saw the king he threw himself to the floor at his feet. Henry raised him up and readied himself to listen to the profession of remorse and the request for forgiveness, only to hear the archbishop say that he would submit to the king's mercy and judgement 'saving God's honour'. In other words, the archbishop's surrender was anything but complete and there remained the point beyond which his loyalty to the king was overridden by his loyalty to God. Becket's position was essentially the same as the one he had adopted as far back as the Council of Westminster in 1163 when he had insisted on limiting his submission to Henry's demands with the phrase 'saving in all respects our order'.[27] Becket's stance at Montmirail shocked the onlookers and incensed King Henry, who left the conference cursing and exasperated; and there seems little doubt that Herbert of Bosham had been instrumental in persuading his master to act as he did. At the very least, this was Herbert's own view. He recalled later how, at the last moment, just as the archbishop was about to appear before the king, he convinced Becket to make only a conditional submission.[28]

Becket's behaviour at Montmirail provoked an almost universally negative reaction and it alienated many, even some within his own household, who had stood by him loyally until this point. For Herbert, though, Becket had simply given further evidence of the rightness of his cause and of his superhuman qualities. The heroic archbishop 'stood among the many and the great pushing and pulling, immovable like a house built upon firm rock, like a city placed on a mountain, like an iron pillar, and like a bronze wall against the land, kings, princes and priests, in heart, voice and deed, as if in the middle of a battlefield'.[29] Presumably Herbert approved in April 1169 when Becket excommunicated Gilbert Foliot and others for their persistent resistance to the archbishop's orders. The bishop of London eventually had to travel to Italy and back to be absolved by the pope from this sentence a year later.

In tandem with such inflammatory conduct, diplomatic efforts to reach a settlement also continued throughout 1169. But, despite their intensity and the likelihood that most on both sides were by now eager for some kind of resolution, they got nowhere. Eventually, a year after the disastrous meeting at Montmirail, Becket met Henry II again, with Louis VII as their chaperone, this time at Montmartre just north of Paris. Henry went further than he had ever gone before when he invited Becket to return to his duties in England without requiring any kind of submission from him, and promised not to take anything that properly belonged to the Church. It was understood too (even by Herbert of Bosham whose record of the meeting is full and clear) that the royal customs embodied in the Constitutions of Clarendon would be abandoned, albeit not explicitly or in writing.[30] Henry also agreed to consider at a later date the issue of compensation for losses suffered during their exile by Becket and his men. All seemed to be going well ('after so many various storms,' Herbert said, 'it seemed and was hoped by all that we were about to enter port'), but at this point Becket demanded a public sign that peace had been made between him and the king, not for fear of Henry, but so that it would be clear to Henry's men that Becket was no longer his enemy. A kiss of peace would make all the difference, the archbishop said.[31] There was nothing unusual about sealing an agreement with such a gesture, but Henry could not make it, he said, because he had previously sworn never to give Becket such a kiss, even if their old friendship was re-established. For Herbert of Bosham, Henry's excuse was a smokescreen behind which he could back out of the promises he had just made: the stalling of the negotiations was the king's fault. It is more likely, however, that Becket knew perfectly well that Henry had sworn never to give him the kiss of peace and that the king would not break his oath. After all of Henry's concessions, Becket had made the one demand he knew Henry would not agree to. Not for the first time, Becket's conduct is difficult to explain away. To Herbert, however, his obduracy was a necessary prelude to his master's impending martyrdom. As he left the meeting at Montmartre (the place itself was the site of the martyrdom of St Denis and named accordingly), Herbert records the brief conversation that took place between Becket and one of the crowd. 'Today the peace of our Church was discussed in the Chapel of the Martyrdom, and I believe it is only through your martyrdom that the Church will gain peace,' the man said. Becket turned and replied, 'How I wish that it were liberated, even with my blood!'[32]

As it happened, the settlement that still appeared so unlikely after the events at Montmartre was now less than a year away. Until the spring of 1170, however, little progress was made. Only then, when Henry II announced his intention to have his eldest son Henry crowned, did the quarrel with Becket enter its final phase. In 1169 Henry II had unveiled his plan to divide his lands between his sons on his death. Richard would become duke of Aquitaine and Geoffrey duke of Brittany, but the biggest prizes, England, Normandy and Anjou, were set aside for the eldest son, Henry. The crowning of the principal heir during his father's lifetime had precedents in France and Germany, although not in England. But this was not really the problem. More difficult was the question of who would perform the ceremony. Not every English king had been crowned by an archbishop of Canterbury, but by 1170 it was a prerogative Becket certainly claimed, and when he heard of the king's plan for Henry junior to be crowned by the archbishop of York instead, he was outraged at the suggestion that anyone other than himself might perform the ceremony. He formally prohibited the English clergy from taking part in the coronation and appealed to the pope. But, undeterred, the king went ahead and his son was crowned at Westminster Abbey on 14 June by Archbishop Roger of York, with nearly all the English bishops, some more reluctantly than others, in attendance.

A storm of official protest greeted news of the coronation of the Young King. Louis VII was furious because his daughter Margaret, young Henry's wife, had not attended the ceremony. Appalled, too, was Pope Alexander, whose envoys warned the king that he would have to end his quarrel with Becket or else England would be placed under papal sentence of interdict. Church services would be suspended and Henry's subjects would be denied the sacraments; in other words, the kingdom would be cut adrift from the rest of Christendom. Under such pressure, Henry agreed to meet Becket once again, this time at Fréteval south of Paris, on 22 July 1170. The wide-ranging concessions that Henry announced were essentially the same as those he had been prepared to make at Montmartre. In addition he apologised for any offence he had caused to the church of Canterbury by having his son crowned at Westminster Abbey in Becket's absence. The archbishop expressed himself satisfied and the two men then embraced. Finally, in a symbolic gesture of humility, the king held Becket's stirrup as the archbishop remounted his horse. In theory, the way was now clear for the exiled archbishop and his followers to return in peace to England. Herbert of Bosham, for one, believed that Becket had won a great victory at Fréteval. The king had given way on just about every issue, and whilst Herbert, with his fellow clerks, had prostrated himself at King Henry's feet, he had also been restored to his possessions. Whether the king had remembered the 'proud fellow' from Angers back in 1166 is unclear. Nevertheless, there were still significant issues left unresolved in the summer and autumn of 1170. Herbert insisted in his account of the meeting at Fréteval that no kiss of peace had been either requested by Becket or given by Henry; and although other versions of the events differ on this point, the lack of clarity about the formal ending of the dispute was ominous.[33] It remained to be seen whether or not the two sides would honour the commitments they had made at Fréteval. In addition, the fate of the bishops who had officiated at the Young King's coronation was also still unresolved, and, more generally, there were many in England who had profited from Becket's exile and who could only lose by his return.

The harmony of the Fréteval conference did not last long. There were problems with the restoration of the exiles' property in England (early in August, Herbert of Bosham and John of Salisbury were sent on an unsuccessful embassy to the king to try and resolve these difficulties), and Louis VII warned Becket that he should not leave France without having received the kiss of peace from Henry II. When Becket met Henry again in September, it was clear to the archbishop's supporters from the king's cold demeanour that the relationship between the two men was close to breaking down once again. It is not surprising that rumours of plots to kill Becket began to circulate within the archbishop's entourage at around this time. These may have been groundless, or perhaps concocted by his biographers later to set the scene for their hero's murder. Nevertheless, there is no reason to doubt that Becket's supporters were nervous as the day of his return approached. And their suspicions were only increased when the king failed to meet Becket at Rouen and accompany him back to England from there. Henry had promised to do this at Fréteval, but instead he sent as a guide the dean of Salisbury, John of Oxford, whom Becket had excommunicated in 1166. The king might have meant nothing by this, but to the archbishop and his followers Henry's behaviour could only have felt dismissive at best and insulting at worst.

At the end of September 1170, Becket sent some of his clerks, led by Herbert of Bosham, to England to make the final preparations for his return. It soon became clear that the situation there remained tense and dangerous. With Henry II in France, the Young King was in charge of the administration and he had orders from his father to deal with Becket's outstanding grievances and restore his and his followers' properties. This was far from easy, however, and Herbert wrote to his master in detail setting out the obstacles and delays he was encountering. Becket's enemies remained in possession of many Canterbury estates, the king was planning to make appointments to a series of bishoprics without Becket's involvement, and there were several high-ranking prelates, not least the archbishop of York and the bishops of Salisbury and London, who remained resolutely opposed to the archbishop's return.

Becket was warned by his clerks not to come to England without 'the unadulterated grace of the lord king', but it was too late to turn back and the archbishop ignored their advice.[34] This was the best chance Becket would get to recover his position in England and reassert his authority over the Church there. He would not return meekly either. Shortly before he embarked Becket had letters dispatched to England announcing that the pope had suspended the archbishop of York and excommunicated the bishops of Durham, London and Salisbury. This was their punishment for having crowned the Young King in Becket's absence.

With Herbert of Bosham at his side, Thomas Becket set sail for England from the port of Wissant in north-eastern France on the night of 30 November 1170. Standing on the beach there before they departed, Herbert urged his master to confront the perils that awaited them in England and press on.[35] Becket agreed, but alert to those same dangers (Becket had been warned about a possible attempt to kill him when he disembarked), his ship made for Sandwich on the east coast of Kent, not Dover some thirteen miles to the south where the official reception committee waited for him. When the archbishop landed at Sandwich, a crowd of locals soon gathered to acclaim his return and receive his blessing. And on the following day his short journey to Canterbury was slowed down by the numbers of people who flocked to see him on his way. When he finally reached the city, the cathedral was filled with music and decorated as if for a major religious festival. As the archbishop and his men entered the cathedral church, Herbert told Becket that it was a day of triumph for the Church and Jesus Christ. Urging him to keep up the fight, Herbert took care to stress that most of the people who had lined Becket's route were poor, and that their fervour was pure, untainted and innocent.[36] There is nothing to suggest that this was not the case, or that the response to Becket's return was not enthusiastic. However, Herbert's account of Becket's approach to Canterbury was clearly supposed to echo Christ's entry into Jerusalem on Palm Sunday, and to provide a necessary overture to the dark events that were to follow over the next month. As Herbert recorded, Becket's own 'Passion' had begun and his martyrdom was 'imminent'.[37]

Herbert's emphasis on the love shown for Becket on his return by the ordinary people of his diocese also served to highlight the selfishness and greed of his richer, higher-status enemies. As soon as they found him after his landing at Sandwich, the king's envoys had badgered Becket to withdraw the sanctions he had imposed upon the bishops who had conducted the Young King's coronation. Becket may have been prepared to do this, as long as the bishops submitted on his terms. But they refused and instead decided to ask the king to intervene on their behalf. Early in December 1170 the archbishop of York and the bishops of London and Salisbury crossed the Channel and headed for Henry II's court in Normandy. When they found him at Bur-le-Roi a few days before Christmas, they were quick to express their full fury at Becket's conduct. The suspension and excommunication of the clerics who had taken part in the Young King's coronation cast doubt on the legitimacy of the whole event, they claimed. And if more was needed to incense the king further, their exaggerated reports of the archbishop's rabble-rousing and of his progress around the kingdom with a huge armed retinue did the trick. Henry was furious: 'A man,' he exclaimed, 'who has eaten my bread, who came to my court poor, and I have raised him high – now he draws up his heel to kick me in the teeth! He has shamed my kin, shamed my realm; the grief goes to my heart, and no one has avenged me!'[38] This outburst, or one like it, was enough to prompt four of the knights at Henry's court to take matters into their own hands. On 26 December they set out for England where they intended to deal with the troublesome archbishop once and for all.

Meanwhile Becket had been attempting to strengthen his position in England. In mid-December he left Canterbury to visit the Young King. His route took him through London where he received a jubilant reception from the clergy and citizens. However, as he was heading off once more he was met by messengers from the prince who instructed him to return to Kent. All the signs suggest clearly that, despite or even because of his popularity, Becket was being frozen out by the royal establishment. He returned to Canterbury for the Christmas festival, at which point Herbert of Bosham picks up the story. In his Christmas Day sermon the archbishop warned the congregation that his death was near and excommunicated some of his most dangerous enemies.[39] For the rest of the day, though, he was in good spirits and jovial. However, on the following day, Becket's mood changed as he received news of the various plots that he was told were being hatched against him. He took Herbert aside and ordered him to go to France to tell King Louis and his other supporters there what was happening in England. Weeping, Herbert protested and declared that, if he went, he knew he would never see his master again. 'Now I see,' he declared, 'that I who was a companion in your struggle will not be a companion in your glory.' Bursting into tears himself, the archbishop replied that Herbert was right about this: they would never meet again in the flesh. However, he insisted that Herbert should still leave for France, perhaps for his own safety as much as anything else. After all, the archbishop said, 'the king sees you as more troublesome than others in the cause of the Church'.[40] So, late on 27 December (in the dead of night, he recalled, because of the traps they suspected lay ahead of them), and in great sorrow, Herbert and a few companions slipped out of Canterbury and headed for the coast.

Two days later the four knights who had left King Henry's court in Normandy arrived in Canterbury. At first, their intention was probably to arrest the archbishop and take him back to Normandy so that he could be made to submit to the king and perhaps resign his position. This plan soon came to nothing, however, as Becket obstinately and defiantly refused to give in to their threats. In the end, they lost patience with him and butchered the archbishop where he stood, in the north transept of Canterbury Cathedral.

Herbert was at Sens, between Paris and Pontigny, when he heard the news of Becket's murder. When he later described the last time he and the archbishop had been together, Herbert portrayed himself as the man who had predicted his master's death.[41] At the time, however, it is unclear just how surprised he was when he heard of the shocking events that had taken place in his absence. Nevertheless, his sorrow was heartfelt and Herbert regretted deeply that he had been unable to defend, and perhaps even to die alongside, his friend. He spent the rest of his life almost entirely in France. As he grew older he became an increasingly isolated and bitter figure. He kept busy, though. Between complaining to the pope that his benefices in England were being unjustly withheld from him and visiting Christ Church, Canterbury, in 1189, Herbert wrote his *Life* of Becket. It is long, complex and sometimes rambling, but of all the contemporary biographies it presents the most intimate and richest portrait of the martyr's life from the outspoken and opinionated perspective of a friend who knew him as well as anyone. Of course, the other man who had once cherished Becket's friendship was Henry II, and Herbert met him at least once more, perhaps during the writing of the *Life* in 1184–6. During their long and frank conversation, Henry admitted that his reckless words in December 1170 had unintentionally caused Becket's death, but he also reminded Herbert of the miracle that Saint Thomas had performed for him in 1174: only a day after the king's public performance of penance before Becket's shrine at Canterbury in July of that year, the insubordinate king of Scots had been defeated and captured by Henry's allies in northern England, thus dealing a decisive blow to the most serious rebellion Henry II ever faced.[42]

Here were two tired and mournful old men remembering their mutual friend. Nothing could have been further from the tense and tetchy meeting between the king and the 'proud one' that had taken place twenty years before at Angers. Yet this was hardly a reconciliation, and it is difficult to escape the impression that Herbert remained a disappointed man. By the time he died in about 1194, probably in the Cistercian abbey of Ourscamp in the diocese of Arras, his master was well on the way to becoming one of the most popular and venerated saints of the Middle Ages. But Herbert had shared neither in the earthly prestige that was quickly spawning an industry centred on Thomas Becket's sanctity nor in the eternal glory that Becket himself had achieved through martyrdom. It is clear from the way in which Herbert describes his own part in the disputes of the 1160s that he saw himself as having been instrumental in the upholding of Becket's cause and, on many difficult occasions, in the reinforcement of the archbishop's own resolve and strength of will. Herbert probably thought he had not been given the credit he deserved for the creation of Saint Thomas, whose 'companion in the struggle' he had been for so long.[43]

CHAPTER FOUR

THE WARRIOR'S TALE
Strongbow and the Invasion of Ireland

B Y THE LATE spring of 1171, Dublin had been under siege for two months. Outside the walls, the Irish besiegers were happy to bide their time and starve the city into submission. Inside the walls, the English defenders were suffering. Food was running out, so was time, and their options were limited. They could stake everything on a charge out of the city gates. Their superior discipline, military techniques and equipment would give them a good chance in a pitched battle against the Irish, but it would be risky nonetheless. Meanwhile, there was little hope of any relief force coming to their aid. King Henry II had banned all voyages to Ireland from any of his lands, and he had also summoned all his subjects in Ireland to return to England and Wales before the following Easter or they would be exiled and disinherited. In this dire situation, with provisions left for only a fortnight, Strongbow ('the valiant earl', as one source called him)[1] tried to negotiate with the Irish one more time, but his offer to accept their leader Rory O'Connor as his lord and to hold Leinster as his vassal was rejected out of hand. The English could keep Dublin, Wexford and Waterford, Rory said, but nothing more. And if they did not accept this proposal immediately, he went on, they would be attacked next day.[2] Strongbow's men reacted furiously and defiantly when Rory's ultimatum was brought back to them in the city. Maurice Fitz Gerald spoke for them all when he said that they should ignore it and seize the initiative with an attack of their own. The Irish were poorly organised and poorly armed, and an assault by brave, well-equipped Englishmen was the last thing they would expect. And after all, what did they have to lose? 'Just as we are English as far as the Irish are concerned, likewise to the English we are Irish, and the inhabitants of this island and the other assail us with an equal degree of hatred,' Maurice declared. 'So let us breach the barriers of hesitation and inertia, for "fortune favours the brave".'[3] Strongbow then joined in. He shouted to Miles de Cogan, the governor of the city: 'Baron! Get all your men armed: you will lead out the vanguard; in the name of the Almighty Father, you will lead out the vanguard.'[4]

Miles had forty knights, sixty archers and a hundred men at arms. Behind him came Raymond le Gros ('the Fat'), and then Strongbow himself, each with the same number of troops as Miles. At about four o'clock that afternoon, the English force slipped quietly and unseen out of the city. They forded the river Liffey, headed north and then turned south-west in order to attack the Irish camp from behind. Most of the Irish troops were relaxing before dinner and over a hundred of them, including Rory O'Connor himself, were bathing in the river. Miles de Cogan began the charge with his shout of 'Cogan! . . . Strike, in the name of the Cross! Strike, barons, without delay, in the name of Jesus, son of Mary! Strike, noble knights, at your mortal enemies.'[5] Behind him, the contingents led by Raymond le Gros and Meiler Fitz Henry also acquitted themselves impressively. Meanwhile 'Richard, the brave earl, also fought well that day; he fought so well that everyone was amazed.'[6] The English attack took the Irish (30,000 of them according to one dubious estimate, 60,000 according to another) completely by surprise and they were quickly overpowered and scattered.[7] Most of the bathers were slaughtered, although Rory O'Connor managed somehow to escape, and over 1,500 Irish were killed in all. The sole English casualty was a wounded infantryman. There was plunder, too, mainly food that would feed the English and their horses for a year. 'The field remained that day with Richard, the brave earl, and the Irish fled, routed and vanquished.'[8] Strongbow's victory was total.

* * * *

Few events in Anglo-Irish history have remained as disputed and controversial as the entry of the English into Irish affairs from the end of the 1160s. Even referring to them as 'English' in this context is problematic. For one thing, Ireland's recent history means that the word is heavily loaded with political significance, and it can be a divisive distraction when discussing the Middle Ages. Another less contentious point, but just as important in many ways, is whether or not most of the men who came to Ireland from England in the mid-twelfth century regarded themselves as English anyway. Their first language was almost certainly French, and their family connections with Normandy and other parts of northern France remained strong and alive. Despite these reservations, however, two things are not in dispute about the newcomers. First, they did come to Ireland from England, or at least from those parts of south Wales conquered and settled by subjects of the English kings after 1066. And, second, they were usually called 'English' by those who wrote about these events at the time. For these pragmatic reasons, but with a recognition that there remains no single satisfactory modern way of describing them, that is what they will be called here.

The English victory at the siege of Dublin in 1171 is a crucial moment in this story. But the account of it given above, whilst it contains many elements common to contemporary descriptions of these events, highlights many of the problems of interpretation. The English are brave and efficient, whilst the Irish are lazy and incompetent. The English are far ahead of the Irish in terms of their military skills, technology and techniques. And in the war cries of Strongbow and Miles de Cogan, with their religious references and appeals for divine assistance, there are hints of crusading fervour as the barely Christian Irish are brought to heel by the loyal sons of the Roman Church. These are stereotypes, of course, rooted in deeply held twelfth-century prejudices; but, like many stereotypes, they also contain germs of truth. The English did succeed in Ireland in the second half of the twelfth century because, whereas the Irish had no armour, cavalry or castles, the English had all three in abundance. The English, at least during the early years after their arrival in Ireland, were a highly motivated and coherent fighting force, bound together by ties of family and locality. And there was indeed a religious impulse behind the arrival of the English in Ireland. The English Church, the English king and the English barons all had much to gain from bringing Ireland under English control and firmly into the mainstream of western European religious orthodoxy.

But there are myths about all of this, too, which need to be dispelled. It has been conventional over the years to characterise the coming of the English to Ireland as an 'invasion' and subsequent events as a 'conquest'. Neither of these words really does justice to what happened after 1169 when a small number of Anglo-Norman barons and their followers crossed the Irish Sea, not to 'conquer' Ireland, but because they had been invited to come by a deposed Irish king who wanted their help to regain his throne. They were serving him and his successors, and their reward for this was land on which they settled men of their own. They were not pirates opportunistically seizing whatever they could get. Nonetheless, they were remarkably successful in a very short space of time, and arguably the most successful and important of them all was Richard Fitz Gilbert, more popularly known as Strongbow. He features in most of the main English and Irish sources for this period, and understandably so. But the two accounts of his career that give the fullest descriptions differ in their emphasis. The first of these, Gerald of Wales's *The Conquest of Ireland*, written in Latin, was finished in 1189. Gerald was archdeacon of Brecon in south Wales and his relatives had played a leading role in Ireland from 1169. His primary aim in *The Conquest* was to give pride of place to the part played by his own brothers and cousins in the Irish adventure. As a result, his attitude towards Strongbow is sometimes rather cool, and he tends to ignore many of his contributions to events and to play down the earl's achievements. The second source, the so-called *Song of Dermot and the Earl*, a poem in Norman-French, had been put into writing by 1225, but that version was based on earlier material, possibly from the 1170s. The writer of the *Song* (his identity is unknown, but it has been suggested that he wrote from within the circle of the king of Leinster himself) was noticeably more positive towards Strongbow than Gerald; Strongbow is frequently styled 'brave', 'bold', 'noble' or 'valiant' by the *Song*'s author. Nevertheless, despite their differences of tone and content, both *The Conquest* and the *Song* tell their stories from the point of view of the invaders, not the indigenous Irish, and both are clearly sympathetic towards the ambitions and the actions of the English.

Such an emphasis underpins the long-held notion that the Irish were the innocent victims of English aggression from 1169 and that

they have remained so ever since. There is more than a little to be said
for this idea, and the arrival of the English marked a turning point in
the history of the British Isles. But to view these events in isolation only
provides a limited explanation of a much more complex and diverse
process. Indeed, the experience of the Irish at the hands of Strongbow
and his men is just one example of trends that defined this period of
European history more generally. The three hundred years between
1000 and 1300 saw rapid population growth, significant economic
expansion and major social change across Europe. And as the pressure
on available resources intensified from within, territorial expansion
followed. On the periphery of Europe, in Scandinavia, the Baltic and
northern Europe, in Spain, southern Italy and the eastern Mediterranean,
territory was brought under the control of men, most of them from
some part of France, who had moved out of their homelands to settle
and make their fortunes. But they acknowledged the authority of
the pope in Rome and they worshipped in Latin like him, and as
their power grew so the structures and institutions of the western
Church were imposed on the areas they now controlled – dioceses were
constructed and monasteries were built to complement the more mili-
taristic approaches of the pioneering settlers. England was not immune
to these trends, and the Norman Conquest provides one case study of
what was happening all around the edges of Latin Christendom at this
time. The English intervention in Ireland, a century after the battle of
Hastings, provides another.

* * * *

'The earl had reddish hair and freckles, grey eyes, a feminine face, a
weak voice and a short neck, though in almost all other respects he was
of tall build.' This is how Gerald of Wales begins his description of
Richard Fitz Gilbert of Clare, earl of Pembroke, later called Strongbow.
According to Gerald, he was also generous and easy-going; he could be
persuasive in argument. But it was in wartime that he came into his
own: 'In civil affairs, removed from the sphere of arms, he was more
inclined to obey than command. In peace time he had more the air of a
rank-and-file soldier than of a leader, but in war more that of a leader
than of a true soldier.'[9] Strongbow was probably born in about 1130. He

was the son of Gilbert Fitz Gilbert, whom King Stephen had made earl of Pembroke in 1138, and Isabella (also known as Elizabeth), daughter of Robert de Beaumont, count of Meulan and earl of Leicester. When his father died in 1148, Strongbow succeeded him as earl of Pembroke and lord of Chepstow, which, in addition to lands in south Wales, gave him extensive estates spread across nine counties of England, as well as lordships in Normandy.

On 7 November 1153, Strongbow witnessed the treaty between King Stephen and Henry, duke of Normandy, which formally brought the war between them to an end.[10] His own position was by no means secure, however. For some reason, probably because he had supported Stephen too loyally for too long, he was not trusted by Henry. By 1153, moreover, Strongbow's Norman lordships were in the hands of his cousin, a result almost certainly of the Angevin conquest of Normandy in the 1140s. According to Gerald of Wales, Strongbow, whilst of noble stock, 'up to this time had a great name rather than great prospects ... and had succeeded to a name rather than possessions'. Another writer, William of Newburgh, gave a similar assessment of Strongbow's circumstances: he had wasted most of his inheritance and wanted to get away from his creditors.[11] This may have been an exaggeration, but Strongbow had lost out at the hands of the Angevins on at least one side of the Channel, and he may have owed money to the great Jewish lender Aaron of Lincoln. These were reasons on the face of it why Strongbow might have been keen to rebuild his career beyond the reach of the new English king and his administration. For a long time at the start of the new reign, to be sure, the two men kept their distance from each other. Strongbow is not found again in the king's company until late 1167 or early 1168.

By this time, events had occurred in Ireland and Wales that were to dictate the course of the rest of Strongbow's career. His tale, in fact, can only be understood in the context of what was happening on either side of the Irish Sea in the middle of the twelfth century. Ireland was a land of political instability and competing rulers. Such men liked to style themselves 'kings', although in reality they were little more than provincial warlords. Power shifted as their individual fortunes rose and fell. There was no single dominant ruler or ruling house, although from time to time one of the more successful kings might assert himself forcefully and long enough to claim the title 'high king' of all Ireland. By the 1160s three Irish kings were inadvertently preparing the ground for what was to follow: the king of Connacht in the west of Ireland, Rory O'Connor; his ally further east Tiernan O'Rourke, king of Breifne (an area covering roughly the modern Irish counties of Leitrim and Cavan); and their common enemy and rival in the south-east, the king of Leinster, Dermot MacMurrough. Such political volatility would have been attributed by Gerald of Wales to the innate character failings of the native Irish who were, he claimed 'a wild and inhospitable people. They live on beasts only, and live like beasts.' When they rode, they did so bareback; when they fought, they did so naked and unarmed, and when they did dress, their clothes were crude and contained 'very little wool'. Their long hair and beards were further evidence that 'all their habits are the habits of barbarians'. Their only estimable skill, Gerald conceded, lay in their flair for music.[12] Gerald is unfair, of course, and bigoted. He was also wrong when he said, for example, that the Irish were lazy and had done nothing to develop their pastoral economy.[13] In the ninth century the Vikings had attacked and settled in Ireland, and towns such as Waterford, Wexford and, above all, Dublin remained centres of Norse influence in the twelfth century. They were also major trading centres and had long-standing commercial connections with English towns such as Chester and Bristol, as well as with Wales and France. English and Norman influence in Ireland was not new in 1169.

Like Ireland, Wales was a land where native local rulers competed with each other for dominance and control. Across Wales, such men had taken advantage of England's internal problems during Stephen's reign to reassert themselves and reclaim some of the power and influence they had lost to the Norman invaders and settlers after 1066. By 1170, when he died, the ruler of Gwynedd (north Wales), Owain ap Gruffudd, was calling himself 'king of Wales' and claiming authority over all native Wales. Meanwhile, the ruler of Deheubarth, Rhys ap Gruffudd (the Lord Rhys), was taking steps of his own in the 1150s and 1160s to dominate south Wales. This, of course, brought him into direct contact, and sometimes conflict, with the descendants of many of those Frenchmen who had settled after 1066 along the coast of south Wales, in Glamorgan, Pembrokeshire and Ceredigion. South Wales had been a frontier zone at the turn of the eleventh century, a place for tough pioneers and hard-bitten opportunists. The new 'marcher' lords at places like Brecon and Chepstow were not exactly given a free hand by the English kings to do as they pleased, but even a notoriously strict ruler such as Henry I was only able to keep half an eye on what his subordinates were up to there. They fought with the native Welsh, took their lands and their tribute, built castles, and made many of their own rules. However, by the 1160s this era was over. The native Welsh recovery under Stephen had put pressure on the marcher lords, and Henry II was determined to rule all his subjects equally firmly and directly. These two forces combined to hem in the marchers and limit their prospects. In 1166, when the Lord Rhys took Cardigan and other lands, he did so at the expense of families with names like Clare, Clifford and Fitz Gerald. The keeper of Cardigan Castle, Robert Fitz Stephen, who was also Gerald of Wales's uncle, was captured and kept in Rhys's custody for the next three years. Rhys then consolidated these gains in 1171 by submitting to Henry II, who confirmed him in all his conquests in return for his cooperation. Rhys had become King Henry's man with royally bestowed authority over all of south Wales. By this time, though, the marcher lords of the region had already realised that they would have to look elsewhere to further their fortunes. Ireland was the obvious place; and the invitation, when it came, was eagerly accepted.

It was Dermot MacMurrough, the king of Leinster, who brought the English to Ireland. According to contemporaries looking for the origins of the saga, it was all because of a woman. Dermot had abducted Dervorgilla, the wife of Tiernan O'Rourke, king of Breifne. Dervorgilla herself was the daughter of another Irish king (of Meath), and one version of the story alleges that she was put up to soliciting Dermot's attention by an ambitious brother with a grievance against Tiernan.[14] More conventionally, Gerald of Wales claimed that Dermot had 'long been burning with love' for Dervorgilla and seized her whilst her husband was away on a military campaign. However, Gerald could not resist reinforcing the violently misogynistic views about women shared by other writers of the period (who were all men and usually clerics): as far as he was concerned, 'no doubt she was abducted because she wanted to be and ... she herself arranged that she should become the kidnapper's prize'. After all, he went on, 'almost all the world's most notable catastrophes have been caused by women'. And in this case, just as Paris and Mark Antony had been destroyed by their infatuations (namely, Helen of Troy and Cleopatra), Dermot's uncontrolled passions resulted in him being chased out of Ireland by a vengeful O'Rourke and his ally Rory O'Connor.[15]

Enticingly scandalous as this story is, however, the political and military realities behind Dermot's flight were certainly more complex than Gerald allows. For one thing, Dervorgilla was abducted in 1152 and returned to Meath in 1153, whilst Dermot did not leave Ireland until 1166. Secondly, there are hints that Dermot was not a popular ruler with all his subjects. Gerald of Wales alleged that many of his followers were quick to make common cause with Dermot's enemies once it became clear he was in trouble: they 'sought to pay him back, and recalled to mind injustices, which they had long concealed and stored deep in their hearts'.[16] This may mean no more than that Dermot had been an efficient and effective lord, but vested interests may have felt excluded by his approach to government. In any event, what eventually prompted his departure was the assassination of Dermot's ally, the high-king Murtough MacLoughlin. This event was followed by the launch of Rory O'Connor's bid for the high kingship. Aided by Tiernan O'Rourke (who may still have felt some lingering resentment over the abduction of his wife), Rory managed to take Dublin from Dermot and turn enough of the men of Leinster, including his own brother, against him. At the start of August 1166, Dermot was forced to flee.

Dermot was not giving up, though; far from it. He had a plan to get his kingdom back, and central to it was Henry II. Dermot probably thought Henry owed him something, after the king had used some of Dermot's ships in 1165 during a campaign in Wales. More than that, Henry was the most powerful ruler in western Europe and, with his backing, Dermot could feel confident of recovering his losses. Dermot's determination to act quickly is clear from his willingness to seek out Henry. Finding him in the first place was difficult. According to the *Song*, Dermot and his wife crossed to Bristol and stayed there for a while with Robert Fitz Harding.[17] He was a prominent and well-connected merchant in the city, who had given staunch support to Empress Matilda during the civil war of Stephen's reign. The future Henry II had got to know him whilst he was based at Bristol in the years either side of 1150, and the strong trading links between Bristol and Dublin, which Dermot had controlled, meant that he and Robert were already well acquainted with each other by the time the deposed Irish king needed his support. Dermot then went to Normandy after it became clear Henry was not in England and, having no luck there either, he had to scour several other territories before finally pinning the king down in Aquitaine, perhaps in Poitiers, where Henry spent Christmas 1166. Finally, Dermot came face to face with the man on whom he pinned all his hopes. He explained his predicament, agreed to become Henry's vassal if the king came to his aid, and waited.

This may not have been the first time that Irish affairs had attracted Henry's attention. There is some evidence that he had contemplated a campaign in Ireland early in his reign, but this never seems to have been a realistic possibility given his other priorities immediately after 1154. However, Gerald of Wales later claimed that Pope Adrian IV had granted Ireland to Henry II in 1155, and that this donation was contained in the papal bull known as *Laudabiliter*, after its opening word.[18] There is now much uncertainty about this document (the first surviving text of it is contained in Gerald's own account), and it has been suggested that any papal support for Henry's ambitions in Ireland was perhaps more cautious than Gerald made it sound. Indeed, Gerald may have falsified an original papal bull, which is now lost, in order to bolster English claims to authority over Ireland and the Irish Church. Nevertheless, it does seem probable that the papacy did endorse English claims to authority over Ireland in some way early in Henry II's reign. No less a figure than John of Salisbury later took the credit for this. 'In response to my petition,' he claimed in his work *Metalogicon*, 'the pope granted and donated Ireland to the illustrious king, Henry II ... Through me the pope sent a gold ring set with a magnificent emerald as a sign that he had invested the king with the right to rule Ireland.'[19] And, according to Roger of Howden, Pope Urban III later sent Henry a crown made of peacocks' feathers, embroidered with gold, which was intended for the king's son, John, whom Henry planned to make king of Ireland.[20]

Whatever theoretical rights he might have been able to claim, when Dermot MacMurrough appeared before Henry II in 1166 the king remained noncommittal about crossing the Irish Sea. He would help later, he said, when he had the time. Nevertheless, Henry was prepared to allow Dermot to recruit assistance from amongst his subjects, and he gave Dermot a letter, addressed to their mutual acquaintance Robert Fitz Harding in Bristol, ordering the merchant to give Dermot and his followers any help they needed as they prepared to return to Ireland. When Dermot later returned to Bristol, it is likely to have been Fitz Harding who suggested that he should approach Strongbow. The two may have had commercial ties of some kind: Strongbow may have owed Fitz Harding money and Nicholas, Robert's son, subsequently held the manor of Tickenham, about ten miles from Bristol, which was attached to Strongbow's honour of Striguil. If this is what happened, however, Strongbow was probably the last resort for Dermot, whose recruiting campaign seems to have been something of a failure by that point. When Dermot and Strongbow finally met, the latter agreed to help Dermot in Ireland and in return Dermot agreed to give Strongbow his eldest daughter, Aife, in marriage, as well as the succession to his kingdom.

Given his indebtedness to and his strained relationship with Henry II, the prospect of military glory and political power must have tempted Strongbow. However, he did not go to Ireland for another three years, by which time other men had begun to cross the Irish Sea without him. Henry may have frustrated him once again here, because in 1168 Strongbow was sent to Germany by the king, to accompany his daughter Matilda on her journey to marry Henry the Lion, duke of Saxony. On the face of it, Strongbow was an odd choice as chaperone. There is no surviving evidence of him having had any direct contact with Henry since the latter became king, and their relationship was hardly friendly. It seems likely, therefore, that, whether because Henry was fearful of what Strongbow might achieve there, or just because he could, the king sent Strongbow to Germany simply to stop him going to Ireland.

Meanwhile, with little to show for his travels apart from Henry's vague permission to recruit and Strongbow's unfulfilled promise to help, Dermot MacMurrough had turned to the dominant figure in south

Wales, the Lord Rhys. But Rhys's initial response was also unenthusiastic and Dermot finally returned to Ireland late in 1167 with only a handful of men. In the winter of 1168/9, in hiding and still desperate for military aid, Dermot sent further requests for such help to west Wales with more promises of land, stock and cash, in particular offering Robert Fitz Stephen and his half-brother Maurice Fitz Gerald the city of Wexford as their prize. Rhys now saw a chance to rid himself of some troublesome English neighbours and he released Robert Fitz Stephen who had been in captivity since 1166, on the understanding that he would lead an army to Ireland and restore Dermot to power. However, it was to be another three years before Robert landed. Dermot had to hang on as best he could until then, and he just about managed to do so from August 1167, when he returned to Ireland and established a bridgehead around Ferns in the south-east, and in May 1169 when Robert Fitz Stephen finally led the first substantial expedition to Ireland from west Wales. This group of pioneers (three ships with thirty knights, sixty men at arms and 300 archers) set sail from Milford Haven and arrived at Bannow Island off the Wexford coast in May 1169. It included Robert's three nephews, Meiler Fitz Henry, Miles Fitz David and Robert of Barry (who was also Gerald of Wales's brother). Gerald proudly associated himself with these men and categorised them as 'Geraldines', as they were all descendants of Gerald of Windsor, his own grandfather. It would have been more accurate, though, to stress their common descent from Nest, Gerald of Windsor's wife. Nest was the daughter of Rhys ap Tewdwr, prince of south Wales, and she had children with several men. One of her lovers had been Robert Fitz Stephen's father and another, no less a figure than King Henry I, was the grandfather of Meiler Fitz Henry. The pioneers also included Hervey de Montmorency, Strongbow's uncle, who was, according to Gerald of Wales, 'a spy sent in the interest of earl Richard [Strongbow]'.[21] There was another landing soon afterwards, in May 1170, when Raymond le Gros, a member of Strongbow's household who later married his sister, crossed with ten knights and seventy archers and set himself and his entourage up near Waterford. So even if he was away on royal business whilst these events were being played out, Henry II's plan does not appear to have extinguished Strongbow's determination to maintain a stake in Irish affairs. He was almost certainly orchestrating events back in Wales. The trailblazers who went ahead of him to Ireland were, or soon would be, related to him in some way, and all had common interests and shared experiences from south Wales. In its earliest stages, therefore, the story of the English in Ireland was very much a family affair.

During 1170, meanwhile, Dermot's resurgence was gathering pace. With the help of Robert Fitz Stephen and his associates, he successfully attacked and captured Wexford (he promptly gave it to Robert, as he had promised to do), reasserted his authority over the leading men of Leinster, and then set his sights on Dublin. It was a violent business. After prevailing in one clash with his opponents, about two hundred severed heads were placed at Dermot's feet; he identified them all as his enemies, but one in particular caught his attention. 'He lifted up to his mouth the head of one he particularly loathed,' Gerald of Wales recorded, 'and taking it by the ears and hair, gnawed at the nose and cheeks – a cruel and most inhuman act.'[22] Perhaps so, but Dermot's performance was enough to bring Rory O'Connor into negotiations. A truce was arranged: Dermot would keep Leinster after acknowledging Rory's position as high king. Later there would be a marriage between Dermot's son (whom Rory took as a hostage along with Dermot's grandson and another kinsman) and Rory's daughter. Dermot also agreed not to bring any more foreigners to Ireland and to send back those he already had with him. Behind these scenes, however, other plans were being discussed. It was at this point, according to Gerald of Wales who also described the truce, that Dermot began to consider doing more than just recovering what he had lost in 1166. His success on his return had been rapid and impressive. Surely the high kingship was now a realistic aim? Fitz Stephen and Fitz Gerald assured him that it was, but they would need reinforcements. They advised Dermot to get in touch with Strongbow once again.

Dermot's messengers must have reached Strongbow quickly. Having heard their pleas, he headed straight for the royal court where, according to Gerald, he gave King Henry a choice: either return to him the lands he should have inherited, or allow him to try his luck in Ireland.[23] This time, it seems, the king gave Strongbow some kind of leave to cross the

Irish Sea. But even this was not straightforward. Gerald claimed that Henry gave 'permission of a sort – for it was given ironically rather than in earnest'. And according to William of Newburgh, as Strongbow was about to sail for Ireland, messengers acting on the king's behalf arrived to stop his departure, threatening him with confiscation of his estates if he set sail.[24] That Strongbow's lands in Wales and England were taken into the king's hands seems to be confirmed by entries in the royal financial records relating to his castle at Chepstow ('Striguil') and his manor of Weston in Hertfordshire; so even in 1170 Henry seems to have been reluctant to allow Strongbow to go to Ireland.[25] Deaf to any such threats, though, Strongbow sailed for Ireland from Milford Haven, having recruited troops on the way in south Wales, and he landed near Waterford on 23 August 1170 with, Gerald claimed, 200 knights and about 1,000 others (the *Song* says he brought 1,500 men with him).[26] He was joined on 25 August by Raymond le Gros, who assisted in the capture and garrisoning of Waterford, and by Dermot, accompanied by Fitz Stephen and Fitz Gerald. The alliance between Dermot and Strongbow was sealed by the renewal of the agreement they had first made at their meeting in Bristol: Aife and Strongbow were married, and his position as Dermot's heir was confirmed. Then, having left a garrison in Waterford, Strongbow set out with Dermot for Dublin where they arrived on 21 September. The city was taken and Asculf, its Norse ruler, was forced to flee. Strongbow remained at Dublin until 1 October, during which time he raided with Dermot into Meath against Tiernan O'Rourke.

News of events in Ireland alarmed Henry II. The success of Strongbow, Fitz Stephen and the rest raised the prospect of Henry's own men setting themselves up independently of him and out of his reach. William of Newburgh refers to Strongbow, who had enjoyed little fortune previously, as 'now nearly a king' and relates how, as a result of his acquisitions in Ireland, he had become celebrated for his wealth and great prosperity in England and Wales.[27] The potential problems for the king were not just confined to Ireland, however. The establishment by an ambitious and ruthless baron of a power base such as Leinster could have ramifications for Henry's position in Wales and even, in time, in England and beyond. After all, Strongbow had not fared well at Henry hands since 1154: perhaps resentful at what he considered to be the unjust loss of both the lordship of Pembroke and his status as an earl, Strongbow could conceivably use his new lands in Ireland (by the summer of 1171 Strongbow controlled the crucial ports of Dublin and Waterford as well as holding the succession to Leinster) to attempt to foment a revolt in Pembroke or seize it by force. This in turn would send tremors across the Angevin world; it is not an exaggeration to suggest that Strongbow's successful intervention in Ireland thus had the potential to destabilise the whole of Henry's dominions.

The king simply could not allow the growth of his barons' power in Ireland to continue in this unfettered way and, in any event, there was money to be made if Henry could get his hands on thriving ports like Dublin, Waterford and Wexford. His first step was to close the ports to Ireland and order all who had gone there to return before Easter 1171 or face seizure of their estates. Gerald describes Strongbow sending Raymond le Gros to negotiate on his behalf with Henry, and proposing that Strongbow hold his Irish acquisitions from the king.[28] But Raymond was still waiting for a reply from the king when news of the murder of Thomas Becket on 29 December 1170 reached the court. Raymond apparently had to return to Ireland without a favourable response from Henry. But when Dermot MacMurrough died about May 1171, there was a good chance that Strongbow would indeed succeed him. Rory O'Connor and his allies responded by besieging Dublin for two months. Trapped 'in a most ill-fortified castle, which was enclosed by a flimsy wall of branches and sods', Gerald of Wales recounted, and with supplies running low, Strongbow, Raymond le Gros and Maurice Fitz Gerald faced defeat.[29] Their desperation, however, combined with news that Robert Fitz Stephen was also being besieged in Carrick Castle by the men of Wexford, led Strongbow to determine on a sudden sortie with three contingents, led by Miles de Cogan, Raymond le Gros and himself, which attacked and routed Rory's army. Contemporaries estimated that their small force overcame an army of between 30,000 and 60,000 men outside the city walls.[30] These numbers are almost certainly exaggerations (estimates like this in medieval chronicles are notoriously unreliable), but this was a significant moment nonetheless. Rory had managed to bring together a coalition from across Ireland and beyond (ships from Orkney and the Isle of Man were used to blockade Dublin Bay), but it had been scattered by the invaders. From this point, it was probably clear to the Irish that the English planned to stay.

Leaving Dublin under the charge of Miles de Cogan, Strongbow set out to relieve the Wexford garrison. By this time, however, Robert Fitz Stephen had been tricked into surrendering by false news of the defeat of his allies at Dublin, and messengers intercepted the relief force with the news that Wexford had been burnt and Fitz Stephen imprisoned. Strongbow then headed to Waterford, where he was met by Hervey de Montmorency who had just returned from the court of Henry II. Messengers from Strongbow had visited Henry at Argentan in July 1171 and offered to surrender Dublin, Waterford, and the lands that he had acquired through his wife to Henry. But it was clear that any deal would only be concluded if Strongbow himself appeared before the king. So he travelled to meet Henry, who had by now almost completed his preparations for his own expedition to Ireland. At Pembroke, after lengthy argument and mediation by Hervey, Strongbow agreed to surrender the city of Dublin and its adjoining territory, the coastal towns, and all fortified strongholds, and to hold the remainder of the land he had acquired in Ireland as a grant from Henry. With this business concluded, and after visiting the shrine of St David to pray for a smooth crossing and a successful expedition, Henry II crossed the sea to Ireland from Milford Haven and arrived near Waterford on 17 October 1171. Accompanying him, according to Gerald of Wales, were 'about 500 knights and many mounted and foot archers'; the *Song* says he brought 400 knights and 4,000 infantrymen, and another source claims Henry came with 400 ships weighed down with warlike men, horses, arms and supplies.[31]

Clearly, whatever the precise numbers, this was a major expedition, and appropriately so. Henry was the first English king (the mythical Arthur apart) to set foot on Irish soil. His first priority was to rein in the activities of his barons in Ireland, but he was also determined to assert his authority over the entire island. Most of the Irish leaders were quick to seek him out, submit, and offer Henry tribute. The men of Wexford appeared before him and handed over a chained Robert Fitz Stephen as a token of their submission. And for men like Dermot of Cork and Donal of Limerick, Henry was a potential ally and protector against the further expansionist ambitions of the English settlers; in any event, they could do little to resist his claims. Even Rory O'Connor, albeit reluctantly, was probably pragmatic enough to accept Henry's supremacy. As for the English, Strongbow surrendered Waterford and Dublin to the king. Royal officials were installed to administer these cities (Wexford too) and their surrounding areas in the king's interests, and a great royal palace, made of wickerwork in the Irish fashion, was constructed just outside the city walls. Henry entertained the Irish leaders there at Christmas 1171, even forcing them to change their eating habits: 'in obedience to the king's wishes,' Gerald of Wales records, 'they began to eat the flesh of the crane, which they had hitherto loathed.'[32]

Within weeks of Henry II's arrival in Ireland, according to Gerald of Wales, 'There was almost no one of any repute or influence in the whole island who did not present himself before the king's majesty or pay him the respect due to an overlord.' He added that 'the whole of the island remained quiet under the watchful eye of the king, and enjoyed peace and tranquillity'.[33] It is hard to know how seriously to take this; Henry had certainly asserted his authority, but the balance of power in Ireland remained in a state of tense equilibrium. There was a power vacuum within the Irish leadership and there were divisions within the ranks of the English barons too. Henry had acknowledged Strongbow as the leading English baron in Ireland, but he was keen to keep him in check. So in Meath and at Dublin, Henry installed Hugh de Lacy, the great lord of Weobley in Herefordshire and Ludlow in Shropshire, who had come with him from England. The appointment of a baron as grand as Lacy was no accident. He had the prestige and the resources to stop either Strongbow or any ambitious Irish leader expanding outwards from the lands the king had allowed them to keep.

Henry's concern with political and military domination extended to the Irish Church too. Ireland lacked centralised political power and the Church was its only national institution. If Henry could stamp his authority on Ireland's ecclesiastical organisation and structures, he would go a long way towards tightening his hold on Irish affairs more generally. In any event, reform of the Irish Church had suddenly become a more urgent personal priority for the king, and in 1171/2 he saw an opportunity to brush off some of the toxic fallout from the Becket dispute by reinforcing his credentials as a loyal and sincere son of the Church. The chronicler Gervase of Canterbury for one agreed that Henry's main priority in going to Ireland was to avoid the effect of any papal punishment imposed on him for his part in Becket's murder.[34]

Henry had papal backing for his plans in Ireland too. Pope Adrian IV may or may not have issued the bull *Laudabiliter* in 1155. But it is clear that the pope in 1172, Alexander III, enthusiastically supported the reform of the Irish Church. He shared many of the commonly held prejudices about Irish religious practice. When he wrote to Henry II in 1172 about the king's expedition, he referred to the Irish as people who 'marry their stepmothers and are not ashamed to have children by them; a man will live with his brother's wife while his brother is still alive; one man will live in concubinage with two sisters; and many of them, putting away the mother, will marry the daughters'. The pope urged Henry on 'to subject this people to your lordship to eradicate the filth of such great abomination'.[35] In fact, whilst the Irish Church was far from exemplary in terms of its organisation and practices (Irish marriage customs were notoriously archaic and loose; divorce was easy and intermarriage between close kin was not uncommon), major changes had taken place during the twelfth century. The Cistercians and the Augustinian canons had established numerous religious houses in Ireland by the 1140s, bringing Ireland into contact with international trends, and a proper system of territorial dioceses was being constructed by the 1150s. Under the leadership of the saintly Malachy of Armagh, a close personal friend of Bernard of Clairvaux, who died in 1148, reforming ideas had gradually begun to take hold. So change was happening before the English arrived in Ireland, but Henry II had political, religious and personal reasons for wanting to speed it up when he summoned a council of the Irish Church to meet at Cashel early in 1172. 'There', according to Gerald of Wales, 'the monstrous excesses and vile practices of that land and people were investigated.'[36] More prosaically, under the supervision of a papal legate, the council dealt with issues such as the proper payment of tithes, marriages and wills. Meanwhile Gerald's account of the council suggests that Henry was finding it hard to change his controlling ways. The aim of the council 'was to assimilate the condition of the Irish church to that of the church in England in every way possible'.[37]

How far or for how long the decrees made at Cashel were implemented is not known. The apparent unity of the Irish religious hierarchy
in signing up to them would not have made their enforcement any
easier. Ireland's social practices and traditions were ancient and deeply
entrenched and it would take more than a few pious pronouncements to
change entire lifestyles. And if King Henry himself planned to oversee
what happened next, he was soon frustrated. The bad weather during the
winter of 1171–2, which interrupted food supplies to his army, was
accompanied by dysentery within the ranks. The king then learned that
papal envoys had arrived in Normandy; they were threatening to impose
an interdict on Henry's lands if he did not come to meet them and settle
his dispute with the Church. So, almost certainly earlier than he had
intended, Henry left Ireland in April 1172. In the following month he
finally brought the Becket dispute to a formal end by making his peace
with the papal legates at Avranches. There was no doubt, in Gerald's
mind at least, that Henry left Ireland with his ambitions unfulfilled. He
was 'particularly grieved at having to take such untimely leave of his Irish
dominion, which he had intended to fortify with castles, settle in peace
and stability, and altogether to mould to his own design in the coming
summer'.[38] If this had indeed been Henry's plan, Strongbow, his collabo-
rators and his competitors must have been relieved that the king was no
longer breathing down their necks. There was some comfort for the king,
though, as he soon began to reap the reward for settling his dispute with
the Church. In September 1172, after hearing reports of the council of
Cashel, Pope Alexander III wrote three letters, one to the Irish bishops,
a second to the Irish kings and leaders, and a third, which has already
been mentioned, to Henry II himself. The three letters together urged
the Irish to accept Henry as their 'king and lord', because Henry had
gone to Ireland as a religious reformer, to rescue the Irish from the state
of religious barbarism into which they had fallen.[39] However genuine his
religious motives really were, by the end of 1172, Henry had rebuilt his
relations with Rome and reinforced his authority over the Irish religious
and political hierarchies at the same time. His stay in Ireland had lasted
barely six months, and he never went there again. But by establishing the
principle of English sovereignty over Ireland, a principle endorsed by
papal blessing, his stay had been highly significant nonetheless.

Following the outbreak of the Great Revolt against Henry in April 1173, the king summoned Strongbow and some of his baronial colleagues in Ireland to fight in Normandy. The earl defended the crucial frontier fortress of Gisors for the king and was present at the siege of Verneuil in August. The king was grateful and Strongbow returned to Ireland in the autumn of 1173, Henry having made him the guardian of all Ireland, including Dublin and Waterford, on his behalf, with Raymond le Gros as his deputy. The king also granted Strongbow the town of Wexford and Wicklow Castle. However, the absence of Strongbow and the other settler barons in Normandy had encouraged a revolt in Leinster; the Irish, after all, according to Gerald, are 'a race of which the only stable and reliable trait is their being unstable and un-reliable'.[40] In south Wales too the Welsh had taken advantage with a great raid on Netherwent on 16 August, which reached as far as the very walls of Strongbow's castle at Chepstow. In 1174 he tried to reassert his authority in Ireland when he led an expedition into Munster against King Donal O'Brien of Limerick. But, assisted by Rory O'Connor, Donal inflicted a heavy defeat on the earl and forced him to retreat to Waterford. There were also tensions within Strongbow's own ranks. According to the *Song*, Raymond le Gros had by this time left Ireland and returned to Wales. Having asked Strongbow for the hand of the earl's sister, Basilia, in marriage and for the vacant constableship of Leinster, he had been refused and had departed 'full of resentment'.[41] Raymond was now recalled by Strongbow, a sure sign of the difficulties he was facing. There was a price to pay for Raymond's renewed support, though, and Raymond was finally offered marriage to Basilia, together with land grants in Fotharta, and Uí Dróna and the coastal site of Glascarrig. Gerald depicts Strongbow as hemmed in and inactive in Waterford and only the timely arrival of Raymond with fifteen ships (or three, according to the *Song*), thirty knights, 100 mounted archers and 300 foot archers prevented Wexford from falling into Irish hands.[42] Raymond celebrated in fine style with his wedding where 'a whole day had been spent in feasting and a night in enjoying the delights of the bridal bed'.[43] Almost immediately, however, Rory O'Connor raided into Meath, which was under the stern rule of Hugh de Lacy, destroying the castles of Trim and Duleek, and threatening to head further north.

Strongbow and Raymond were quick to respond (the latter 'not in the least slowed down by the effects of either wine or love', Gerald says), forcing Rory to withdraw.[44]

Such events demonstrated that the English grip on Ireland was far from secure by 1174. The Irish themselves, not least Rory O'Connor, remained determined to resist the further spread of English influence and, where possible, to destroy it. The continuing vulnerability of the settlers' position in Ireland, and of Henry II's own newly established power there, probably lay behind the so-called Treaty of Windsor, an agreement the king made with Rory O'Connor in October 1175. Under the terms of this deal, Rory was to rule Connacht as Henry's 'liege man'. In other words, whilst Rory owed personal service and tribute to the king, he did not hold Connacht from him as a feudal vassal, but 'as fully and as peacefully as he did before the lord king entered Ireland'.[45]

Henry recognised Rory's high-kingship over those parts of Ireland not explicitly reserved to English control. In practice, this meant that Rory was left to do what he could to assert himself in the north and south-west, whilst English control over Dublin, Leinster, Meath and Munster from Waterford to Dungarvan was pragmatically acknowledged. What Strongbow and the other settler barons made of all this is unknown (the treaty certainly didn't put any stop to their further advances in the following years), but the earl was with the king at Marlborough and witnessed a number of his charters at about the time the treaty was negotiated. Meanwhile in Ireland, Raymond le Gros was leading an Anglo-Norman force to capture Limerick, a command which, according to the *Song*, had been handed to him by Strongbow.[46] Hervey de Montmorency complained to the king that Raymond was acting against the king's interests and aspired to seize control, not only of Limerick, but of the whole of Ireland. Henry responded by sending four messengers to Ireland early in 1176, two of whom were to escort Raymond to him, while the other two were to remain with Strongbow. As Raymond was about to depart with the royal envoys, news came that Donal O'Brien had besieged the Anglo-Norman garrison of Limerick. Strongbow, according to Gerald, prepared to go to the assistance of the garrison, but his men asserted they would only fight under the leadership of Raymond. Strongbow agreed with the envoys that Raymond should return to Limerick.[47] The Anglo-Norman garrison was relieved on 6 April, but news then broke of Strongbow's death.

He probably died in Dublin, but the precise date of his death is unclear. Gerald of Wales says it was about 1 June 1176, but other sources put it as early as April.[48] Strongbow was buried at the church of Holy Trinity, Dublin, where he was commemorated every 20 April. The cause of Strongbow's death is rather obscure too. Gerald says that the earl had been taken seriously ill some time, perhaps several weeks, before his death. Other sources vary in their graphic details: according to one, an ulcerated foot killed him, whilst another described him dying 'an unholy death . . . after a long wasting sickness'. Both agree that his demise was the revenge of the saints whose churches he had plundered.[49] Strongbow had not been blind to the needs of his soul, however. He founded a nunnery at Usk and made grants in favour of numerous religious houses in England, Wales and Normandy. In Ireland he made grants to Holy Trinity, Dublin, and St Mary's Abbey, Dublin, and to the Knights Hospitaller.

It is arguable that Strongbow died at the right time. The signs are that, by 1176, his grip on power in Ireland was starting to loosen. A man like Hugh de Lacy was able to consolidate his position by constructing castles such as the one at Trim, which nailed down his control of Meath, and by installing his tenants from England, and to do so with royal backing for his attempt to build up his lordship. By the time he died in 1186, an Irish chronicler felt it appropriate to describe Lacy as 'king of Meath and Breifne, and Oriel' (in other words, mid-western Ireland), and to note that the neighbouring kingdom of Connacht paid him tribute. 'He it was that won all Éirinn [Ireland] for the foreigners,' the chronicler proclaimed.[50] Strongbow could not match this kind of power and influence. And even within his immediate family there are signs of tension by the end. When Strongbow's sister Basilia sent news of her brother's death to her husband Raymond le Gros, her coded reference to Strongbow is not hard to decipher: 'that large molar tooth which caused me so much pain has now fallen out,' she declared.[51] Had Strongbow lived longer, it is hard to see how his relationship with Raymond could have prospered. Strongbow was a remarkable man, but his support in Ireland had never been deep or particularly influential. After Henry II's intervention in 1171, and despite his appointment by the king as governor in 1173, Strongbow had struggled to recover his earlier dominant position among the English elite. He was ultimately unable to establish members of his own family in important positions for any length of time, and those men who can be identified as his followers (the witnesses to his charters or the recipients of his land) were not generally men of substance. He left only infant heirs (his only son, Gilbert, was a minor in 1176), and so Leinster came into royal custody when he died. Strongbow's legacy did survive, though. Gilbert died in his teens, but Strongbow's daughter Isabel married William Marshal in 1189. Through his wife, William succeeded to the lordships of Chepstow and Leinster, and in 1199 he regained the earldom of Pembroke.

In 1177, meanwhile, Henry II made another attempt to organise Ireland's political landscape. Perhaps in response to complaints from those English settlers who felt that the Treaty of Windsor had been too generous to Rory O'Connor, at the Council of Oxford in May of that year Henry announced that he would keep the cities of Cork and Limerick for himself. The kingdom of Cork, meanwhile, was carved up between some of the leading settlers, whilst the kingdom of Desmond was given to Robert Fitz Stephen and Miles de Cogan and the kingdom of Limerick to Philip de Briouze. Most important for the future, however, was Henry's decision to make his youngest son, John, king of Ireland. To confirm this he asked the pope to provide John with a crown. John was not yet ten years old, and his appointment was the cornerstone of a long-term plan to bring Ireland securely into the Angevin territorial fold. John did not travel to Ireland until 1185, but his entrance onto the stage of Irish affairs began a new act in the drama.

CHAPTER FIVE

THE YOUNG KING'S TALE
Henry Fitzroy and his Troublesome Family

IT WAS SUPPOSED to happen in August 1179. Louis VII, king of France, had decided that his son, Philip, should be crowned. The boy would be fourteen by then, old enough to start playing a role in government. And it was customary for the French kings to have their sons formally installed as heirs whilst the reigning monarch was still alive. But things were more urgent than usual this time. King Louis was ill when he made the announcement in Paris, and he must have been acutely worried about the future. Philip was his only son, so there was no doubt about his position as heir; nevertheless it was essential to solemnise this once and for all, and a coronation would do just that. But it was Philip who nearly died, not his father. The young prince went hunting and got lost. By the time he was found and taken to safety, he had been out all night and had not eaten for two days. He fell ill, it looked like he would not survive, and the coronation was postponed. King Louis, now in his sixties and with doubts still lingering over his own health, boarded a ship for England. On landing at Dover, he was met by King Henry II, who escorted him to Canterbury. Louis spent two days there praying for his son at the shrine of Thomas Becket. It worked: Philip recovered rapidly and was crowned at Reims on 1 November 1179. Louis was too sick to attend the ceremony. He may have suffered a stroke after returning from England, but whatever was wrong with him, he was incapable of governing anymore. Less than a year later, in September 1180, Louis was dead, and his fifteen-year-old son had become 'the most Christian king', as the Capetians liked to style themselves.

In the congregation at Reims in November 1179, amongst the magnates and prelates of France, were three of Henry II's sons – Geoffrey, Richard, and the eldest surviving legitimate son, Henry, known as Henry 'the Younger' or Henry 'the Young King'. His own coronation had taken place in 1170, and it had confirmed his position as his father's heir to the kingdom of England, the duchy of Normandy and the county of Anjou. One day he would become arguably the most powerful ruler in western Europe, certainly more powerful by far than the king of France. But, after nearly a decade of waiting, that day had still not yet come, and the Young King had to be content with carrying Philip's crown at the head of the coronation procession and leading the shouts of 'Vive le roi!' for the next French king. He probably enjoyed this, as it kept his profile high and his image polished. The Young King was the closest thing to an international celebrity that the twelfth century could produce – handsome, dashing and brave, he was courtly glamour personified. So he would also have been looking forward to the celebrations after the ceremony. There would have been feasting, of course, but there was also sport. At Lagny a few miles east of Paris, a great tournament was arranged to mark the occasion. The Young King arrived there with a retinue of more than two hundred knights, at least fifteen of whom brought companies of their own. This was a huge and impressive body of fighting men, but also a very expensive one – Henry paid for his own knights' expenses, but he also paid twenty shillings a day for each knight brought by his senior commanders. The whole occasion must have cost Henry over £200 a day, the size of a rich baron's annual income. 'It was a source of wonder where this wealth was to be found,' remarked one incredulous contemporary.[1]

In 1179 the Young King was ten years older than Philip. So in terms of age and experience, he was the senior of the two. Admittedly, the French king was the overlord of the lands Henry would inherit in France, and the Young King was required to observe the ceremonial niceties and play the deferential vassal at Philip's coronation. But this would not matter in the end, Henry probably thought, because his promised lands dwarfed Philip's in size. And, above all, Henry would have England, where the king had no superior and Philip had no authority. Unlike Philip's, Henry's kingdom would be large, rich and easy to rule, and in time he would tower above his French counterpart, just as Henry II had overshadowed Louis VII. But this particular future never came to pass and the careers of these two heirs to great inheritances could not in the end have been more different. Within a year of his coronation, Philip was ruling his kingdom. Henry, by contrast, never got his inheritance at all. He rebelled against his father twice in an effort to make him surrender some power, but he failed both times and he was dead at twenty-eight, his last years spent as a bitter man, unfulfilled and ignored. Philip II, by contrast, or Philip 'Augustus' as he would later be called, reigned for another forty years after the Young King's death. During that time he would destroy the achievements of Henry II and change the shape of Europe.

* * * *

With hindsight, it is possible to see the essential hollowness of the Young King's position in the events of 1179 and 1180. He attended Philip's coronation as his father's representative, not in his own right, and his performance at the Lagny tournament was funded mostly by credit that he never repaid. He put on a splendid show both times, but on these occasions, as on many others, he was unable to hide his lack of real military, political and economic power. But his story is not important just because it is a sad one of unfulfilled promises and potential. There were many other sides to aristocratic life in the twelfth century, and the Young King's story opens a window onto these. He has often been seen as the epitome of the feckless heir-in-waiting. But life was more complex and difficult than this for someone in his position. There was glamour and glory, of course, at court and on campaign, and there was music, literature and philosophy. But more typical were the everyday inconveniences of travelling and the mundane necessity of paying the bills. And whilst young Henry was the most famous of his kind, there were whole hosts of young noblemen like him with little to do. Some were waiting for their fathers to die so that they could step into their shoes and become great lords. Before this happened, though, they lived on credit, on their winnings from gambling and tournaments, and on what their parents were prepared to give them. Others, second or third sons from poorer families with few prospects of their own, hung around the heirs, served them, drank and feasted with them, whored with them, and fought alongside them in taverns, at tournaments and, occasionally, in a real battle, in the hope of picking up money and lands of their own in due course. The Young King, privileged though he was, still inhabited a ferociously competitive and unforgiving world. There was a limit to what a man could do on his own account, whoever he was.

But most importantly, the Young King's story provides a reminder that, even at the highest level, national and international politics was also family politics. Henry II's fraught and troubled relationship with his wife and their sons dictated the course of his reign to a significant extent; how he managed his children's upbringings, their education, their marriages and their inheritances was a crucial factor in causing wars and bringing them to an end. Other rulers were happy to get involved in the quarrels that beset Henry's family and to play on the tensions within it for their own gain and advantage. The stability of England and France depended on such things regularly from the 1160s onwards; in the 1170s they nearly led to disaster for Henry II in the greatest rebellion he ever faced, and the Young King was at the heart of it all until his death in 1183.

* * * *

Young Henry was the second son of Henry II and Eleanor of Aquitaine. Born in London on 28 February 1155, he became his parents' eldest surviving son after the death of their first, William, in December 1156. Almost from the start, Henry was a focus for controversy. He was only three years old when his engagement to Margaret, the six-month-old daughter of King Louis VII of France, was arranged by Thomas Becket, Henry II's chancellor. The reasons behind this betrothal were purely political and territorial. Straddling the lands of the dukes of Normandy and the kings of France was the strategically vital frontier zone known as the Vexin. In the tenth century it had been split into the western Vexin, which became part of the duchy of Normandy, and the eastern Vexin, which had been annexed by the French kings when its own line of counts died out in the 1070s. After that William I, William II and

Henry I had campaigned there frequently, and control of the Vexin had become central to the ongoing struggles between the Norman kings and their French adversaries. The area's importance was obvious. The line between the western and eastern parts of the Vexin ran roughly north to south along the river Epte, a tributary of the Seine. The junction between these two rivers was roughly equidistant between the cities of Rouen and Paris, which were themselves only seventy miles apart. So domination of the Vexin by one ruler would inevitably endanger the chief city and wider territories of the other. The Vexin consequently became one of the most heavily militarised areas of twelfth-century Europe: a series of great castles lined the banks of the Epte, and three of these, Gisors, Châteauneuf and Néaufles, were set aside to form Princess Margaret's dowry as part of the 1158 marriage agreement.

There was no suggestion in 1158 that Henry and Margaret might actually marry any time soon. Even by twelfth-century standards, they were far too young for this and in no position freely to give their consent. So until they were old enough Margaret would be brought up at Henry II's court. However, events soon made the need to control the castles of Gisors, Châteauneuf and Néaufles even more pressing than before. In 1159, Henry II went south and attacked Toulouse in an attempt to make something of his wife Eleanor's long-standing claims to the county. He was unsuccessful, and Louis VII campaigned against him there in person; the relationship between the two rulers was only temporarily mended by a truce in May 1160. The 1158 marriage arrangements were confirmed as part of that truce and the Knights Templar were given custody of the three dowry castles. Later in the year, though, this finely balanced peace was compromised when Constanza of Castile (Margaret's mother) died in childbirth in September 1160. Within a fortnight of his wife's death King Louis had announced that he was to marry again, this time Adela of Blois-Champagne. News of an alliance between the French kings and the house of Blois-Champagne was not well received by Henry II, who saw it as a threat to the balance of power in northern France. In October 1160 young Henry did homage to Louis VII for Normandy. The French king had now accepted the child prince's position as heir. Almost immediately after that, however, in order to secure his position in the Vexin by getting his hands on the three frontier castles, Henry II had Henry and Margaret married. Fortunately, there were three cardinals travelling through France at the time, seeking support for the new pope, Alexander III, against his rival for the papal throne, the schismatic Victor IV. Presumably in return for Henry's agreement to back Alexander, they were prepared to overlook the obvious irregularities and grant a dispensation for the marriage of two children. The couple became husband and wife at Neubourg in Normandy on 2 November 1160; Henry was five years old, his new wife only two. In the words of Roger of Howden, they 'were still little children, crying in the cradle'.[2]

The Templars in possession of the three castles readily handed them over to a delighted Henry II who, it was said, 'enriched them with many honours'.[3] King Louis' response, meanwhile, was predictably furious. He and his new brothers-in-law from Blois-Champagne attacked Henry in Touraine, but he responded by seizing the castle of Chaumont on the Loire. Stalemate followed and another truce, finally arranged in October 1161, was inevitable. Henry had been scandalously bold in pressing ahead with the marriage, but his seizure of the tactical initiative had paid off. By the time Henry celebrated Christmas 1160 at Le Mans, the Vexin castles were his and his eldest son had been recognised as the heir to Normandy by a French king whose daughter was now part of Henry's family. That King Louis had been duped, outmanoeuvred, and left with a strong sense of grievance was probably regarded by King Henry as a price worth paying. In the longer term, however, Henry was storing up trouble: Margaret's marriage, the status of the Vexin, and the way Henry handled his eldest son would all in future be skilfully exploited by Louis and his own heir. Henry II may have won the political and diplomatic battle in 1160, but the war was only just beginning.

King Henry had probably developed other plans for his son by now. It seems likely that, by the early 1160s, he was keen to have young Henry crowned. The transmission of a royal title would mark him out clearly as his principal heir. Although this was a common practice in the French kingdom, nothing like it had happened in England since the eighth century. Henry II was certainly not inspired by this example. It would have been his predecessor's predicament that he had in mind. Stephen had tried to have his son Eustace crowned in the early

1150s, but the English bishops' refusal to cooperate had signalled their rejection of Stephen's dynastic ambitions and mortally damaged his cause. Henry II would not have wanted any such uncertainty to surround his own plans for the succession, and it is not surprising that Alexander III sent a letter to Archbishop Roger of York in 1161, when the archbishopric of Canterbury was vacant, ordering him to crown young Henry whenever he wished to do so, and that in the following year a crown and other regalia were made for the prince.[4] It is tempting to think that Thomas Becket, the king's chancellor, was central to these arrangements. According to one of Becket's biographers, the chancellor was sent back to England by the king in 1162 'especially to gain the fealty and subjection of all to his son, then to be crowned and sworn in as king'.[5] It was also in 1162, if not a little earlier, that young Henry was placed in the chancellor's household. This was to be his school. The prince may have begun to pick up some reading and writing skills before then, but in Becket's household he would be grounded in 'honest education and doctrine'.[6] Precisely what William Fitz Stephen meant by this is not clear, but young Henry would have continued to learn to hunt and fight, and, in time, he would have been introduced to the workings of royal government, politics and diplomacy. He would have done so, moreover, alongside the sons of other noblemen, from England and beyond, who had also been entrusted to the care of Becket and his staff. It may also have been Becket who gave young Henry something of the taste for luxury, extravagance and display for which the prince became famous later in life. The splendour of Becket's embassy to Paris in 1158, when he had negotiated Henry's betrothal to Margaret, was already legendary, and the chancellor's own daring military exploits, in Toulouse in 1159 and in Normandy in 1161 (a campaign on which young Henry accompanied him) were striking and exciting. His military household in 1161 was said to have consisted of 700 knights, 4,000 foot soldiers and 1,200 mercenaries. Such conspicuous showmanship must have made an impression on the young prince.

The importance of the relationship between young Henry and Becket was summed up by an event in May 1162. At a council in London, it was to the young prince that the bishop of Winchester presented the petition asking that Becket be appointed archbishop, and it was Henry who gave formal consent. Not surprisingly, he was present at Becket's consecration in Canterbury too. So, at the very least, it makes sense to think that the plans for Henry's coronation and education went hand in hand to some extent. With Becket overseeing both, young Henry would be well prepared for the duties that he would have to perform. When the English barons paid homage and fealty to him in January 1163, followed by the Scottish king and the princes of Wales in July of that year, this was an early taste of what was to come. In the end, however, Henry II's relationship with Becket quickly worsened after his chancellor became archbishop, the coronation was postponed and young Henry was withdrawn from Becket's care in October 1163. Young Henry's presence at Clarendon in January 1164, when his father published the Constitutions, also suggests that the king was trying to drive a wedge between the prince and his former teacher. Whether the nine-year-old Henry appreciated it or not, he was no mere bystander at Clarendon, and he was explicitly associated with Henry II's stance on royal customs and privileges when the Constitutions noted that they were drawn up 'in the presence of the lord Henry, and of his father, the lord king'.[7]

For the next six years the dispute between Henry II and Thomas Becket rumbled on. We can only speculate what young Henry made of it all as he went from boyhood into adolescence and as his political sensibilities developed. Any lingering fondness the young man might have felt for the archbishop must have been overridden by the need to support his father's position, and by a growing awareness of the complex and conflicting demands of royal rule. For one thing, Henry II had more to think about than just his troublesome archbishop. There were problems in Wales, Brittany and Aquitaine in the second half of the 1160s, all of which required the king's personal attention. In addition, the Becket dispute was not self-contained, and it was used and exploited by Henry II's rivals. Louis VII had finally had a son of his own, Philip, in 1165, so he was looking to the future when he pointedly offered Becket shelter and support in 1166. Louis had already encouraged the disgruntled Welsh and Bretons in their struggles against King Henry, and he was keen to use the latter's treatment of Becket as further evidence of the harsh and tyrannical rule that Henry's critics were complaining of with ever more frequency and volume. Then, in 1167, open warfare broke out. Henry accused Louis of interfering in the affairs of the county of Auvergne in Aquitaine. In fact, the new count, William VIII ('the Old'), who had seized power from his nephew, William VII ('the Young'), had simply appealed to Louis for justice; arguably, the new count was entitled to do this given the French king's position as overlord of the ruler of Aquitaine. Louis could play the role of the honest broker and concerned lord, so when Henry decided to deal with the problem by marching into the Auvergne and laying waste to the count's lands, Louis responded by sending raids into the Norman Vexin. Henry immediately went north and sacked Louis' arsenal at Chaumont-sur-Epte (in the French Vexin) and Louis returned fire by burning the town of Andelys on Henry's side of the river Epte. After a short truce, the war resumed in 1168, and a final peace was only arranged after Henry had systematically destroyed more than forty villages along the Norman frontier that belonged to the count of Ponthieu, Louis' vassal.

Whether young Henry played any part in these campaigns is unclear. He may have remained in England, either for his own safety or, more likely, to help keep the peace in the kingdom and along its internal frontiers. Wherever he was in 1167–8, however, he was central to the peace discussions of 1169, which took place at Montmirail in the county of Maine in January 1169. King Henry took this opportunity to announce his plans for the succession to all his territories. What they amounted to was the dismantling of his 'empire' and its redistribution amongst his sons. Young Henry would succeed to England, Normandy and Anjou, and Geoffrey would rule Brittany as a vassal of his eldest brother; Richard would become duke of Aquitaine and marry King Louis' other daughter, Alice. Of the four brothers, only the two-year-old John was left without an inheritance. This was no ploy by Henry II and, even though it was an arrangement Louis VII enthusiastically accepted, the English king seems to have been quite sincere in his wish to divide his lands. Geoffrey took the homage of the barons of Brittany at Rennes in May 1169. In the same year Richard was proclaimed count of Poitou (the northern part of the duchy of Aquitaine) and in 1170 he was accepted as future lord of Aquitaine in grand assemblies at Niort and Limoges. Moreover, when King Henry fell ill and almost died in August

1170, his priority was to confirm the arrangements first announced at Montmirail.

By then, buoyed by his new status as heir apparent, young Henry's career had entered its next phase. He had performed homage to Louis VII for Anjou and Brittany at Montmirail (having already done homage for Normandy in October 1160) and then, as the acknowledged heir to Anjou, he was made seneschal of France by Louis. In February 1169, Henry was in Paris to perform his duties at the French king's table. These were purely ceremonial, to be sure, but the symbolism of Louis as master and Henry as servant was significant. And Louis also took this opportunity to have Henry perform homage to his three-year-old son, Philip. This new relationship between young Henry, Louis and Philip, that of vassal, lord and lord-to-be, was to become increasingly important over the next few years and would challenge the centrality of that other relationship in the young prince's life, the one with his father. Nevertheless, that relationship remained close for the time being. Indeed, King Henry's focus on his eldest son appears to have been resharpened by events at Montmirail, and the idea of having him crowned king in England, which had been abandoned in the early 1160s, was soon revived. On 24 May 1170 the young prince became the Young King when he was crowned at Westminster Abbey. On the following day Malcolm, king of Scots, and his brother David, along with all the English barons, paid homage to him.

On one level, the objective here was clear and understandable, and the same as it had been ten years before: to clarify and formalise young Henry's position as heir to England, just as he had been confirmed heir to Normandy and Anjou the previous year. On another level, though, the coronation of the Young King is a perplexing episode. Henry II must have known it would be provocative and controversial, simply because the ceremony was performed by the archbishop of York and not by the archbishop of Canterbury, who claimed the exclusive right to consecrate the king. Becket was still in exile (attempts by Louis VII to force a reconciliation between Henry and his archbishop at Montmirail had failed) and nothing could have been more calculated to add to Becket's wounded pride and outraged feelings than this deliberate insult to his position. Moreover, until the Young King was consecrated by the archbishop of Canterbury, it would be open to his rivals and critics to question the legitimacy of his position and, more specifically, because the Young King's wife Margaret was not crowned with him, the event imperilled the good relationship established with her father Louis VII in the previous year. It has been suggested that this whole affair was a ploy by Henry II to force through a resolution to the Becket dispute; in other words, Becket would make any compromise in order to recover his lost prestige. Alternatively, perhaps the absence of Margaret from the coronation was an essential part of the scheme. There are suggestions that she was deliberately delayed at Caen so that she missed the ceremony.[8] Louis would now have to put pressure on Becket to heal his rift with Henry so that his daughter could get the legitimate coronation she needed. If this was Henry's strategy, however, it was complex and high-risk to say the least. It enraged the monks of Canterbury and many of the English bishops. It also provoked Pope Alexander III, who until this point had been cautious about publicly supporting Becket, and it led him to threaten England with a sentence of interdict and Henry II with excommunication. It seems more likely that King Henry had simply overreached himself and he was probably taken aback by the vehemently angry response the coronation caused. So, rather than backing Becket into a corner in which the archbishop had no choice but to compromise, it was the king who was forced to offer Becket an olive branch. Henry and Becket met at Fréteval on 22 July 1170 and the archbishop accepted the king's offer of a peaceful return to Canterbury and the chance to re-crown the Young King. By the time Henry and Margaret were eventually crowned together, however, at Winchester on 27 August 1172, Thomas Becket had been dead for nearly two years.

All of this still lay ahead when Henry II left England for Normandy after his son's coronation in June 1170. The Young King's position as his father's principal heir had been secured, it seemed, and now, at last, he was actually being allowed to rule. As his father travelled to Normandy to try and appease Louis VII, the Young King was left in England with the authority to make 'all rights and judgements by his new seal'.[9] Then, full power seemed within his reach for a time between July and September as news of Henry II's grave illness reached England. It was even rumoured at one point that the king had died. He recovered, of course, and perhaps the Young King was relieved: he must have thought his time would come soon enough. As it turned out, however, this was as close as he ever came to succeeding his father. His new seal, the one made for him in 1170, may hint more credibly at the reality of his position after his coronation: it described him as 'King of the English and Duke of the Normans and Count of the Angevins', but it shows him holding a globe and a rod, not a sword, the true symbol of royal authority.[10] The Young King was soon to learn that, for all his titles, he had been given no real power.

As Henry's eighteenth birthday approached at the start of 1173 he was finding it hard to conceal the unhappiness he felt at the way his father was treating him. He was now a grown man with a wife and an entourage to support. He needed resources if he was to live like the king he was supposed to be: cash to meet his domestic expenses and support his lifestyle, and land from which to draw an income and with which to reward his followers. Just as importantly, for the sake of his image and his reputation, he needed to rule territory of his own and start making decisions that had an impact on the lives of subjects who acknowledged him, not his father or one of his brothers, as their lord. He had been under the restrictions placed upon him by his father when he went to England after his coronation, and his continuing frustration was still evident a year later in 1171 when he held a Christmas court at Bur near Bayeux. Henry II was in Ireland and as the Young King held court in Normandy for the first time, he was anxious that the celebrations should be memorable. Henry was determined to impress his future Norman subjects, but there was still more style than substance to the show, and there was something almost desperate about his desire to stage a spectacle; just as there was at the great banquet of Christmas 1172, which featured a room containing more than a hundred knights, all called William! Henry's second coronation in August 1172 and his birthday knighting by his friend William Marshal in February 1173 were major events in the prince's life. However, they may only have reinforced the impression in his own mind and in the opinions of others that he was little more than a decorative luxury, not to be taken seriously as a hard-headed, forceful and formidable leader. The contrast with his father was obvious: by the end of his eighteenth year, Henry II was already ruler of Normandy, Anjou and Aquitaine, and he was about to conquer England.

No doubt the Young King was being urged to stand up to his father by those around him. When he and his wife visited Louis VII at the end of 1172, his father-in-law told him to demand a meaningful share of his inheritance. If Henry II refused, Louis said, the Young King should return to him in France. Louis' influence over his son-in-law was clearly becoming a problem for Henry II.[11] The members of the prince's own household, too, were becoming frustrated at their lord's lack of substantive power. The Young King's surviving charters reveal a group of knights more or less permanently in his company; young men like their lord, and like him impatiently waiting for land of their own and the independent standing this would give them. Some of them were even removed from the prince's entourage by Henry II, almost certainly a result of the father's concerns about the ideas these ambitious young men were putting into his son's head. Despite Henry's efforts, however, these ideas were firmly lodged by the time the old king revealed his new plan in February 1173. Almost as if to coincide with young Henry's coming of age, Henry II announced his intention to hand over to John (his youngest son, only five years old) three important castles in Anjou: Chinon, Loudun and Mirebeau. The plan was to make John a more acceptable candidate for the marriage alliance Henry was arranging with the Count of Maurienne (John would marry the count's daughter, Alice). However, the lands set apart for John were to be taken from the county of Anjou, which was part of the Young King's inheritance.

So not only had young Henry not been given anywhere to rule after 1169, these particular lands would now be lost to him forever. He was understandably outraged by what he must have seen as his father's deliberate insult: he didn't even have a place where he and his wife could live together, he pointedly remarked.[12] But, whilst genuine, his angry response was probably not spontaneous, and Roger of Howden's view that Henry 'thirsted for the blood of a father, the gore of a parent!' was perhaps a little far-fetched.[13] The Young King may have had some inkling of his father's scheme before its details were made public. It gave him the set-piece matter of principle he had been looking for in his ongoing struggle for power with the elder Henry. Emboldened by the advice he had received from King Louis ('and by the counsel of the earls and barons of England and Normandy, who hated his father,' Howden alleged),[14] he demanded that King Henry immediately give him England, Normandy or Anjou. But his father refused and the pace of events accelerated quickly enough to suggest a degree of forward planning by the prince and his supporters. In March 1173 he slipped away in secret from his father's court and fled to Louis' in Paris. The French king was probably not surprised to see him, and Henry was soon joined there in open rebellion by his brothers Richard and Geoffrey. Their mother, Queen Eleanor, also tried to follow them, but her disguise as a man was unsuccessful and she was intercepted by her husband's men and imprisoned. Then, when Henry II sent envoys to Paris to negotiate, they were treated dismissively. On requesting the Young King's return, King Louis enquired 'Who asks?' They replied, 'The king of England'. 'Nonsense,' Louis said, 'the king of England is here; his father may still pose as king, but that will soon be fixed, for as all the world knows he has resigned the kingdom to his son.'[15]

What on the face of things looked like an internal family dispute soon developed into something much more significant. In fact, between 1173 and 1174 Henry II faced the biggest and most serious rebellion of his reign. The Young King actively set about recruiting support as soon as it became obvious that war was inevitable. A council of French barons met at Paris and pledged him their loyalty, in return for which he promised not to make peace with his father without their consent. King Louis had a new seal made for his young protégé and Henry used it on charters with which he bought the support of important French lords. The count of Boulogne, who was married to King Stephen's daughter, was promised the county of Mortain in Normandy and extensive estates in England; his elder brother, the count of Flanders, was promised the county of Kent and an annual pension of £1,000 from English funds; the count of Blois-Champagne was promised lands and revenues in Anjou and Touraine; whilst the king of Scots was seduced by the offer of all Northumbria as far south as the Tyne. The coalition was further strengthened by the addition of leading earls and barons from England and Normandy, who defied the king after tolerating nearly two decades of being denied what they saw as their rightful claims to inheritances, estates, offices and castles. Henry's aggressive centralising policies had alienated many of these men. On both sides of the English Channel he had inquired repeatedly and intrusively into his barons' affairs, gathering information about their lands, incomes, rights and their relationships with their own vassals. There were rebels in Anjou, Maine, Brittany and Aquitaine, too, some simply opportunistic, others with their own personal axes to grind. The chronicler Ralph of Diss summed up the attitude of those who jumped on the Young King's bandwagon. They did so, he said, 'not because they regarded his cause as juster, but because the father was trampling upon the necks of the proud and haughty, dismantling or appropriating the castles of the country, and requiring, even compelling, those who occupied royal lands to relinquish them, and be content with their own patrimony'.[16] The revolt spread quickly into every corner of Henry II's lands, and even if men were not prepared openly to join in the fight against him, many were reluctant to give him their active support.

The war began in May 1173 with a five-pronged assault on Normandy led by the counts of Flanders and Boulogne (supported by the Young King and his brothers), the count of Blois, King Louis and the rebellious Bretons. Meanwhile in England, William, king of Scots, invaded the north in an effort to link up with the rebel earls in the Midlands. Luck was on the king's side, however: the count of Boulogne was mortally wounded by a stray crossbow bolt, and the death of his brother persuaded the count of Flanders to pull out of the war altogether. Henry now struck a decisive blow against King Louis' army, which had advanced into southern Normandy and, after a surprise attack at Verneuil, he chased him ignominiously back across the frontier in August. Then, in a lightning march west, he took the Bretons by surprise, scattered their forces and captured their leaders, amongst them the earl of Chester. Back in England, Henry's faithful justiciar, Richard de Luci, had captured the rebel stronghold of Leicester in July, driven the Scots back across the border, and then defeated a large force of Flemish mercenaries that had landed in Suffolk. These troops had been led by the earl of Leicester, but they had also been joined by the earl of Norfolk, Hugh Bigod, who had decided to side with the Young King. Bigod was by now in his seventies, but his energy seems to have been as great as ever. His castles at Framlingham, Walton and Bungay made him a formidable ally for young Henry and access to the Suffolk coast would allow the rebels to bring in supplies and mercenaries from Flanders. Perhaps the temporary loss of the first two of these castles in 1156–7, and the money he had been forced to pay the king before he could build the third one, still rankled with Hugh, and this gave him a chance to take his revenge. More immediately, however, the price young Henry paid for Hugh's support was a promise of the constableship of Norwich Castle and the honour of Eye. These had both been given to Bigod's old rival, William of Blois, King Stephen's son, in the closing stages of the civil war. The chance to get them for himself, after so many years during which they had challenged his position in East Anglia, must have been too tempting for Hugh to resist. When Robert, earl of Leicester, and his wife, Petronilla, landed at Walton in Suffolk at the end of September 1173, they stayed for some days with Bigod at Framlingham. Together, the two earls then captured the small fortress at Haughley, about fifteen miles east of Bury St Edmunds. However, their attack on Walton Castle and the town of Dunwich failed, and after a brief return to Framlingham, Earl Robert and Countess Petronilla were captured (the latter dressed in armour and carrying a shield and lance, according to one chronicler) when they tried to force their way out of East Anglia and return to their estates in the Midlands. So by the end of 1173, despite the size of the coalition against him and the geographical extent of the revolt, King Henry had retained the initiative and looked to be on course for victory.

The war resumed in the spring of 1174. King William attacked northern England again in April, although his campaign soon petered out. And so Philip of Flanders, by now recovered from his brother's death, declared his intention to invade England. At the end of June he was at Gravelines with the Young King, preparing his fleet for launch. Count Philip may have meant this seriously, or it may have been, at least in part, a ploy to get Henry II out of Normandy so that Louis could undermine his position there. Philip did send a force of Flemish merce-naries to England. After landing at Orwell in Suffolk and joining 500 of Hugh Bigod's soldiers, they captured Norwich Castle, massacred a large number of the inhabitants, and sacked and burnt the city; but this was the limit of their achievement. Meanwhile, the prospect of his eldest son returning to England with powerful military support was enough to persuade Henry II to cross the Channel himself at the start of July. His first priority on his return, however, was not military. After landing at Southampton, the king made straight for Becket's new shrine at Canterbury. Barefoot, and clad just in a plain woollen smock, Henry walked the last part of the journey into the city. Once in the cathedral itself, he prostrated himself in front of Becket's tomb and was publicly lashed by the monks. Then, on the very next day, 13 July, after Henry had spent the night in prayer before the remains of his old friend, the king of Scots was captured by loyalist northerners at Alnwick in Northumberland. This was surely Becket's doing: pacified at last by Henry's abasement and humiliation, it was clear to his supporters that the king had regained divine favour and that he would now go on to defeat his enemies. In the event, King William's capture did indeed signal the effective end of the rebellion in England, but Henry felt it necessary to deal personally with Hugh Bigod first. The king mustered a large army at Bury St Edmunds in preparation for an assault on Bungay and Framlingham, but Hugh decided to submit before the attack began. At the end of July 1174 he swore an oath of homage to Henry II, and he was fined heavily. Hugh may have hoped that this would be the worst of his punishment, but his castles at Framlingham and Bungay were demolished in 1176. Whether Hugh witnessed their destruction is unknown. In 1176 he embarked on a pilgrimage to Jerusalem, but he died on the journey, some time before 9 March 1177. His body was brought back to England and he was buried at Thetford Priory, to which he had granted numerous estates during his long and eventful life.

Meanwhile, taking advantage of Henry II's absence from Normandy, King Louis had moved up the Seine to besiege Rouen in the middle of July 1174. He was joined there by the Young King and the count of Flanders, who had put their plans to invade England aside once Henry II had reasserted his authority over the kingdom in person. The great Norman city had been the rebels' principal target all along: if they could take it, as Geoffrey of Anjou had done in 1144, the rest of the duchy would be at their mercy. By the time Henry returned to confront them there in August, however, Louis' army had not even managed to surround the whole city. The French king retreated, leaving the Young King and his brothers isolated. With England pacified and Normandy back safely under Henry's control, the game was up for his opponents.

Richard submitted quickly when his father confronted him in Poitou in September. The best he, his brothers and their erstwhile allies could do now was sue for peace and throw themselves on the old king's mercy.

At Montlouis, on 30 September 1174, Henry and his sons were formally reconciled. The grant of lands to John (the Young King's reason for rebellion in the first place) was confirmed, but the king did grant his eldest son two castles in Normandy and 15,000 Angevin pounds for his upkeep. Richard and Geoffrey were awarded revenues from Poitou and Brittany respectively. The other rebels were treated leniently (too leniently, some thought). They were allowed to have the lands and castles they had held before the revolt; Henry had wiped the slate clean. Only Queen Eleanor, who remained in royal custody, and William, king of Scots, who was compelled to submit to his English counterpart, do him homage and, in effect, give up Scotland's status as an independent kingdom, were treated harshly. Henry's generosity was a reflection of how total his triumph had been in 1173–4. From having seemed so vulnerable at the start of the war, by the time it ended he was more dominant than ever. Even so, those fundamental tensions within Henry's family that had provoked the revolt in the first place remained unresolved. The official peace terms certainly left no doubt about who was still in charge of the family business: 'King Henry, the king's son, and his brothers, returned to their father, and to his service, *as their lord*.'[17] But this, indeed, was the problem. The Young King's ambitions had been thwarted once again, and a couple of castles and a few thousand pounds were not likely to satisfy him for long. And he could now add another item to the list of empty gestures his father had made towards his supposedly royal status: having taken the homage of his sons Richard and Geoffrey at Montlouis, Henry refused to accept the offer of a similar submission from his eldest son 'because he was a king'.[18]

It is fair to assume that young Henry felt anything but regal at this point. Some contemporaries were inclined to blame others for his failure. The Young King had acted 'unadvisedly, by the counsel and suggestion of a treacherous faction', and 'on the advice of wicked men', claimed the courtier and prolific letter-writer Peter of Blois.[19] Such arguments may have been designed to absolve Henry from blame for what had happened, but they also inadvertently perpetuated the image of the impotent, passive prince unable to take his fate into his own hands. Even during the war of 1173–4 (the Young King's war, it should be remembered), the surviving accounts leave a strong impression that others were doing most of the fighting, and that he played a supporting role at best. Perhaps paradoxically, however, for as long as he continued to evoke sympathy rather than inspire respect, the likelihood of the Young King raising his banners in revolt once again remained high.

And it is clear enough that the reconciliation of 1174 did not improve the relationship between father and son for long. To be sure, there were times when the two Henries worked together on royal business: great councils were held at Northampton in 1176 and at Windsor in 1179, and the important decisions announced there about changes to the English legal system were explicitly stated to have been made by the king and his son. But despite such examples, the two men struggled to get along. Young Henry's request to leave England and go on a pilgrimage to Santiago de Compostela was turned down by the king, who suspected that his son's untrustworthy advisers had put him up to this as a way of getting him out of his father's reach. However, the Young King was instructed by his father to escort Joan, his sister, to Poitou in 1176, the first stage of her journey to Sicily where she would marry the king, William II. Once he had arrived in southern France, Henry joined his brother Richard in his struggle with the local nobility, over whom Richard had been trying to exert his authority since the early 1170s. Henry may have spent less of his time there fighting, however, than he did getting in touch with others who nurtured grievances against Henry II. Perhaps as an act of defiance and as a further attempt to demonstrate his independence, whilst in Poitou young Henry brought a group of men into his household whom, Roger of Howden reports, his father hated.[20] The king's concerns about their character were probably confirmed after they apprehended Adam of Churchdown, the Young King's vice-chancellor, who had attempted in secret to tell Henry II about this, and tried him for treason. Found guilty, he was spared from execution only because he was a clergyman. Instead he was whipped naked through the streets of Argentan in Normandy and imprisoned. Adam had to be rescued by the personal intervention of Henry II himself. It is only possible to guess at the kind of atmosphere and ethos prevailing within the Young King's household at this time: certainly it must have been nasty, spiteful and cruel. For his part, whether he actively encouraged such conduct or was too weak to rein in his friends, this event shows young Henry at his worst. It is important to know, however, that Adam of Churchdown had been placed in the Young King's household by his father: Adam's treatment at young Henry's hands was really an attack on Henry II.

It was soon after this, Ralph of Diss noted, that 'Henry the son of the king of England, leaving the kingdom, passed three years in French contests and lavish expenditure'.[21] The 'contests' Ralph had in mind were tournaments. Tournaments were war games or mock battles between different groups of knights. Fighting men had always found ways to practise their vocation, but meetings like this are first mentioned only in the early twelfth century. They were designed to provide the warrior aristocracy of western Europe with meaningful training in combat. They certainly did this, but there was more too. In the tournament a knight could make a name for himself through his displays of martial skill and valour. He could also make a living and even get rich by capturing and ransoming his opponents. Successful knights were sought after by rival teams and lured into their company with promises of money and other rewards. Some of the greatest nobles of the day (the count of Flanders and the duke of Burgundy, for example) would take part in tournaments, but they would also sponsor and arrange them, hosting and feasting their most honoured guests and offering prizes, as a way of burnishing their own leadership credentials. Tournaments were banned by the kings in England for reasons of public order, and the Church strongly disapproved of them, too. But by the 1160s and 1170s something like a full-blown tournament circuit was operating in parts of France. Late autumn was the height of the tournament season and an enthusiastic knight might take part in one every couple of weeks. Often these events were not large (forty or fifty knights perhaps, divided into two teams), but some were major occasions that attracted hundreds of combatants from all over France and England.

Tournaments were thrilling and exciting, but also dangerous and brutal, and an encounter at a tournament differed little from real warfare. The participants would be fully armed and armoured and, at a given signal, the knights from the different companies or teams, often dressed in the same colour and arranged in national or regional groups, would charge at each other on horseback and the mêlée would begin. The fight would then tend to degenerate into running battles between groups of knights and might spread over several square miles within the area that defined the tournament zone. The winning side was the one that eventually secured control of the field or took the largest number of captives before the day's fighting ended. In fact, hostage-taking and ransoming were the major concerns for the participants whilst the fighting was going on. A captured combatant was expected to promise to pay a ransom to his victorious adversary although, once this had been arranged, the vanquished man would probably be allowed to re-enter the battle.

The prospect of riches and glory, as well as the chance of a good scrap, were bound to entice a man such as the Young King. After all, to put it bluntly, in the second half of the 1170s he had little else to do with his time, he needed the money, and he craved the status that success in tournaments would bring. As a result, Henry became one of the most well-known and prominent participants on the tournament circuit. In this he was encouraged, once again, by the members of his entourage and, probably, by one man in particular, William Marshal. The Marshal (as he was known) had joined the Young King's household in 1170, having transferred there from the household of Henry's mother, Queen Eleanor. His special responsibility was to train the prince in arms. Before entering royal service the Marshal had been brought up in Normandy in the household of William, lord of Tancarville, and he had been on the tournament circuit with his lord after 1166. When the Marshal arrived at young Henry's side, aged about twenty-three, his reputation as a successful tournament knight was already growing. The prince, by contrast, was only fifteen, just crowned and, as yet, inexperienced in warfare. He had also already acquired a reputation for extravagance and for reckless spending. Henry II's hope was probably that the older man would act as a mature, steadying influence on his eldest son and keep his youthful spirits within the bounds of royal propriety. Any such hopes, however, were soon disappointed. The Marshal was strong, dynamic and charismatic. If anything, his tales of the tournament field and his accounts of his adventures would have spurred the Young King on to emulate him. It was the Marshal who knighted the Young King in 1173 (something Henry II had wanted Louis VII to do), and he joined the Young King's rebellion in 1173–4. In due course, moreover, the Marshal would become the most famous and successful tournament knight of them all and, it has been said, the 'player-manager' of the Young King's own tournament team.

From 1176 until 1182, if the Young King was not actually taking part in a tournament, he was preparing for one. There was much travelling of course, but this may have suited the prince's own restless nature. After all, as the Marshal's biographer wrote, 'a long period of rest is a disgrace to a young man', and young Henry himself is reported to have argued that 'it could be a source of much harm to me to stay idle for so long . . . I am no bird to be mewed up; a young man who does not travel around could never aspire to any worthwhile thing, and he should be regarded as of no account.'[22] Peter of Blois, who lived and worked in Henry II's court for over a decade from the mid-1170s, painted a famously unappealing picture of life on the road for the average royal servant. The food and drink were terrible, lodgings were appalling, and there was no settled routine: 'The life of the court,' he said, 'is death to the soul.'[23] On a smaller scale, things were probably not very different for the followers of the Young King as he moved around France in search of the next tournament. But for young Henry himself, the rigours of such a life were probably not so great. Travelling was done in comfort and luxury. The finest food and accommodation were available as money was spent freely and seemingly without scruple as to the lavish expense involved. Not surprisingly, since many of them were landless and without funds of their own, men were keen to serve alongside the young prince. At the great tournament held at Lagny in 1179, where his company contained more than two hundred knights, Young Henry paid a daily cost of about £200, an enormous amount at the time. He had his allowance from his father, of course, but this would not have been enough to pay for everything, and much, it seems, was borrowed. As he was about to move out of one place and on towards another, 'debtors would appear, men who had supplied him with horses, garments and victuals. "This man is owed three hundred pounds, this one a hundred, and that man two hundred, and the total debt is six hundred."'[24] Even allowing for some exaggeration, this startling description shows a young man living far beyond even his considerable means. However, there may have been another side to this. Open-handed generosity was one of the hallmarks of a truly noble lord, and Henry's spending served to develop his image as the soul of knightly largesse. It is easy to assume that Henry II must have disapproved of his son's conduct as frivolous and trivial, but he may actually have tolerated it as good public relations that gave outsiders the impression of a splendid and magnificent Angevin court. At the very least, tournaments gave the Young King something to do. For as long as he could exorcise his frustrations on the tournament field, he was unlikely to vent them on men like Adam of Churchdown. More importantly still, any thoughts of another rebellion might remain dormant.

For Henry II, then, whilst the financial price of his son's activities was heavy, the political gains were potentially considerable. As well as keeping him busy, young Henry's friendship with Count Philip of Flanders, which was based on their shared enthusiasm for the tournament, may have been something Henry II was prepared to allow in the hope that diplomatic benefits would follow in its wake. Count Philip had succeeded his father, Count Thierry, in 1168 just as Flemish dominance of the European cloth trade was reaching a peak. Increasing prosperity was complemented by the counts' prudent administrative and legal reforms, and by the time young Henry had come of age, Count Philip was a major political figure and an ally worth having in the ongoing struggle between the French and English kings. One English contemporary said of him that 'Of all the princes of these days, except our own king, he is the mightiest in arms and in the art of ruling.'[25] And with enormous wealth to draw on, his court became a centre of chivalric and knightly culture. It is not surprising that the Young King was attracted by all of this. Philip was twelve years older than him and, if not quite old enough to be a father figure, he would have made an impressive big brother. To Henry, it must have seemed that Philip had everything he lacked: land, money, power and influence, as well as renown and martial prestige. Philip had supported young Henry during the revolt of 1173–4, and it was at Philip's court in 1176–7 and 1178–9 that Henry developed his military skills in lavish tournaments and built up, largely at Philip's expense, his reputation for chivalrous extravagance. In the end, however, Philip did not prove to be a reliable collaborator. He had become the dominant figure at the French royal court as Louis VII's health had worsened in the late 1170s, and after Louis' death in 1180, the count arranged the marriage of the new king, Philip II, to his niece Isabella of Hainault. Count Philip looked set to direct the start of the new reign just as he had the end of the old one. Soon enough, however, the two Philips, count and king, fell out as the young man tried to assert himself and extend his own power at the expense of his over-mighty subject. This allowed Henry II to play the sympathetic elder statesman and establish a new, reasonably sincere relationship with the French king. Once again, young Henry was left isolated. His relationship with the count of Flanders was over and he may have thought that he, rather than his father, was best placed to develop the new approach to King Philip. After all, they would be ruling alongside each other soon enough.

By 1182, the Young King had lost patience with his father once again and he restated his demand 'that he be given Normandy or some other territory, where he and his wife might dwell, and from which he might be able to support knights in his service'.[26] When Henry II again refused, his son left immediately for the French royal court to put his grievances to Philip II. King Henry was certainly worried by this development, but his refusal to hand over any lands to his son held firm. His only concession was to increase the Young King's allowance to a hundred pounds a day (along with a further ten pounds daily for his wife), but while this calmed the prince down for a while, the deal did not last long. Young Henry had already seen an opportunity to make his point in Aquitaine, where the barons were growing increasingly unhappy with Duke Richard's imperiously harsh ruling style. And when he started agitating there in support of Richard's rebellious subjects, his claim that this was justified by Richard's seizure and fortification of Clairvaux, which arguably lay within the borders of Anjou rather than Poitou, was convenient at best. In January 1183, Henry II called his sons together at Le Mans, and, apparently having accepted the Young King's assurances about his future good conduct, demanded that Richard perform homage to the Young King for Aquitaine. At this point the accounts differ about precisely how Richard responded to his father's order. All agree, however, that he was outraged by the suggestion that he should submit to his brother. He promptly left court and, according to Roger of Howden, 'returned in haste to his own territory and fortified his castles and towns'.[27] The Young King, accompanied by his brother Geoffrey, followed him. Henry II may have hoped that this would force Richard and his barons to make peace. However, it was never the Young King's intention to encourage any kind of settlement. Quite the opposite; he planned to capitalise on Richard's unpopularity and encourage further resistance from the Aquitainian nobility. And all seemed to go well at first. When he arrived at Limoges he was received enthusiastically by the citizens as a liberator, and his gifts to the shrine of St Martial there were characteristically extravagant.

By the end of February 1183, however, the family was at war. Young Henry and (for obscure motives of his own) his younger brother Geoffrey were lined up against Richard and, having finally realised that his eldest son's word could not be trusted, against Henry II himself. The king, of course, was concerned that another revolt along the lines of 1173–4 might develop. But he need not have worried. Even within Aquitaine itself, support for young Henry and Geoffrey was patchy and unreliable. And whilst King Henry besieged Limoges, Richard criss-crossed his duchy dealing quickly and brutally with any opposition he encountered. The Young King managed to slip out of Limoges after plundering that same shrine of St Martial which he had only just patronised so generously, but he was soon back there pleading with the townsfolk to let him in once again. Not surprisingly they refused and, throwing stones at him from the walls, shouted 'We will not have this man to rule over us.'[28] He was now a fugitive on the run, forced to resort to plundering monasteries and shrines as he moved aimlessly around the countryside. By the start of June 1183 he had fallen ill with dysentery and developed a fever. He wrote to his father begging for forgiveness, but Henry II, suspecting another trick, kept his distance, merely sending a ring as a token. The fading prince, meanwhile, summoned his spiritual advisers to gather around his bed and hear his last confession. He gave a cross to William Marshal, with instructions that it be taken to Jerusalem in recognition of the dying man's unfulfilled crusading vow.

After this he had his fine clothes removed and he was dressed instead in a hair shirt. He also had a cord tied around his neck to symbolise his surrender to the Church, and then he gave orders that he should be dragged out of his bed with the cord and placed on another bed that had been strewn with ashes. When this had been done two large square stones were placed under his head and feet. Finally, having received the sacraments for the last time, on 11 June 1183 the Young King died. He had asked for his body to be buried at Rouen and his entrails at Limoges, but as it passed Le Mans, the townsfolk seized his corpse and buried it in their cathedral. The outraged citizens of Rouen threatened to take the body back by force, and the king's intervention was needed to insist that his son's wishes be observed by his reburial there.

The Young King's final weeks had revealed once again the emptiness of his position and the flimsiness of his power. To a large extent his life had been a triumph of image over substance. However, the struggle for possession of his corpse does at least reveal how popular he was. So, more remarkably, does the attempt to construct a posthumous cult around him, which briefly hinted at a very different kind of eternal fame. His body, in this context, became much more than a prize to be competed for between rival towns keen to stage a celebrity burial. It was briefly seen as a holy relic, and a list of miracles that occurred after physical contact with his remains was compiled: ulcers, facial sores, fevers, even leprosy and blindness were cured, it was claimed. The cult never really took off and in the end was short-lived. However, there is no denying the extent of the admiration the Young King had inspired. He was charming, courteous and generous, and 'reckoned to be the finest of all the princes on earth, be they pagan or Christian', according to the biographer of William Marshal, and 'the most beautiful of the men of our time', in the opinion of his chaplain, who also claimed that his early death was not a result of his sins, but of his father's and the latter's role in the death of Becket.[29] Not all contemporaries were so flattering or keen to excuse the Young King, however. Walter Map, for example, who knew him from the court of Henry II, extravagantly bemoaned the waste of the Young King's talents. On the one hand, he had 'roused chivalry from something like slumber, and raised it to the height . . . He was fairer than the children of men in stature and in face, richly endowed with eloquence and charm of address, blest with love and favour of his fellow men.' But 'all these gifts he turned to the wrong side, and that mighty man, corrupting his blessings, became a parricide of such baleful soul that his dearest wish was for his father's death . . . he befouled the whole world with his treasons, a prodigy of unfaith and prodigal of ill, a limpid spring of wickedness, the attractive centre of villainy, a lovely place of sin'.[30]

Modern historians, albeit in more moderate tones, have tended to agree with Walter's view of Henry's abilities and achievements and have seen him as frivolous and incompetent, an irresponsible youth who never grew up. And, to be sure, it is easy to be critical of him. His conduct in 1173 and 1183 reeks of disloyalty and selfishness, whilst his extravagant lifestyle and his passion for the tournament lay bare the trivial parts of his character. Having said all this, however, Henry was not the only heir to the throne who has found it difficult to define a meaningful role whilst waiting to succeed. And it is certainly arguable that he was badly treated by his own father, who must bear some of the responsibility for creating the uncertainties and insecurities that bedevilled his eldest son. The Young King's brothers, Richard, Geoffrey and even John, were given real authority by Henry II, whilst, for reasons that remain obscure, the eldest of them all was left with no more than a promise of power in the future. And as his father continued to frustrate him, Henry's attempts to find alternative sources of advice and encouragement all failed in their turn. One after the other Thomas Becket, Louis VII, William Marshal and Philip of Flanders had all offered the tantalising prospect of prestige and power of some kind, but in the end all had been disappointments. Young Henry may have had his faults, but, at crucial moments in his life, he was let down by those who could have helped him.

CHAPTER SIX

THE PRINCESS'S TALE
Joan, the Crusade and the Politics of Europe

THE LATEST JOURNEY had been long and difficult. It started in captivity following the death of her husband. Since then there had been riots, interminable negotiations and, finally, a family reunion on board ship. Joan, daughter of King Henry II of England and widow of King William II of Sicily, was safely back in the care of her lion-hearted brother, King Richard I. This must have been a happy meeting, unlike the one that took place between them six months later. By then, October 1191, Joan and Richard were in the Holy Land, in the great port city of Acre, and Richard had a new plan. It concerned Joan and he needed to break the news to her. She was to be married, he told her. Joan might just have shrugged her shoulders in resignation. She was a princess after all and a valuable diplomatic and political asset – getting married and married again was only to be expected of her. This marriage proposal was different, however, and the widow of the king of Sicily was taken aback by its audacity. There would be no king for a husband this time. Such a loss of royal status would have been aggravating but ultimately bearable. But Joan's new partner was not even to be a duke or a count; most shockingly, he was not even to be a Christian. No, the name gave it away. This time Joan was to marry al-Adil. Also known as Safadin, he was the brother of Richard's greatest enemy, Saladin. But, and more to the point, he was a Muslim.

The use of marriage to end military conflict or set the seal on negotiations was nothing new. Once irreconcilable opponents could become family before the altar. But this was no ordinary proposition. It is tempting to think of a tense, silent pause as the meaning of Richard's words sank in, the only noise the uncomfortable shifting of feet as Joan's attendants eyed each other nervously. Alternatively, brother and sister might have been alone, the proposition deemed too sensitive to be heard at this stage by anyone else. Either way, true to her Angevin instincts, Joan reportedly flew into a rage, swearing that she would never consent to be the wife of an infidel and demanding to know how she could possibly allow a Muslim to have carnal knowledge of her.[1] The legendary warrior Richard, for once in his life, probably made a swift retreat out of Joan's tent. Nevertheless the idea, however outrageous it seemed, had been broached, and Richard sent word of Joan's response back to her intended husband. Of course, he told al-Adil, Joan had been shocked, but this was not necessarily fatal to the plan: if al-Adil would consider becoming a Christian, he said, 'I will finish the business'.[2]

In the end, there was no marriage between Joan and al-Adil, and it has never been clear just how genuine the proposal was. On the face of things, it looks far-fetched. However, the idea of a Christian princess marrying a Muslim prince, even with crusading fervour at its height, was not completely fantastic. After all, Christians had been known to marry Muslims in eleventh-century Spain. And just over a hundred years before Richard put his proposition to Joan, in 1086, the Muslim sultan of Baghdad had written to the Christian emperor of Byzantium in Constantinople suggesting an alliance to be sealed by marriage between the emperor's daughter and the sultan's eldest son.[3] Nor was Richard's idea of al-Adil converting to Christianity completely out of the question. There were rumours that Saladin himself had offered to convert when he had proposed a marriage between one of his sons and a daughter of Emperor Frederick Barbarossa in 1173. And even before the idea of conversion to Christianity was put to him, al-Adil seems to have been prepared to accept the plan if Saladin agreed. Muslim sources record that Saladin did indeed give his consent, although this was on the assumption that Richard would not in the end keep his word and that the proposal was some kind of trick or practical joke, worth playing along with for the time being.[4]

Richard may have meant what he said. In November 1191 the proposed marriage was discussed again in a diplomatic exchange between Richard and Saladin. Richard's plans had come under fire from his leading barons, it seems, who were complaining that he had promised Joan to al-Adil without seeking the pope's consent (not, it is worth noting, because the marriage was in itself an unacceptable idea). Accordingly Richard was sending an envoy to the pope: 'If he gives permission and she is happy about it, well and good, otherwise I shall marry you to my niece, for which I do not need his permission.'[5] Once again, therefore, the possibility of a Muslim-Christian marriage was raised as a realistic option, if not between Joan and al-Adil then between him and Eleanor, the daughter of Richard's late brother, Duke Geoffrey of Brittany. Richard did not need the pope's permission to marry off his niece, the Muslim sources tell us, because she was a virgin; papal agreement to Joan's marriage was required, not because she was a Christian, but because she had already been married.[6] In other words, there was no bar in principle to a marriage between Christian and Muslim, unusual though that would be, and there is enough evidence to suggest that both sides gave the notion at least some consideration. To be sure, al-Adil baulked at the idea of marrying Eleanor of Brittany, but that was because she was not Joan: 'we have already talked of her,' he said of Joan, 'and we do not go back on our word. If it cannot be managed, we are not concerned with any alternative.'[7] This was effectively the end of the matter and there is no evidence to suggest that the marriage proposal was ever mooted again. But the failure of the plan probably had as much to do with other issues (territory and resources were at stake too, as will be seen) as with its inherent implausibility. And remarkable though the tale is, it was only the latest chapter in Princess Joan's extraordinary story.

* * * *

Joan's story is one of journeys and marriages. She had two husbands and, as the tale of al-Adil's proposal suggests, she might have had more. She travelled back and forth across western Europe, but she was familiar with the eastern Mediterranean too, and the Holy Land. She knew Christians and Muslims and, as far as we know, lived comfortably alongside both. Few women of her time can have seen as many different parts of the known world or met a more diverse range of people. In this sense, in the scale and scope of her experiences, Joan was probably unique, and that alone makes her story worth telling. But in other ways she was a typical aristocratic woman of the twelfth century. She was born to be married, so that relationships between families could be established and dynasties merged. Lands and resources changed hands when marriages took place, and this was the conventional way of transferring assets and building zones of influence. Such was the case with any marriage in the twelfth century, whatever the social standing of the bride and groom. What marked out Joan's marriages, however, was their elevated status. Her first husband, William of Sicily, ruled the most dazzling kingdom in Europe; her second, Raymond of Toulouse, was one of the richest and most prestigious princes anywhere.

Joan was certainly not the only member of her family to marry at this level. One of her sisters, Eleanor, married a Spanish king, Alfonso VIII, whilst the other, Matilda, became the wife of a Saxon duke, Henry the Lion. Such matches gave entry into a world of trans-continental diplomatic and political manoeuvring in which the family of Henry II and Richard I played a central role. England and France were their main concerns, of course, but the security of their dominions relied as much on good relations with their neighbours and on delicately balanced alliances with other rulers further away as it did on the military and political power they wielded closer to home. It is a commonplace to say that medieval men and women rarely travelled far from their homes, and in many cases that would be true. At the highest levels, however, politics was an international business and family organisation was a vital tool of diplomacy and a cosmopolitan affair. Joan's story reveals the wide-ranging and diverse nature of her family's connections and concerns.

But Joan was not just a token in a game of diplomatic chance. It is clear from what can be gleaned about her relationships (and admittedly such information is limited and elusive) that she was capable of establishing long-lasting and firm bonds with the people she knew. Everything suggests that she was close to her mother, Eleanor of Aquitaine, and to at least two of her brothers, Richard and John. As for her two husbands, there is no sign that they tired of her. Other women, too, played important roles in her life, from ladies of the highest status like Richard I's queen, Berengaria, to Joan's own servants, whom she clearly cherished. It is of course impossible to know the everyday details of these loves and friendships – the letters and diaries that bring later periods to life simply do not exist for this one. Nevertheless, a close reading of the evidence that does survive provides much more than just an outline of Joan's life. It reveals a woman who, through her own efforts and force of will, had an impact, not just on great affairs of state, but on the lives of all those with whom she came into contact.

* * * *

Joan was born in October 1165 at Angers, the chief city of her father's county of Anjou, and she would have spent much of her early life at nearby Fontevraud, the family church and mausoleum. She was an Angevin through and through. However, as the third daughter and seventh child of Henry II and Eleanor of Aquitaine (only one sibling, her brother John, born in 1167, was younger than her), she features hardly at all in the chroniclers' accounts of the period until her time came to enter the international marriage market. The matches arranged for her older sisters at a young age reveal the kind of future that Joan would have grown up to expect. In 1167 her eldest sister Matilda, age twelve, left for Germany where, early in the following year, she was married to the duke of Saxony, Henry the Lion, age thirty-nine. Two years later, in 1170, nine-year-old Eleanor, Joan's second sister, was betrothed to the young King Alphonso VIII of Castile, and the couple were finally married in 1176. Joan's fate was to be no different. As early as 1168 (Joan was only three), as a way of bolstering his position in Pyrennean France, her father attempted to arrange her marriage to another Spanish prince, in Aragon or Navarre.

Nothing came of this plan in the end, and while she was waiting to be allocated a husband of her own, Joan's education and training would have focused on preparing her for that marriage. Young aristocratic girls would usually be kept safely apart from the temptations of the outside world. In their seclusion they would have been instructed in the skills and refinements deemed appropriate for their gender and status. Joan would have learnt how to sew and weave, sing and perhaps play an instrument like the harp; she would have been taught how to ride (she mentions her horse in her will), but not how to fight. Falconry was a popular pastime for aristocratic women of this period, though, and Joan may have learned how to handle a hawk. Her lessons would have been as much moral as practical, however. There would have been constant reminders of the need for a young lady of her rank to behave virtuously. In practice this meant chastity, obedience, humility and silence. When Joan did speak, she was expected to do so well and carefully. Temptation was to be avoided, the flattery of young men was to be politely ignored, and material extravagance was to be shunned. She would have attended Mass every day and confessed regularly; the battle against evil and the consequences of sin were without end.

Above all, though, Joan would have been primed in the responsibilities of a loyal, dutiful wife and in how to deal with a husband, a mother-in-law, children and servants. Much of this instruction would have been in the form of stories. Some of these tales would have been taken from the Bible, or from histories of the deeds of kings, queens, heroes and heroines; others would have been folk tales passed on orally from generation to generation and retold at her bedside or dressing table by the young girl's nurse, maid or even her mother. Some of these instructive, edifying tales would have described the triumph of virtue and the defeat of vice. Others may well have been quite lurid and graphic, even frightening, warning as they did of the eternal punishment that would flow inevitably from a life of worldly vanity and lax morality. Joan probably read many of these stories herself, of course, and the idea of the learned princess was by no means unheard of. In the late twelfth-century romance *Partonpeus de Blois*, the heroine, Melior, is the daughter of the emperor of Constantinople. Her father prepares her for governing the empire after his death by hiring teachers from whom Melior learns not just reading, but also medicine, divinity, astronomy and necromancy. By the time she is fifteen she surpasses all her teachers in knowledge. Nothing suggests that Joan became as erudite as this, but she would certainly have known how to read. She would have learnt the alphabet at an early age and carried on with reading practice, probably from religious texts – the Psalms were a common teaching tool. Joan would therefore have been able to pronounce and recite Latin correctly; this was necessary in order to hold one's own during religious services and the performance of penance, if nothing else. That Joan understood the texts she was reciting is less likely. She may have learnt some elements of Latin grammar, but, in the manner of aristocratic society more broadly in the second half of the twelfth century, she may also have moved quickly on to French, the increasingly dominant language of courtly literature and romance. Joan would have been able to read and understand the language, perhaps even in its several different forms, from the French of the north, the *langue d'oil*, to that of the south, the *langue d'oc*.

It is tempting to give the credit for Joan's education to her mother. Queen Eleanor's interest in literature has given rise to the popular image of her as 'the queen of the troubadours'. Her court at Poitiers has also come to be seen as the birthplace of the rituals, conventions and systems of 'courtly love'. Eleanor's tomb effigy at Fontevraud depicts her holding a book (indeed, it is the earliest image of this kind to survive), surely an indication of her interest in the written word. However, her mythical reputation is harder to substantiate with further clear evidence. To be sure, Eleanor, like her daughters Marie de Champagne and Matilda of Saxony, and like her son Richard I, was an enthusiastic literary patron – lyrics, poems, songs and romances were all composed by artists with connections to the Angevin court in England, Normandy and Aquitaine. Eleanor and her family were also connected with perhaps the most important literary phenomenon of the twelfth century, the development of the story of King Arthur and his Knights of the Round Table. Stories of Arthur had been in circulation long before Geoffrey of Monmouth wrote his *History of the Kings of Britain* in the 1130s. But it was Geoffrey's work that placed Arthur at the centre of aristocratic consciousness. His account of the all-conquering Arthur's life and death, obviously fictional and fantastic to a modern reader, was accepted as inspirational historical reality by its twelfth-century audience. The surviving number of manuscripts of the *History*, moreover (over two hundred in all, with some in languages other than the original Latin), testifies to its huge popularity. It is more than likely that versions of these stories were in even wider circulation, transmitted orally or adapted, amended and embellished in written form by singers and storytellers, and that they stirred the emotions of Joan's generation. Most importantly, in 1155 the Jersey-born historian and poet Wace completed his *Roman de Brut*, the oldest surviving Old French chronicle of the early kings of Britain. It was based largely on Geoffrey of Monmouth's *History*, but it also included material not found there as well as the earliest reference to King Arthur's round table. There is even some evidence, problematic though it is, to suggest that Queen Eleanor herself was presented with a copy of Wace's work.

Certainly, the latter half of the twelfth century saw a boom in Arthurian literature. Arthur and his court were mentioned, for example, in two of the *lais* of Marie de France, a series of twelve short narrative poems written in Norman French in the later 1100s. The 'noble king' to whom the poems were dedicated was almost certainly Henry II or his son the Young King.[8] And the earliest surviving account of Arthur in English, by the poet Layamon, dates from about 1200. But it was the work of Chrétien de Troyes that did most to cement the Arthurian stories in the western imagination. Geoffrey of Monmouth had concentrated on the figure of Arthur himself and, to a lesser extent, his teacher and sorcerer Merlin. But in a series of stories probably written down in the 1170s and 1180s, Chrétien placed the other Arthurian characters centre stage for the first time. Lancelot and Guinevere, Percival, Tristan and Isolde; their stories of bravery and betrayal, of love and sacrifice were to dominate and frame the concerns of European literature for the rest of the Middle Ages. It is known that Chrétien wrote for Joan's half-sister, Marie de Champagne, and it is easy to imagine the young Joan listening rapt and excited to stories like these for the first time. Could they also have been told to her by Chrétien himself? Perhaps, although there is no evidence to show that he ever visited Henry II's court. But at the very least, it is impossible not to wonder whether an early copy of these adventures was included amongst the treasured possessions Joan took with her as she prepared to leave home and family for good.

In May 1176 an embassy from Sicily visited Henry II's court in London. King William II wanted Joan as his bride. As the largest island in the Mediterranean, situated more or less in the middle of that great watery corridor connecting Europe, Asia and Africa, Sicily's strategic importance had been obvious since pre-classical times. Its climate and its volcanically enriched soil also made it fertile and productive: the island's abundance of grain meant that it was one of the richest places in Europe, but it also produced oranges, lemons, tomatoes, cheese, olives and wine. The Spanish Muslim, Ibn Jubayr, visited Sicily over the Christmas and New Year of 1184–5. Although, according to him, the prosperity of the island 'surpasses description', he still tried to describe it: it is 'a daughter of Spain in the extent of its cultivation, in the luxuriance of its harvests, and in its well-being, having an abundance of varied produce, and fruits of every kind and species'.[9] Sicily was therefore a tempting, even a necessary target for those seeking to dominate the Mediterranean, and for centuries the island had been fought over, won and lost by a variety of occupiers. The Greeks had been replaced by the Romans; the Germanic invaders who threw out the Romans in the fifth century were themselves removed by the Byzantines in the sixth; they in turn lost out to Muslim invaders from north Africa. By the middle of the eleventh century, Sicily was still largely Muslim-controlled. However, it was also cosmopolitan and culturally diverse. Christians from western Europe and Constantinople, Jews and Muslims, coexisted largely peacefully.

So languages and beliefs were already and uniquely mixed together when adventurers from Normandy fixed their greedy stare on the riches of Sicily in the decades either side of 1100. These men originally came to southern Italy as pilgrims en route to and from the Holy Land. Having become mercenaries in the pay of the aspiring native rulers of southern Italy, they soon decided to take power into their own hands. The most spectacularly successful of them all were two of the many sons of the Norman lord Tancred de Hauteville: Robert 'Guiscard' (the nickname means 'crafty' or 'cunning') and Roger.

By the time he died in 1085, Robert Guiscard had carved out a territory for himself that stretched across most of southern Italy. In 1059 he had been formally recognised as duke of Apulia and Calabria by the papacy, and in 1061 he had invaded Sicily with his brother Roger, so beginning a prolonged but inexorable takeover of the island. After they had captured Palermo in 1072, Robert made Roger count of Sicily, but it was not until the early 1090s that the Norman conquest of the island was completed. In 1105, Roger's second son, also called Roger, became count of Sicily, and in 1112, at the age of sixteen, Roger II started to rule the island in his own right. Then, when Roger's cousin, William II of Apulia, died in 1127, Roger claimed all the Hauteville family possessions in southern Italy and, during the 1130s, when there were two claimants to the papal throne, he managed to have himself recognised as king of Sicily by both of them. Roger had to face internal revolts and foreign invasions during his reign, but he dealt with every challenge and he was able to harness and increase Sicily's economic strength to complete a remarkable piece of state-building and become one of the greatest rulers in Europe. At the time of his death in 1154 the kingdom of Sicily comprised the island itself as well as most of mainland Italy south of Rome. It was Roger's grandson William, who became king of Sicily in 1166 at the age of eleven, who asked for the hand of Princess Joan in 1176. If the marriage went ahead, Joan would become queen of one of the most dynamic, successful and wealthy kingdoms of the Middle Ages.

After meeting his councillors to discuss the marriage proposal, Henry II agreed to allow the Sicilian envoys to visit Joan, who was at Winchester. At great cost to the city authorities and to the bishop of Winchester personally, the embassy was entertained lavishly when it reached the city. But this was not just a courtesy call; it would have been quite normal for the prospective groom's officials to have a formal 'view' of the nominated bride so that they could make a report on her appearance, her voice, her manners and her conduct to their master. The visitors were delighted with what they found and impressed by Joan's beauty; and after discussing matters with King Henry, the latter gave his consent to the match.

After the Sicilian deputation returned home, Joan was prepared for her long and arduous trip, and for the rest of her life. Money had to be raised for the journey and her wedding. The king imposed a tax 'for the marriage of his daughter', and the royal records of the later 1170s are full of entries setting out the contributions of the English shire communities to the collection. Joan's wedding dress alone, it seems, cost well over £100, an enormous sum at the time.[10] She eventually left England in August 1176, sailing from Southampton to the Angevin territories in northern France. She was received there by her eldest brother Henry, the Young King, and he escorted her on the next part of her journey to Poitou, where she was met and taken through his territories by another brother, Duke Richard of Aquitaine. Then, the final leg of the trip took her to St Gilles in Toulouse, where in November the marriage party found twenty-five Sicilian galleys awaiting them. The voyage to Sicily was rough and unpleasant. Winter storms in the Mediterranean made Joan so ill that her ships had to stop at Naples for Christmas so as to continue the journey by land, and she finally arrived in Palermo late in January 1177. Night had already fallen when she landed, but the city's inhabitants were still waiting to meet her. The streets were dazzlingly illuminated by torchlight. So many and so large were the lights, one account claimed, that the city almost seemed to be on fire, 'and the rays of the stars could in no way compare with the brilliance of such a light'.[11] Mounted on one of King William's horses, Joan processed to her new apartments through the cheering crowds that filled the Palermo streets. A few days later, on 13 February 1177, she and William were married in the Palatine Chapel at Palermo, and Joan was crowned queen and given a golden chair for her own use.

But why did William II want to marry Joan at all? Certainly not out of love; the two had never met. No, there were pragmatic political considerations behind the union. The traditional enemies of the kings of Sicily were the Byzantine emperors in Constantinople, who, with their own interests in the Balkans and the southern Mediterranean, had struggled since the days of Robert Guiscard (largely without success) to hold back the advancing tide of Norman rule in southern Italy. However, by the 1160s, the political dynamic in Italy had changed and the king in Sicily faced a new threat. Since becoming king of Germany in 1152, Frederick I (or 'Barbarossa' because of his red beard) had made his ambition to rule Italy himself very clear indeed. He had come to Italy with an army no fewer than four times by the end of the 1160s and during the latest expedition, in 1166–7, he had nearly achieved his objectives, and had been foiled only by an outbreak of malaria in his army. For the other rulers of Italy, in particular King William of Sicily and Pope Alexander III, the dangers were obvious; but for the pope they were particularly acute. Since 1159 there had once again been rival claimants to the papal throne. Alexander III had the backing of the kings of England, France and Sicily whilst his opponents (first Victor IV and then Paschal III) were supported by Barbarossa. The emperor's grand ambitions in Italy required for their fulfilment a compliant pope, and in

1167 Frederick had even managed to have Paschal III installed in Rome. However, the ultimate failure of his expedition on that occasion was a significant setback and, by the time Barbarossa returned to Italy with an army for the fifth time, in 1174, Alexander III had managed to regain some lost ground and shore up his own network of alliances. It was against this background that the negotiations for Joan's marriage to William II were conducted.

The idea of an Angevin-Sicilian marriage was not new. It had been floated by August 1169 at the latest, when the exiled Thomas Becket mentioned it in a letter to one of his supporters.[12] The friendship between Henry II and William II was still obvious in 1173 when the Sicilian king wrote to his English counterpart to sympathise with him over the behaviour of his rebellious sons.[13] However, by 1176, the situation in Italy meant that a formal union between the two ruling families had become a political and diplomatic necessity. Pope Alexander was desperately keen for the marriage to go ahead, so as to reinforce the anti-German connection between two of his most important supporters. And when Frederick Barbarossa was defeated at the Battle of Legnano by the army of the Lombard League (a loose alliance of about twenty Italian cities looking for freedom from imperial control) in May 1176, the emperor was forced to negotiate. He made peace with Alexander III at Anagni in November of that year, agreeing to abandon the anti-pope and recognise Alexander. And then at Venice in July 1177 a more general peace was made that covered most of Italy. It included a truce for fifteen years with the recently married King William of Sicily.

Joan was not yet twelve years old when she married, and her new husband was twenty-two. The dowry granted to Joan by William was generous, and doubtless the negotiations surrounding it had taken up much of the Sicilian ambassadors' time when they had proposed the marriage to Henry II. Joan was to receive the county of Monte Sant' Angelo, along with the cities of Siponto and Vieste, on the Gargano peninsula in north-eastern Apulia. Other estates were also set aside for Joan in King William's charter, in which his new wife was described as 'the maiden Joan, of royal blood, and the most illustrious daughter of Henry, the mighty king of the English'. The charter also made explicitly clear (not, presumably, that it needed to be spelt out) just what was expected of the new queen: the marriage had taken place in order that 'her fidelity and chaste affection may produce the blessings of the married state, and that by her a royal offspring may, by the gift of God, hereafter succeed us in the kingdom'.[14] Joan's first duty was to give William a son. There is evidence to suggest that a boy, Boamund, born in 1181 or 1182, was immediately proclaimed duke of Apulia by his father. But if he ever existed at all, the boy died in infancy. Joan had produced no surviving heir by the time King William died in 1189.

There is little to show how Joan spent her twelve years as queen of Sicily, but the accounts of the Spanish traveller Ibn Jubayr give some indication of the kind of life she might have led. Ibn Jubayr believed that Sicily would eventually become a Muslim island once again, but his resentment at Christian rule did not stop him being impressed by what the Christian rulers were doing. He had been brought to the island after his ship ran into trouble offshore from Messina in December 1184. King William himself took part in the rescue operation, going so far as to give the stranded Muslim passengers the money they required to pay the captains of the rescue boats. This must have contributed to Ibn Jubayr's generous appreciation of the king: he was 'admirable for his just conduct' and whilst 'no Christian king is more given up to the delights of the realm, or more comfort and luxury-loving', he did not neglect his royal duties and he ruled his kingdom 'in a manner that resembles the Muslim kings' – high praise indeed![15] Once ashore, Ibn Jubayr made his base at Palermo, where relations between Christians and Muslims were peaceful and even progressive. The king himself had Muslim servants at his court. His pages in particular, from whose ranks he drew his ministers and chamberlains, kept their religion secret, but they were Muslims, Ibn Jubayr insists.[16] The royal cook was too, and the king's tailor; and William II made much use of the services of Muslim doctors and astrologers. Most remarkably, William could read and write Arabic, and his 'alamah', or personal motto, was strikingly Islamic in form and tone: 'Praise be to God. It is proper to praise him.'[17] William's wife could hardly have escaped such influences herself. Indeed, Ibn Jubayr remarks how the Muslim presence at the royal court was more than just male. The 'handmaidens and concubines' of the palace were Muslims, he says, and there were rumours that the Christian ladies who came to the court were converted secretly to Islam by these women. Perhaps this was an exaggeration, but Ibn Jubayr saw for himself how the Christian women of Palermo followed Muslim fashions: they went to church, he says, veiled and 'bearing all the adornments of Muslim women, including jewellery, henna on the fingers, and perfumes'.[18] Joan, of course, may have resisted such trends or found the practices of the royal court distasteful. But on the other hand, and given her husband's apparently sympathetic attitude towards Islam, it is easy to imagine her dressed in this way, walking in the gardens of her splendid palace above Palermo, accompanied by her ladies in their silk robes, elegant cloaks and coloured veils.

It is also easy to picture Joan visiting one of her husband's greatest creations – the cathedral church at Monreale, about ten miles west of Palermo. William II may have tolerated Muslims, but he was always a devout Christian. The church was built between 1174 and 1182 as a mausoleum for William's family (he had his father's remains moved there, his mother was buried there in 1183, and his own tomb is in the church too) and it was designed to be appropriately lavish and splendid. It is decorated throughout in a single, unified mosaic scheme that includes depictions of William II himself and stories from the Old and New Testaments. But amongst the 162 saints also portrayed around the walls is the earliest known artistic representation of Thomas Becket anywhere in the world. Of course, by the late 1170s when the mosaics were being made, Becket's fame as a saint was already widespread, and there is every chance that his image would have been included in the scheme anyway. But it is worth wondering whether the Angevin influence present at the Sicilian court after 1177 might have had something to do with the inclusion of the saint's image in the decoration. Some of those who had travelled with Joan might even have known Becket or seen him in the flesh; perhaps they were able to help the mosaicists with the likeness.

By the early 1180s it must have been clear to Joan and William that the chances of them producing a legitimate heir together were fading. In similar circumstances, another king might simply have divorced his unproductive wife and taken a new one (the rulers of France did this regularly during this period), and it might say something about his relationship with Joan that William never seems to have contemplated this. However, the king did need to make alternative provision for the succession and he announced that, if he died without a son or daughter of his own, his heir would be his aunt, Constance (she was the daughter of King Roger II). And to reinforce her position William had arranged her marriage to Frederick Barbarossa's son and chosen heir, Henry, in 1184. This reversal of Sicilian policy towards the German Empire, which gave rise to the prospect of a German emperor succeeding peacefully to most of southern Italy, caused great consternation at the papal and Byzantine courts, and probably at King Henry II's too; but it fitted in with William's wider ambitions in the Mediterranean. Even before he married Joan, in 1174 William had sent his large and powerful fleet to attack Alexandria in Egypt, and in 1182 he had threatened Majorca. His most significant campaign, however, saw the revival of the traditional hostilities between the Norman rulers of southern Italy and their Byzantine rivals.

Dynastic squabbling and political instability within the Byzantine Empire followed the death of Emperor Manuel Komnenos in 1180. This and the death of Pope Alexander III in 1181 gave William some leeway to pursue policies of his own and attack his Greek neighbours. Eventually, just as his ancestor Robert Guiscard had done a hundred years before, William crossed the Adriatic with his army and seized Durazzo in June 1185. He then marched across country to Thessaloniki, and sacked it with a fleet that had sailed all the way around the Peloponnese, capturing the islands of Corfu, Cephalonia, Ithaca and Zakynthos on its way. William found it impossible to hold on to Thessaloniki after his forces were defeated by a Byzantine army in November 1185, and eventually in 1189 he made peace with Emperor Isaac Angelus and agreed to abandon all his conquests. Nevertheless, his military achievements in 1185 had been strikingly impressive, whilst his pro-German, anti-Byzantine policies had destroyed the fragile balance of power established in the region by the Peace of Venice in 1177.

King William's arrangements for the Sicilian succession, however, would plunge the island into chaos on his death and leave his widow isolated and in danger. When he died in November 1189, there were few in Sicily who looked forward to the arrival of a new German king, albeit one with a Sicilian wife. Further north, Pope Clement III also viewed the prospect of being surrounded by Henry VI's territories with dismay. So in the struggle that inevitably followed William's death, power was seized by Tancred of Lecce, an illegitimate cousin of the late king. Joan, now a widow, was caught up in these turbulent events. But because of what was happening at the same time on the far side of the Mediterranean, in the Holy Land, they acquired an even greater significance.

On 4 July 1187 the Muslim warlord Saladin had defeated the army of the Christian kingdom of Jerusalem at the Battle of Hattin. So crushing was Saladin's victory that the defenceless kingdom, which had been established after the success of the First Crusade in 1099, was subsequently overrun by his forces. The holy city of Jerusalem itself fell into Muslim hands in October 1187. News of the catastrophe at Hattin hit western Europe like a thunderbolt. Pope Urban III died of shock on hearing of the defeat. His successor, Gregory VIII, was pope for only two months, but he was responsible for launching a new crusade to recover Jerusalem. In his encyclical of late October 1187, *Audita Tremendi*, he wrote of God's desire that the Holy Land and the True Cross (the kingdom's most holy relic that had also been captured at Hattin) should be recovered.[19]

In November 1187, Duke Richard of Aquitaine, Joan's brother, was the first prince north of the Alps to take the cross and commit himself to going on crusade. At this stage, however, the man who struck contemporaries as most likely to revive the fortunes of the Latin East was that scourge of Italy, Frederick Barbarossa. Putting aside his ambitions in southern Europe, he left on crusade at the head of a powerful and well-equipped force, made his way through Byzantine territory using a mixture of force and diplomacy, and inflicted a significant defeat on the Turks at Iconium (now Konya) in May 1190. Frederick drowned, however, probably the victim of a heart attack, whilst trying to cross a river at Silifke in southern Cilicia. Leadership of the Third Crusade thus passed to two other western princes – Duke Richard of Aquitaine and King Philip of France. Richard did not leave for the Holy Land until Barbarossa's expedition was well under way. His relationship with his father, Henry II, had deteriorated during the 1180s, and neither trusted the other. Richard was worried that, if he left on crusade, Henry would take the opportunity to dismantle his power base and install his younger and only surviving brother, John, in his place. Richard eventually joined forces with King Philip in order to secure his position in southern France, but only the death of Henry II in July 1189 reassured Richard that he could begin to think about leaving western Europe. On 13 September 1189 he was crowned king of England in Westminster Abbey, and in December he left England for France.

Going on crusade was no simple undertaking, however, especially not for a great prince like Richard. Huge efforts were made to build a fleet and to provide it with food and war supplies. Massive sums of money were raised by the sale of offices, lands and privileges. Scottish independence from England was guaranteed for a payment of £6,666 by King William the Lion, for example. Historians have traditionally been quick to criticise Richard for his attitude towards England and its affairs at the start of his reign: England was exploited for its wealth, it has been argued, and Richard deserted and neglected his kingdom. Recent reassessments have shown how carefully Richard's arrangements were made, however: that he did not see England simply as a source of money. Moreover, contemporaries would have agreed that Richard's highest duty was to attempt the recovery of Jerusalem. Nor was this just religious duty. Queen Sibylla of Jerusalem was Richard's cousin and her husband, Guy de Lusignan, was one of Richard's vassals from Aquitaine. Richard was acting as a good lord and kinsman should.

Richard spent the first half of 1190 touring his lands in France and making arrangements for their safekeeping during his absence on crusade. It was probably during this period that his marriage to Berengaria, daughter of King Sancho VI of Navarre, was planned. The arrangements had to be handled delicately, however, as Richard had been betrothed for nearly twenty years to Alice, the sister of King Philip II of France. Richard and Philip met twice during this period to make plans for their departure (Philip had taken the cross in 1188) and, finally, three years to the day after the Battle of Hattin, on 4 July 1190, their two armies set off from Vézelay. Richard and Philip divided their forces before they reached the Mediterranean coast, Richard finally setting sail from Marseilles and Philip from Genoa.

On 23 September 1190 (a week after Philip II had arrived on the island), Richard reached Sicily and made a grand public entrance into

Messina. Once the flamboyant parade was over, however, Richard turned his attention to his sister. Joan was in captivity, the prisoner of the new ruler of the island, Tancred of Lecce. Joan's treatment gave Richard cause enough to intervene on her behalf. However, there was money at stake as well as family pride. On King William's death, the extensive territories reserved for Joan by her husband at the time of their marriage should have been granted to her as her widow's 'dower'. However, Tancred had withheld them. Moreover, King William had left a generous legacy to Richard's father, Henry II, in his will, which comprised cash, an enormous amount of supplies, a hundred ships and, amongst other things, a golden chair, a golden table twelve feet long, a silken tent large enough to seat 200 knights at a time, twenty-four golden cups and the same number of golden plates![20] None of this had been forthcoming. Richard would not tolerate this, and he needed the money to help defray the costs of the crusade. As soon as he had arrived on Sicily, Richard sent messengers to Palermo demanding Joan's release. Tancred grudgingly gave in and Joan (carrying 'the mere furniture of her bedchamber', Richard of Devizes noted) was reunited with her brother at Messina on 28 September.[21] According to Roger of Howden, the sight of her made King Philip so cheerful that rumours soon spread of his wish to marry her.[22] Joan had only been released with a relatively small sum of money, though, nothing like as much as Richard claimed she was entitled to. So he seized the Calabrian town of Bagnara at the end of September, installing Joan and her household in the fortified monastery there; and on 4 October, Richard took Messina itself. Tancred was forced to come to terms: he agreed to pay Richard 40,000 ounces of gold, half of which was in lieu of Joan's dower, and to betroth his daughter to Richard's nephew and current heir, Arthur. To ease any irritation King Philip felt at Richard's behaviour, however, he was given one-third of all the money Richard had received from Tancred. Tancred remained king of Sicily until his death in 1194, when Henry VI finally secured his inheritance and brought an end to the Norman kingdom of Sicily.

With winter approaching and the weather worsening, Richard decided to stay on Sicily until the new year. Christmas 1190 was celebrated splendidly at his fortified base. Philip II was his guest, and it is tempting to wonder whether the French king's initial delight at meeting

Joan lasted through the festive season. Certainly, Philip's relationship with her brother was deteriorating. Philip had been angered by the way Richard (who was the French king's vassal after all) had upstaged him with the capture of Messina, and by his conspicuous displays of generosity to the rank and file of the crusading army. Moreover, early in 1191, Richard formally ended his long-standing betrothal to Philip's sister, Alice. Richard's bride-to-be, Berengaria of Navarre, was on her way to Sicily, accompanied by Richard's mother, Queen Eleanor, and Richard certainly planned to marry Berengaria as soon as he could. As will be seen, this marriage was central to Richard's plans for shoring up his defences in south-west France during his absence on crusade and against any attack by Count Raymond V of Toulouse. So, at Messina, during the early weeks of 1191, Richard told Philip that he could never marry Alice because she had been his father's mistress and borne him a son. When Richard added that he could produce witnesses to support this story, Philip had little choice but to give in for the sake of his sister's honour.[23] Humiliated and furious, Philip left Sicily on 30 March, just a few hours before Eleanor and Berengaria arrived.

Richard spent ten more days on Sicily with Berengaria before setting sail himself. In that time, Queen Eleanor, her duties as an escort completed, began her journey home, leaving Berengaria with Joan. As the widow of a great king, Joan was well placed to act as companion and chaperone to her future sister-in-law and to advise her on the demands and responsibilities of her life to come. She would also have contributed greatly to the plans for the royal wedding, which was due to take place after the end of Lent. But first there was further travelling to do. Richard's fleet consisted of over 200 ships and carried over 15,000 men, as well as horses, arms, money, heavy siege equipment and food. The weather in the Mediterranean was not good, however, and two days into the voyage the fleet was hit by storms. When the fleet regrouped at Crete on 17 April 1191, twenty-five ships were missing and one of these was carrying Joan and Berengaria. Richard sailed on to Rhodes, unaware that some of the missing ships, including the one carrying his sister and his fiancée, had sailed ahead of the main fleet. On 24 April they arrived off the south-western coast of Cyprus, near Limassol. Some of these vessels (although not Joan and Berengaria's, which remained anchored offshore) ran aground and were plundered. Some crew members and passengers were robbed and imprisoned.

Cyprus had been ruled by the 'tyrant', Isaac Komnenos, since 1184. He was a member of the former imperial ruling family of Byzantium and an ally of Saladin. The strategic importance of the island for the crusader states in the Holy Land was obvious. If it was held by Latins rather than Greeks, it could be used as a reliable source of renewable supply and as a launch pad for future crusades. Thus, whilst Richard's first thought on hearing of the plight of his shipwrecked family and followers was probably their recovery, the conquest of Cyprus itself was an attractive idea. Richard arrived on the island on 6 May 1191, and on the same day Joan and Berengaria landed at Limassol. His demands for redress and for restoration of the seized goods were rejected by Isaac. This was a mistake, and by 11 May surrenders were being made to Richard, and Isaac was forced to sue for peace. On 12 May, doubtless with Joan looking on, Richard and Berengaria were married in Limassol and Berengaria was crowned queen. Richard had conquered Cyprus, but he soon sold his rights over the island to the Templars for 100,000 saracen bezants. Cyprus remained under Western control until it fell to the Turks in 1571.

Whilst on Cyprus, Richard had been met by the king of Jerusalem, Guy de Lusignan, and his brother Geoffrey. They had come to complain about King Philip, who had arrived at Acre on 20 April. Philip planned to force Guy off the throne and replace him with Conrad of Montferrat. King Guy had been imprisoned by Saladin for a year after his defeat at Hattin, during which time the crusaders' presence in the Holy Land had been maintained largely by the efforts of Conrad, who had put up a staunch and successful defence of the principal remaining Christian outpost in the Holy Land, the city of Tyre. When Guy was released in June 1188, Conrad refused to hand Tyre over to him and began to act as if he were the real king of Jerusalem. To make matters worse for Guy, his claim to the throne came through his wife, Sibylla, the heiress to the kingdom, and she had died along with her two daughters in 1190. The alternative claimant was Sibylla's younger sister, Isabella, and, not surprisingly, Conrad thought that it would make sense for him to marry her. Undeterred by the fact that his own wife and Isabella's husband were still alive, Conrad had Isabella abducted from her tent in the camp outside Acre. In 1183, Isabella had been married when merely eleven to Humphrey (himself only a teenager), the lord of Toron between Tyre and Damascus. But he and Isabella had had no children by 1190; what is more, Humphrey was an Arabic speaker and allegedly effeminate. All of these factors were used to justify the hasty annulment of their marriage and on 24 November 1190, Isabella and Conrad became husband and wife. That this marriage was itself both bigamous and incestuous meant little when King Philip arrive at Acre and recognised Conrad as 'king elect'. Inevitably, therefore (and because of his family connections with Sibylla and the Lusignans), this meant that Richard would support Guy. It was into this diplomatic minefield that Richard sent his new wife and his sister. They arrived at Acre on 1 June 1191; the king himself landed a week later.

Prior to its capture by Saladin's forces in July 1187, Acre had been the largest town and chief port of the kingdom of Jerusalem. The siege of Acre had been begun by Guy de Lusignan in August 1189 as a way of reasserting his authority within the kingdom after his release from captivity. Almost immediately, however, Guy's forces had become sandwiched between the Muslim garrison in the city on one side and Saladin's relieving force on the other, and stalemate ensued. Guy could not take the city, but Saladin was unable to dislodge him. King Philip's arrival on the scene, with fresh troops and new siege engines, began to tip the balance in the crusaders' favour, but Richard's contribution was decisive. On his way to Acre he had already sunk a huge ship laden with reinforcements and supplies, intended for the relief of the Muslim garrison of the city, and Muslim commentators disconsolately remarked on his arrival there in great pomp with twenty-five galleys 'full of men, weapons and stores'; and this was only a part of his fleet.[24] After landing, Richard's siege engines were brought up to the city walls and gradually the bombardment of Acre was stepped up. The final capitulation of the garrison was delayed by illnesses suffered by Richard and Philip, but the defenders were exhausted. Saladin planned night attacks on 4 and 5 July 1191, but these came to nothing, and on 5 July a large part of the wall, undermined and set alight by Richard's sappers, collapsed. Finally, on 12 July the garrison surrendered and on the following day Acre and all its contents were divided between Richard and Philip. A few days later, on 21 July, Richard, Berengaria and Joan moved into the royal palace.

As for the competing claims of Conrad and Guy, Richard and Philip announced a compromise on 28 July. Guy would remain king for his lifetime but, whether he married and had children again or not, the throne would pass on his death to Conrad and Isabella and their heirs. Meanwhile the kingdom's revenues would be shared between them. On 29 July, King Philip appointed the duke of Burgundy commander of the French forces and gave his half of Acre to Conrad. On 30 July the Muslim prisoners were divided between the two kings and on 31 July, Philip left Acre for Tyre, taking his prisoners with him. He was going home, and although he had left Hugh of Burgundy in charge of the remaining French forces, there was now no doubt who was in command of the crusade.

Amongst the most important spoils of the victory was the Egyptian galley fleet, an acquisition that put an end once and for all to Muslim thoughts of dominating the Mediterranean. As far as the peace terms were concerned, it was agreed that the lives of the Acre garrison, and of their wives and children, would be spared in return for a ransom of 200,000 dinars, the return of 1,500 Christian prisoners and the return of the True Cross. Negotiations with Saladin about the precise implementation of these terms soon broke down, however. When the due date arrived for the payment of the first instalment of the ransom (11 August 1191), Saladin's attempt to impose new conditions was rejected. Negotiations continued in an atmosphere of mutual mistrust until 20 August. What is more, the crusaders were keen to press on south to Jerusalem and could not delay indefinitely; they felt that Saladin was spinning out the negotiations deliberately. On 19 August a rumour spread through the crusaders' camp that Saladin had killed all of his prisoners, and on 20 August, in full sight of Saladin's army still encamped near Acre, Richard's men put to death their own hostages, at least 2,600 men and perhaps over 3,000. Muslim reaction to the massacre was predictably hostile (they killed their Christian prisoners), whilst Christian writers regarded it more neutrally, and as the inevitable consequence of Saladin's failure to abide by the peace terms. Later historians have tended to condemn Richard for what today would be viewed as a war crime, but it would arguably be anachronistic to view such acts in modern moral terms. The prisoners were bargaining counters in a diplomatic and military game. If Richard wanted to leave for Jerusalem, he could not take 3,000 prisoners with him and nor could he leave them indefinitely in the hands of his men at Acre. Something had to be done, and Richard was not afraid to be ruthless. As it had been with his great-great-grandfather, William the Conqueror, perhaps this is what enabled him to succeed to the extent that he did.

Richard now faced a dilemma: should he try to capture Jerusalem or not? At first glance, this seems like an odd question. After all, the crusade had been launched in large part to recover the Holy City. However, matters were not as straightforward as this. Richard could march on Jerusalem and try to take it, but even if this worked, who would garrison Jerusalem and defend it after its capture? It would remain isolated, exposed and vulnerable to Muslim counter-attack. Alternatively he could turn his attention to Jerusalem after taking Ascalon. Ascalon was the key to the road between Egypt and Syria. If it was held by Christian forces, it could disrupt the links between the two halves of Saladin's empire and protect Jerusalem too. So when Richard set out from Acre on 22 August 1191, leaving Berengaria and Joan safely behind in the city, Ascalon was his target. First, though, he had to take Jaffa, on the road to Ascalon and Jerusalem's nearest port. It was eighty-one miles from Acre to Jaffa and the march took nineteen days. It was during this journey, however, that Richard's reputation as military leader and strategist was secured. His march along the coast and his victory over Saladin's troops at the battle of Arsuf on 7 September were outstanding military achievements. Richard reached Jaffa on 10 September to find that Saladin had destroyed it. Saladin now decided to demolish Ascalon too, to prevent the crusaders finding a serviceable base there. The dismayed Muslim reactions to Saladin's conduct at this point suggest that this was not the sort of behaviour expected of a great warrior.

As for Richard, his wider ambitions at this time are hard to determine. For many of those with him, their first and only objective was to visit Jerusalem, pray at the holy places and return home. Richard, though, it has been suggested, was already looking beyond Ascalon by October 1191 and formulating plans for an invasion of Egypt. The kings of

Jerusalem, especially Amalric I in the 1160s and 1170s, had attempted such an invasion in the hope of securing Egypt's huge wealth for themselves (William II of Sicily had done something similar in 1174). It is difficult to know whether Richard was serious about following their example, however, and even if he was, it did not stop him attempting to reach a settlement with Saladin between October 1191 and January 1192. It was during these negotiations that the marriage between Joan and Saladin's brother al-Adil was proposed.

Joan and Berengaria had left Acre and rejoined Richard at Jaffa by the middle of October 1191. On 18 October, according to Muslim sources, Richard held detailed discussions with al-Adil's secretary about the terms of a possible peace deal.[25] The possession of Jerusalem and the True Cross were the initial sticking points; but a few days later fresh proposals were put on the table. Richard suggested that Saladin should grant Palestine to al-Adil and that Joan would then marry him, taking as her dowry the coastal cities held by the Christians. This new territory would be part of Saladin's empire, whilst Joan and al-Adil would live at Jerusalem, which would be freely accessible to Christian pilgrims. The True Cross would be returned to its Christian owners and both sides would release their prisoners. Joan's allegedly outraged response to this scheme has already been described. However, there is some evidence to suggest that she was not opposed to it as strongly as some of the sources make out. After all, Joan's twelve years on Sicily would have accustomed her to Muslim customs and lifestyle. One writer alleged that some of her servants there had been Muslims too, albeit secretly. Moreover, another Muslim observer, who was privy to the negotiations, believed that Joan had been happy enough with the idea, and was only forced to reject it under severe pressure from her religious advisers.[26]

While Richard's attempts to find a diplomatic solution to his problems in the Holy Land continued throughout October and November 1191, he kept his military options open. By mid-November he had taken his army ten miles inland from Jaffa to Ramleh. He spent Christmas at Latrun and then advanced to within only twelve miles of Jerusalem. Many with Richard were now excited at the prospect of retaking the city, but others (principally the Templars and the Hospitallers, who knew the country well) drew Richard's attention to the dangers of such an enterprise. The crusaders could be trapped between the garrison and a relieving army, as King Guy had been at Acre; and, unlike Guy, they would have no access to the sea for reinforcements and supplies. Moreover, what would happen if they did take the city? Who would defend it? Their advice was to turn away from Jerusalem and make (as Richard had originally wanted) for Ascalon. On 13 January 1192, Richard gave the order to withdraw. For most of the ordinary soldiers, this was a bitter blow.

Richard's forces returned to Ascalon towards the end of January 1192 and spent the next four months rebuilding the city. During the first half of the year, however, the necessity of finding a satisfactory way of resolving the stalemate in the Holy Land was brought home to Richard when he received two separate pieces of news from England. In the first, he was told that his brother John had removed Richard's representatives in England and was attempting to take over the government. In the second, he was told that John had also formed a conspiracy with King Philip of France. Richard needed to return home before the situation got even worse. But before he could do this, the ongoing feud between Guy de Lusignan and Conrad of Montferrat had to be settled. The earlier judgement Richard and Philip had made on their respective claims was abandoned as support for Guy amongst the kingdom's nobility began to dissolve, and, in April, Conrad was recognised as king of Jerusalem. As compensation for his lost crown, Guy was allowed to buy Cyprus from the Templars, and his family remained in control of the island until 1489. Unfortunately, this new arrangement was undermined by Conrad's assassination at Tyre on 28 April. He was stabbed to death on his way home from dinner, and there was plenty of contemporary gossip to the effect that Richard had been involved in the killing in some way. Was Richard so alarmed at Conrad's elevation to the throne of Jerusalem that he was prepared to have him killed? King Philip of France, unhappy at the bad publicity he had received as a result of leaving the crusade early, was certainly prepared to support the view that Richard was responsible. Whatever the truth, Conrad's death left Jerusalem without a king, but on 5 May 1192 his widow, Isabella, married Count Henry of Champagne (the nephew of both the kings of England and France). Although Henry was never crowned king, the political situation in Jerusalem was stabilised for the time being.

All this time, the fighting and the campaigning continued. At the end of May 1192, Richard's forces captured the fortress of Darum, twenty miles south of Ascalon. This added to the length of coastline in Christian hands and put further pressure on Saladin's line of communication between Egypt and Syria. And at the beginning of June, Richard reluctantly agreed to take part in another siege of Jerusalem. By early June the crusaders were back where they had been six months before. Richard was even able to ride to a hilltop from which he could see the Holy City. It was the closest he ever got to Jerusalem as familiar differences resurfaced within the crusaders' camp about what to do next. The French were in favour of pressing on with a siege, whilst Richard and the locals pointed out the problems once more. Richard was not prepared to risk his reputation when the chances were that any besieging force would be cut off by Saladin, and a committee (five Templars, five Hospitallers, five French barons and five from the kingdom of Jerusalem) eventually voted to opt for an invasion of Egypt instead. Despite the problems back home, Richard declared his willingness to lead it. A final decision was frustrated, however, by news that Muslim reinforcements were on their way from Egypt. On 24 June, Richard's troops attacked their caravan and scattered it, capturing men, horses, camels and plunder in the process. This was one of Richard's most underrated military successes. But for most of the crusaders, it was no substitute for a successful siege of Jerusalem, and the decision not to mount such a siege was profoundly unpopular. Contemporaries as well as later historians have criticised Richard for his reluctance to try and take Jerusalem. At the very least, it has been thought, he should have completed his pilgrimage. Others have excused him by saying that he wanted to besiege the city, but was unable to do so because the duke of Burgundy, acting on instructions from the French king, who did not want Richard taking credit for capturing the ultimate prize, refused to join him.

Meanwhile the threat from Saladin remained immediate and significant. On 28 July his forces attacked Jaffa in an effort to divide the recovering kingdom of Jerusalem in two. The city was heroically defended by its garrison long enough to allow Richard to come to its relief. He arrived offshore on 1 August and, having learnt that the citadel was still in Christian hands, led the efforts to construct a beachhead. He took off his leg armour, jumped into the water and waded ashore, heading an advance that pushed the Muslims back inland and enabled his forces to enter the city. Negotiations followed, but Saladin had one last card to play. On the night of 4 August he launched a surprise attack on Richard's camp and nearly succeeded in routing it. The defenders were heavily outnumbered by the Muslims, but they managed to organise themselves in ranks, the front made up of kneeling men holding a shield and a spear pointing at the enemy, and behind them cross-bowmen working in pairs. After eight hours of defending, during which time the Muslims broke into the city and were cleared out by Richard himself and a handful of knights, the Christians were able to go on the attack. Contemporaries rated this victory outside the walls of Jaffa as perhaps Richard's greatest military feat. None of them had any doubt about how crucial his personal contribution had been. In the words of one of them, the crusaders' victory was 'the great miracle that all the whole world wonders at'.[27]

It was clear by now that there was little chance of either side inflicting a decisive defeat on the other. Richard fell ill at this point, but even this development did not convince Saladin or his advisers that they could better the Christians. So negotiations to end the stalemate resumed, and on 1 September the final terms of a settlement were agreed and embodied in a document, the Treaty of Jaffa. There was to be a truce for three years and eight months from 2 September 1192. The coastline from Tyre to Jaffa was to remain in Christian hands. Ascalon, the main bone of contention throughout the negotiations, was returned to Saladin, but only after its fortifications (laboriously and expensively reconstructed by Richard's men), along with those at Gaza and Darum, had been destroyed. Jerusalem was to remain in Muslim hands but Christian pilgrims would be allowed to visit the city. Richard did not take advantage of this concession: ill, and doubtless concerned about what was happening in France and England, he set sail for home on 9 October 1192.

By the time he did so, Joan and Berengaria had already left the Holy Land. They would return to France slowly through southern Italy. After landing at Brindisi, they headed for Rome. Such a journey, across 300 miles or so of her former kingdom, must have stirred strong feelings in

Joan; but at least she was tolerably safe, now that Tancred of Lecce was a loyal ally of her brother. This was more than could be said for Richard himself who, on his journey home, was captured by Duke Leopold of Austria, whom Richard had offended at the siege of Acre, and handed over into the custody of Emperor Henry VI. There was no love lost between Richard and Henry: the latter wanted the kingdom of Sicily, of course, whilst back in Germany, the biggest thorn in Henry's side, Duke Henry 'the Lion' of Saxony, was Richard's brother-in-law. Of more immediate importance, though, was the money the emperor could demand for Richard's release. Richard was only freed in 1194 after a huge ransom of £100,000 had been paid. This windfall allowed Henry to relaunch his Italian plans. He returned to Italy in May 1194 and, aided by the opportune death of Tancred of Lecce in February, completed his conquest of Sicily at the end of the year when he was crowned *Rex Sicilie* in Palermo Cathedral.

All of this lay in the future, though, when the two queens arrived at Rome early in 1193. They were honourably received by Pope Celestine III and they stayed there for almost six months. They were at the Lateran Palace in April when they issued a charter in their joint names, and it was presumably whilst they were there that they heard the news of Richard's imprisonment.[28] Indeed, the chronicler who records their stay at Rome says quite clearly that the two queens remained there so long out of fear of the emperor who was holding Richard captive. They eventually left Rome, however, travelling first to Pisa, then to Genoa and Marseilles. There they were met by King Alfonso of Aragon who escorted them for a while; and finally they were conducted through his lands by Count Raymond of Toulouse. At last, they reached Poitiers.

For the next three years or so Joan disappears from sight. However, it is reasonable to think that she spent most of this time in and around Queen Berengaria's entourage. And she would almost certainly have spent some time with her mother, Queen Eleanor. After Eleanor had helped mediate a settlement between Richard and John in 1194, she had retired to Fontevraud, and it is fair to imagine Joan as a regular visitor to the abbey over the next couple of years. Joan's will, written in 1199, also gives some indications of the kind of life she might have led during this otherwise obscure period.[29] It records bequests of significant sums to her chaplain, Joscelin, to two of her clerks who were presumably responsible for all her letters and documentary administration, and to several male servants. The largest gifts, however, were reserved for her ladies-in-waiting: £40 to Philippa (also referred to, tantalisingly, as Joan's 'kinswoman'), just under £70 and £95 to Elisabeth and Alice respectively, and, the biggest personal legacy of all, £133 to Beatrice. Joan's relationships with these women were clearly close and significant. One account records how, when she and Berengaria left Acre in October 1191, they did so 'with their ladies'. And as a further sign of the particular importance of Beatrice and Alice, Joan left them 'her two coffers at Verdun and all their contents', whatever they were. The will also hints at Joan's piety. There is a long list of bequests to various religious houses – commonplace in an aristocratic will of this time, but still notable given the size and nature of some of the gifts. Joan's three hangings (tapestries, perhaps; how revealing it might be to know what these depicted) were given to three different churches and just under £270 went to the Cistercians. But the family church at Fontevraud was favoured above all. It was to receive various gifts, including Joan's body for burial, but also the enormous sum of £600, expressly earmarked for the payment of the abbess's debts. Joan's saltpans were obviously important to her too, the income from these being divided between various beneficiaries.

The writing of the will was still three years away when Joan once more caught the chroniclers' attention. At Rouen in Normandy in October 1196, around her thirty-first birthday, she married Count Raymond VI of Toulouse. He was approaching forty, and Joan was his fourth wife. This was a predictably political arrangement in which Joan, yet again, probably had little say; but it was no less striking for that and marked a clear change of direction in the policy of Joan's family towards southern France. For nearly forty years since the late 1150s the rulers of Aquitaine had been at loggerheads with the counts of Toulouse over territory and status. The city of Toulouse itself was of crucial strategic and economic importance, placed as it was on the main trade routes between the Mediterranean and the Atlantic. For the dukes of Aquitaine it was the link between Bayonne, Bordeaux and La Rochelle on the eastern seaboard and Narbonne, Arles and Marseilles and the maritime commerce of the west. The counts of Toulouse had their own concerns:

they acknowledged the authority of the kings of France only loosely, their main preoccupations being with the rulers of northern Spain (the kings of Aragon and Navarre and the counts of Barcelona) and Provence, which was part of the German Empire; and with the dukes of Aquitaine, of course, who were rivals and competitors, not just neighbours. When Henry II married Eleanor of Aquitaine in 1152 he acquired through her a hereditary claim to the county of Toulouse, which he first tried (largely unsuccessfully) to make good by force in 1159. In the early 1170s the affairs of southern France and northern Spain again featured heavily in Henry's diplomacy. His daughter Eleanor, Joan's elder sister, was betrothed to King Alfonso of Castile in 1170, and in 1173 Henry was able to intervene and act as peacemaker in an ongoing conflict between the count of Toulouse and the ruler of what was by this time the joint kingdom of Aragon-Barcelona. The price exacted from Count Raymond by Henry for this assistance was the former's homage, performed before the barons of Aquitaine at Limoges in February 1173. This may have resolved the thorny questions at issue between Aquitaine and Toulouse for a while, but the settlement did not last. The second half of the 1180s was a period of almost constant warfare between Count Raymond and Richard, in his capacity as duke of Aquitaine. King Philip of France was dragged into this struggle as the overlord of both men, and the conflict was only prevented from escalating further between 1188 and 1190 when both kings became preoccupied with their preparations for the Third Crusade.

It is only in this context that Richard's marriage to Berengaria of Navarre can be understood. Richard knew Aquitaine intimately from his twenty years of campaigning there. He understood the wider political dynamics of the area, and he was well aware that, given the chance, Raymond of Toulouse would attempt to increase his own power and extend his territories at Richard's expense. Particularly in dispute were the lands around Cahors and the Quercy, which Henry II had managed to seize during his campaign of 1159. Now that Richard was going on crusade, Raymond would have the time and opportunity to undermine Richard's control of the area, and Richard needed to reinforce his own position before he left. The kings of Navarre made good allies, therefore, and Richard's marriage to Berengaria was a price worth paying for security on his vulnerable southern frontier. The alliance proved its worth in 1192 and 1194 when Berengaria's brother Sancho helped put down revolts in Aquitaine that might otherwise have allowed Count Raymond to intervene. By the mid-1190s, however, circumstances were different. For one thing, Richard and Berengaria had failed to produce an heir, and husband and wife had rarely been together at all since the end of the crusade. It seems that the marriage had failed. What is more, the regional situation had also changed with the deaths of Count Raymond V of Toulouse in 1195 and King Alfonso II of Aragon in 1196. Navarre and Aragon had been allies against Castile, but following the death of King Alfonso the Aragonese made their own peace with the Castilians, leaving the new king of Navarre, Berengaria's brother, Sancho VII, isolated. Navarre, therefore, was rapidly losing its usefulness as an ally, and Richard seized the chance to capitalise on the diplomatic upheaval that was taking place in Spain to abandon his hostility to Toulouse and arrange the marriage of the new count, Raymond VI, to Joan. There was a price to be paid, of course. Richard had to abandon his family's claim to Toulouse; he returned the Quercy to Count Raymond and added the county of Agen as Joan's dowry. But with this new understanding firmly in place, Richard could look confidently ahead to a period of prolonged peace and stability on his southern frontier. The alliance with Navarre, by contrast, had run its course and Richard's relationship with King Sancho soon deteriorated. By 1198, Sancho was holding on to castles which Richard claimed he was entitled to as part of Berengaria's dowry, and no less a figure than the pope himself promised to intervene to help resolve the dispute.

It would be fascinating to know what Berengaria and Joan made of these developments in 1196 and whether they discussed them. They had been in each other's company for most of the time since the royal marriage on Cyprus, and they must have known each other well by the time Joan heard she was to marry once more. Whether they were fond of one another is a different question, of course; but even if they were, Joan's marriage to Raymond and the end of the Navarrese alliance might well have driven a wedge between them. Richard had practically abandoned his wife already, but now he had abandoned her family, too, and in favour of an ally whom the Navarrese had been fighting to keep at bay for Richard only a few years before. By the end of 1196, Joan was remarried, Berengaria was more alone than ever, and Navarre was cut off as well: two queens and a kingdom, all three victims of Richard I's ruthless diplomacy. If Berengaria attended Joan's wedding to Raymond (and perhaps she did – there is no evidence either way), she cannot have felt much like celebrating.

Joan had never been able to provide her first husband, William of Sicily, with a surviving heir. The same did not happen this time. In July 1197 at Beaucaire, between Avignon and Arles, Joan gave birth to a son, the future Count Raymond VII of Toulouse. Then, the following Easter she was with her husband and her brother Richard at Le Mans, further evidence that the old enmity between Aquitaine and Toulouse was finally at an end. Soon after this, Joan embarked upon another of her remarkable journeys, and during it she revealed aspects of her character that had not been seen before. This journey was much shorter than others she had made, but this time it was at the head of an army. Some of Count Raymond's subjects had rebelled and, rather than wait for him to return and deal with them, Joan took it upon herself to handle the situation and besiege the rebels in their castle of Les Cassés, about thirty miles south-east of Toulouse. Unfortunately for her, though, the siege did not go well. Joan was betrayed by some of her own men, who smuggled arms and equipment into the castle. Forced to abandon the siege, she had only just escaped when her camp was set on fire by the traitors in her own ranks. Outraged by these insults, Joan's first impulse was not to seek out her husband, but to find her brother and tell him what had happened: Richard would surely not let such an incident pass. Before she could find him, however, Joan learnt of Richard's death. He had been besieging a castle at Châlus-Chabrol near Limoges when he was struck in the shoulder by a crossbow bolt shot from the battlements. The wound turned gangrenous and after ten days, on 6 April 1199, he died.

Joan headed for Fontevraud, where Richard's body was buried on 11 April. The sheer length of this journey (the abbey is about 300 miles from Toulouse) suggests that Joan was deeply affected by news of Richard's death. And the trip must have been even more gruelling for her because she was pregnant again. The depth of her grief and anger at her brother's death can also be gauged from one particularly gruesome story. Before he died, Richard forgave the man who had shot him; others, however, were in no mood to be so generous. Roger of Howden describes how Richard's mercenary captain, Mercadier, had the king's killer flayed alive once Richard was dead. But another version of the same story alleges that it was Joan who could not bring herself to forgive. The most direct route from southern France back to Anjou passed through or near Limoges, close to the site of Richard's death. It could have been around here that the man who had shot the fatal bolt was brought before Joan. Having been seized by Mercadier and sent to her, the story goes, it was on Joan's orders that the nails of his hands and feet were pulled out, he was blinded and then skinned before, still breathing, he was drawn by a team of horses. It was behaviour such as this that led the writer of this graphic account to describe Joan as 'a woman whose masculine spirit transcended the weakness of her sex'.[30]

Joan stayed at Fontevraud for some weeks, to recuperate and pay her respects at Richard's new tomb. However, by late summer she was travelling again, this time north to Normandy. She was probably keen to establish contact with the new king, her younger brother John, and she was reunited with her mother by then too. There was certainly some family business to conduct. At Rouen at the start of August 1199, Joan (described as 'our dearest daughter' by Eleanor) was the first witness to one of her mother's charters.[31] Then, at the end of that month, John agreed to grant his sister an annual pension of £67 to use charitably as she saw fit; John also granted her the enormous sum of £2,000 in consideration of all the debts that had been owed to Joan by Richard. This is the only evidence that she had helped her late brother financially, but it suggests that there was a strong bond between them. And it is surely significant that John named two of his daughters Joan – the first, one of his illegitimate children, went on to marry Llywelyn ap Iorwerth, the ruler of north Wales, in 1203–4, while the second, John's eldest legitimate daughter, became queen of Scotland when she married King Alexander II in 1221.

There is no sign of anything amiss with Joan in the documents of 1199, and there is no evidence that she was unwell or that there were problems with her pregnancy. However, by the end of September 1199 she was dying. By the time she arrived at Rouen, Joan was entering the final stages of her pregnancy, but the birth went badly: the child survived long enough only to be baptised and Joan was left fatally ill. Seeing no chance of recovery, she decided to take the veil and become a nun. At first she wanted to send for the prior of Fontevraud, but he was too far away and would not arrive in time. So she asked the archbishop of Canterbury, Hubert Walter, who was also in Rouen, to administer the vows. Hubert told Joan that she couldn't become a nun while her husband was still alive, but so zealously and fervently did she press her case that he relented and took her vows in the presence of her mother, Queen Eleanor.[32] Before she died, Joan left money to Fontevraud, for her own soul and for that of her brother Richard. The first witness to this charter was 'our dearest mother'. Eleanor had already seen three of her sons predecease her; now her youngest daughter was on her deathbed.[33] The old queen had one last task to complete for her daughter: it was her job to take Joan's will to Count Raymond so that he could carry out its terms. Joan's body was carried to Fontevraud, as the will required, and she was buried at the feet of Henry her father and by the side of Richard her brother. These two men had held the Angevin territories together through a combination of military skill, political cunning and sheer force of character. However, by the time Joan was laid to rest in their company the struggle for her family's inheritance was already under way and the Angevin Empire was only five years away from catastrophic collapse.

PART THREE

The Death of an Empire

CHAPTER SEVEN

THE NEPHEW'S TALE

Arthur of Brittany and the Collapse of Angevin Power

Lᴀᴛᴇ ᴏɴ Sᴀᴛᴜʀᴅᴀʏ, the night before Palm Sunday, the courier reached the castle at Rouen with news of the king's death. Two weeks before, on 26 March 1199, Richard I had been inspecting his siege works at the castle of Châlus-Chabrol near Limoges. It was a routine military operation and Richard was wearing no armour. But a crossbow bolt shot from the battlements of the castle punctured his unprotected shoulder, the wound festered and its poison killed him on 6 April. The courier (his name was Thierry) went straight to William Marshal, earl of Pembroke, and delivered the message. The Marshal was taking off his boots and about to go to bed, but on hearing the news he dressed quickly, left his quarters and went to find the archbishop of Canterbury, who was staying with the monks at the priory of Notre Dame du Pré outside the city walls. At first alarmed by the Marshal's appearance at such an hour, and then shocked by what he was told, it took Archbishop Hubert a while to compose himself. But soon enough the thoughts of both men turned to the future. The archbishop was gloomy and pessimistic. 'What solace is there for us now?' he wondered. 'None, so help me God! With him gone, I can think of nobody to choose to rescue the realm or come to our aid in anything. The realm is now on the road to destruction, grief and destitution. We can be sure it won't be very long before we see the French rush upon us to take everything we have, because there will be nobody able to stand in their way.' The Marshal had no time for such despair and urged on the archbishop the need to choose the next king quickly. 'My understanding and view of the matter,' the archbishop replied, 'and I'm sure of this, is that by right we ought to make Arthur king.' 'Oh! My lord,' warned the Marshal, 'my feeling is that that would be a bad course to take, and I do not recommend or advise it: Arthur has treacherous advisers about him and he is unapproachable and overbearing. If we call him to our side, he will seek to do us harm and damage, for he does not like those in our realm. My advice is that he should never be king. Instead, consider the claim of earl John: to the best of my knowledge and belief he seems to be the nearest in line to claim the land of his father as well as that of his brother.' 'Marshal,' the archbishop asked, 'is this what you want?' 'Yes, my lord, for that is right, since the son is indisputably closer in the line of inheritance than the nephew is, and it is right that that should be made clear.' 'So, Marshal, that is how it shall be. But this much I can tell you,' Hubert stated ominously, 'that you will never come to regret anything you did as much as what you're doing now.' To this the Marshal replied, 'Thanks for the warning! Nonetheless, my advice is that it should be so.'[1]

This conversation was not written down until more than twenty years after it was supposed to have happened. So the accuracy of the account is open to question. On the other hand, it was recorded by William Marshal's biographer, who knew him well, and he may have got this description of the meeting directly from the Marshal himself. Either way, it describes a predicament that was very real for the ruling elite of the Angevin Empire in 1199. Richard I's death was sudden and unexpected and it was by no means clear who should succeed him. Should it be his brother, John, or his nephew, Arthur, the only son of Richard's late brother Geoffrey of Brittany? Which of the two had the better claim – John was the younger brother of the previous king whilst Arthur was the son of a dead older brother? And anyway, even if the legal situation had been clear (which it was not), there was much more to consider than this. Which of the two would the barons of England and Normandy support? What would be the response to Richard's death in the rest of the Angevin lands in France? Would John or Arthur receive the backing of King Philip II of France? Which of the claimants would act most decisively in the circumstances?

The dilemma in England and Normandy was resolved quickly. None of the barons on either side of the Channel had any desire to be ruled by a Breton and support for John was widespread. He was installed as duke of Normandy on 25 April 1199, and just over a month later, on 27 May, Archbishop Hubert (the man who had reportedly wanted Arthur to succeed Richard) crowned him king of England in Westminster Abbey. In other parts of Angevin France, though, things were less straightforward. On Easter Day, 18 April, in the city of Angers an assembly of barons from Anjou, Maine and Touraine, led by the most powerful lord in Anjou, William des Roches, had acknowledged Arthur as Richard's lawful successor. What was more, an army of Bretons was on the march and King Philip had declared unequivocally for their prince.

* * * *

Like William Atheling and Henry the Young King, Arthur of Brittany was a king of England who might have been. His life was even shorter than theirs (Arthur was only just sixteen when he died), and there was little time for him to make an impact. Nevertheless he managed to do so. To be sure he was used and exploited by men more powerful than he was, but he was also a potent symbol of independence to his people and a serious threat to the ambitions and claims of his rivals. And he is important here because he stands at the centre of the political and military storm that convulsed northern France in the early years of the thirteenth century. In 1199 the king of England was arguably the most powerful ruler in western Europe. Only the German emperor could compare in terms of status and political strength. Because the king of England was also the ruler of most of France: as duke of Normandy, count of Anjou and duke of Aquitaine, he controlled lands that stretched from the English border with Scotland to the northern frontiers of Spain. The king of France, by contrast, ruled only notionally over most of his kingdom and controlled directly only a small area of territory around Paris. By the end of 1204, however, this situation would be transformed. The English king had by then lost nearly all his continental lands, and his French counterpart had begun the process of adding them to his own territories. A rapid and dramatic rebalancing of power in Europe was under way.

Historians still argue fiercely over how this happened and why. Some claim that the Angevin Empire was an artificial entity, created by chance when Henry II became king of England in 1154. Never designed to survive for long, it was destined to break apart sooner or later. It had few institutional, political, cultural and linguistic ties holding its elements together; nor were its two most important parts, England and Normandy, bound by a common aristocracy with interests on both sides of the English Channel as they had been in the generations immediately after 1066. Others suggest that Richard I had placed intolerable strains on England and Normandy with his constant warfare and financial demands, or that French power was rising and French wealth was increasing well before Richard's death. In other words, one way or the other, the Angevin Empire was already doomed by 1199. It has also been argued that the collapse of 1203–4 was all King John's fault. After inheriting a strong position, he alienated important people needlessly, he did not take the lead in confronting the French threat, he used unreliable mercenaries to fight his wars, and he did little to win the support of the Norman people. And, in the midst of all this, he (allegedly) murdered his nephew, Arthur of Brittany.

Now it is by no means certain that this is what happened. And anyway, Arthur's disappearance did not lead directly to the loss of the English king's lands in France. Nonetheless, John was deeply implicated in whatever happened to Arthur, and his treatment of his dead brother's son served to loosen further the ties of loyalty and trust that bound together the king's relationships with his leading subjects, and his territories. Arthur's death also came to represent something rotten at the heart of John's regime – a casual brutality and a contempt for accepted norms of aristocratic conduct and behaviour. It bred and fostered an atmosphere of suspicion in which nobody could feel safe in the company of a volatile and unpredictable king. So when men had to choose between rival rulers in 1203–4, there were plenty who abandoned John with relief.

* * * *

Arthur's tale has its origins in the complex and sometimes bewildering history of Brittany itself, a history shaped by the impact of external forces, whether geographical, climatic or human. Brittany is essentially a peninsula, the largest in France, with a coastline nearly 1,800 miles long. To the north it faces the English Channel, to the south the Bay of Biscay, to the west the Atlantic Ocean. With neighbours on land only to the east, the Bretons were and are jealous of their autonomy and proud of their distinctive culture. Having said this, that culture was itself a blend of different ethnic and linguistic elements. Central to the Bretons' notions of their unique identity was their own language, Breton, which had evolved over centuries as a mixture of indigenous dialects, namely Latin (Brittany had been a province of the Roman Empire known as Armorica) and, most interestingly in this context, British influence. From the mid-fifth century, for reasons that are still ultimately obscure, migrants from southern and western Britain had come to this region of north-western France in increasing numbers. They brought their own habits and idioms with them, and gave the area a new name, Brittany. The resulting fusion of customs and tongues was deep-rooted by the twelfth century, when Gerald of Wales was able to state confidently that the Bretons, the Cornish and the Welsh spoke essentially the same language.[2] And it was most likely in that common language that the first stories of King Arthur were shared and developed. The hard evidence for a historical King Arthur is extremely thin and highly prob-lematic, but the first recorded references to him by name were made in Wales in the ninth century and described events that were supposed to have taken place in the late fifth and early sixth centuries, precisely the time when British settlers were arriving in Brittany. What is more, these written accounts almost certainly derived from a much older oral tradi-tion, in which travelling bards and storytellers had transmitted their tales to succeeding generations by word of mouth alone. So myths surrounding Arthur must have been developing in and between Wales, south-western England and Brittany long before Geoffrey of Monmouth turned the legendary Celtic warrior into a model Anglo-Norman aris-tocrat in the 1130s. By then the Bretons had their own ideas about who Arthur was, and his name was loaded with political significance.

By then, too, political and military connections between Brittany, Normandy and England were well established. The post-Conquest English kings used Bretons as mercenaries in their armies. Brittany, indeed, was well known in the twelfth century as a source of paid troops. In one of her *lais*, Marie de France told the story of the handsome, brave and wise Eliduc and of his relationship with the two women who loved him.[3] It is romantic and poignant stuff, but there is no getting away from the fact that the hero is a soldier of fortune. More prosaically, William of Malmesbury wrote of the Bretons in the 1120s:

> As a race they are penniless at home, and happy to earn the rewards of a laborious life elsewhere at the expense of strangers. Pay them, and they will throw justice and kinship to the winds, and not refuse to fight even in a civil war; and the more you give, the readier they will be to follow wherever you lead. Henry [I] knew this habit of theirs, and if ever he needed mercenary troops, spent a great deal on Bretons, taking a short lease of that faithless people's faith in return for coin.[4]

Many such men fought for Duke William of Normandy at Hastings in 1066 and some had been richly rewarded with English lands. Alan 'the Red', for example, the nephew of Duke Alan III (1008–40), was given estates across England by the Conqueror, most notably those in the north centred on the great castle at Richmond in Yorkshire. Eventually, in 1136, the descendants of this junior branch of the ducal line were given the title 'earl of Richmond'. Meanwhile another Alan, Duke Alan IV (1084–1112), had married Constance, one of the Conqueror's daughters, and his intervention at Tinchebrai in 1106 proved crucial to the victory of his brother-in-law, King Henry I. One of Henry's own illegitimate daughters, Matilda, married Duke Conan III (1112–48), Alan IV's son and successor.

Personal links aside, however, the precise nature of the political relationship between Brittany and Normandy is harder to assess. The Norman dukes liked to think that Brittany was a dependency of theirs, and later, Henry II thought the same. However, there is no evidence to suggest that the position was as clear-cut as this and much depended on the circumstances and personalities of the individual rulers. The situation had become particularly fraught, and not a little complicated, by the middle of the twelfth century. Shortly before he died in 1148, for reasons that have never been clear, Duke Conan III had disowned his only son, Hoël, allowing his daughter, Bertha, to succeed him. She had been married first to Alan of Brittany, a Breton count who was also earl of Richmond in England, and they had had a son, who would eventually become Duke Conan IV. Before this, however, Bertha's second husband, Eudo, viscount of Porhoët, acted as duke in right of his wife, probably with the intention that his rule should end when his stepson Conan reached his majority. However, the displaced Hoël continued to dispute Eudo's authority until his death in 1158. In the ensuing confusion over the Breton succession, the Angevins, who had long coveted the port of Nantes at the mouth of the Loire, were able to seize it, and Henry II installed his younger brother, Geoffrey, as count there. At the same time, in September 1156, the king permitted young Conan, who was now of age and had been restoring order to the English lands he had been allowed to inherit from his father, to cross the Channel and challenge his stepfather. Conan besieged and took Rennes, expelled Eudo and took his place as duke. Conan attempted to extend his authority further after Geoffrey of Anjou, count of Nantes, died in July 1158. However, Conan quickly came to regret his seizure of the county. Henry II confiscated Richmond and when the king crossed to France, Conan hurried to submit to him and hand back Nantes. After this, Conan remained obedient and dutiful and spent much of his time between 1156 and 1164 in his English lands. He was also a regular visitor at the royal court and witnessed a number of Henry's charters. And it is hard not to see Henry's hand in Conan's marriage to Margaret, sister of Malcolm IV, king of Scots, in 1160.

Conan did have duties in Brittany, though. As far as Henry II was concerned, the duke's job there was to keep the peace on the border between eastern Brittany, Normandy, Maine and Anjou. In this, Conan was notably unsuccessful. Baronial unrest and disobedience remained endemic and there seems to have been little respect for the duke's authority amongst the frontier nobility. So in 1166 Henry II returned to Brittany to deal with the problems there in person. Conan agreed to betroth his only daughter and heir, Constance, to Henry's fourth son, Geoffrey. There was nothing extraordinary about that; but the rest of the arrangement was strikingly one-sided, as Conan also agreed to stand down as duke of Brittany in favour of his new son-in-law. Not that he had much choice: Conan had been deposed and, since Geoffrey was only seven in 1166 (his marriage to Constance didn't take place until 1181), Henry II was now directly in charge of Brittany. At Rennes, Henry took possession of the duchy in Geoffrey's name and later in 1166 the barons of Brittany performed homage to him at Thouars.

Over the next few years real power in Brittany remained in the hands of Henry II and the men he appointed to positions of authority in the duchy's government and Church. By 1173, though, Geoffrey was fifteen and old enough to play a role in Breton affairs. He did this by choosing to join with his brothers Henry and Richard, and with his mother Eleanor, in the revolt of 1173–4 against their father. Geoffrey certainly displayed some soldierly skill during the war, but his subjects found themselves on the wrong end of Henry II's angry response to the uprising when he attacked the duchy in August 1173 and again in September 1174. The revolt soon ended with Henry triumphant and for the rest of the 1170s he and his sons coexisted in a state of uneasy and fragile truce. Henry came gradually to rely on Geoffrey more and more, however, to keep the ever-restive Breton nobility in line. On 6 August 1178 he was knighted by his father at Woodstock near Oxford, and, probably in July 1181, Geoffrey finally married Constance and took over full control of his duchy.

The last stage of Geoffrey's life was dominated by the conflict between him and his brothers Henry and John on the one hand and his brother Richard on the other. Henry II struggled with little success to keep the peace between his warring sons. The death of the Young King on 11 June 1183 brought the first phase of these hostilities to an end, but in the following year, with the succession to the Angevin lands uncertain once again, Geoffrey and John attacked Richard, who retaliated by invading Brittany. The war continued into 1185, and in pursuit of his aims (the main one was to take control of Anjou) Geoffrey looked to Philip II to help him. The two men appear to have got on well (they were almost the same age) and Philip was determined to use whatever opportunity presented itself to cultivate tensions in the Angevin family. Significantly, it was in Paris rather than London, Rouen or Rennes that Geoffrey died on 19 August 1186. The cause of his death remains unclear. Perhaps wounds he received in a tournament proved fatal, or complications resulting from those. One chronicler claims he had a fever, another a bowel complaint. He was buried with great pomp in the choir of Notre Dame, where according to some accounts a distraught King Philip II had to be restrained from throwing himself into the grave.[5]

When Geoffrey died, he and Constance had one surviving daughter, Eleanor (a second girl, Matilda, had died in infancy), and another child was on the way. Their only son was born at Nantes on Easter Day, 29 March 1187. Usually he would have been given a family name, just as his sisters had been: Henry or Geoffrey from his father's side, perhaps, or alternatively Alan or Conan from his mother's. The chronicler William of Newburgh claimed that King Henry fully expected his grandson to be named after him. However, the boy was named Arthur, and this decision was almost certainly his mother's. His choice of name might conceivably have been little more than a product of courtly fashion and the popularity of Arthurian literature. But this seems unlikely. Boldly and defiantly, and perhaps with the encouragement and backing of the Breton nobility, Constance had associated her son directly with the legendary hero and symbol of Breton independence. The message to Henry II was clear: Brittany would not be dominated or subordinated, and this new leader, under what William of Newburgh called 'the mighty omen of his name', was the saviour they had been waiting for.[6] It was his destiny to defend the duchy from greedy predators, revive the glories of its past, and take it to greatness in the future. Unfortunately, however, during his short and tragic life, Arthur would do little to fulfil these expectations or emulate his mythical namesake.

Arthur and his family remained very much at the mercy of their Angevin neighbours. After Richard I succeeded Henry II in 1189, Arthur and Eleanor were used repeatedly as pieces in the new king's diplomatic chess game. When he was on Sicily in 1190, the settlement Richard made with Tancred of Lecce concerning Queen Joan's dower also included a provision that Arthur (still only three years old, of course) would marry one of Tancred's daughters. More significantly, perhaps, it also stipulated that, should Richard die without children of his own, Arthur would be his heir. One English chronicler suggests that Richard had made this decision before he left Normandy, so it is possible that the king was simply using the chance he got on Sicily to confirm his plans and reassure Tancred about his daughter's prospects.[7] But, whenever Richard decided to make Arthur his heir, it is hard to know how seriously he took his nephew's chances of succeeding him. Given that the king was about to be married to Berengaria of Navarre, presumably with the intention of producing plenty of potential successors, Arthur still remained an unlikely heir in 1190. Nevertheless, he was at least seen by his uncle as a plausible nominee, and less than ten years later he would indeed be fighting to obtain Richard's lands. As for Arthur's sister Eleanor, she was first promised to a son of Duke Leopold of Austria in 1193, as part of the deal agreed for the ransom of King Richard who had been captured on his return from crusade by the duke. But this scheme was thwarted by news of Leopold's death. Then, in 1195 plans for marrying Eleanor to Louis, Philip II's son and heir, were discussed, but again the match never happened.

Soon after this the political situation in Brittany deteriorated significantly, and Arthur's importance was highlighted once again. On Duke Geoffrey's death in 1187, his widow and Arthur's mother, Constance, had taken control of the duchy. However, she was still subject to the oppressive influence of Henry II, and it was on his orders in February 1188 or 1189 that Constance was required to marry Ranulf III, earl of Chester. Constance was an able and assertive ruler, and perhaps this was part of the problem Henry planned to address by marrying her off to one of his loyal followers. However, there are also hints of instability and unrest in Brittany following Duke Geoffrey's death that would have concerned Henry. It was not clear after 1186 just where the loyalties of the Breton barons lay – with Constance, Henry, King Philip or themselves. In 1187, Henry visited Brittany, ostensibly to meet his new grandson, but also to discipline some rebellious Breton lords. So Ranulf's job, as far as Henry was concerned, was probably to keep the Bretons in line, rein in his ambitious wife, and prevent the spread of Philip II's influence into the duchy. Almost inevitably, however, this was not a happy or a successful relationship. Constance was about ten years older than her new husband (Ranulf was only eighteen in 1188), and there must also have been significant differences between them both culturally and perhaps even linguistically. Ranulf did have estates along the Breton frontier, and his lands in England were close to those of the honour of Richmond. But the northern English lord and the proud Breton lady can have had little in common. They spent most of their married life apart, Constance in Brittany with her son, Ranulf on his estates in England or Normandy. There is little if any evidence of their acting together in the government of Brittany and the marriage produced no children.

In 1196, however, the marriage did take on an unexpected political significance. In the spring of that year, having just agreed a truce in his ongoing struggle with King Philip, Richard summoned Constance to his court. Richard already had custody of Eleanor, Constance's daughter. Now, it seems, after several years of crusading and fighting against Philip, during which Constance had been left to rule Brittany in her own way, Richard thought it was time to reassert his authority over the duchy and get Arthur out of his mother's reach as well. Perhaps Constance smelled a rat, because she left Arthur in the care of her Breton supporters. She was abducted by her husband Earl Ranulf as soon as she entered Normandy and taken to his castle at St James-de-Beuvron. Whether Ranulf was acting on Richard's instructions or with his approval is unclear. Perhaps this was simply a clumsy attempt by the earl to assert some kind of authority over his wife. But in any event, news of Constance's kidnapping was received with outrage back in Brittany and Richard was blamed for what had happened. The Bretons protecting Arthur appealed for help to King Philip and renounced all their ties with the duke of Normandy; Richard responded by demanding that the Bretons hand over Arthur to him. When they refused, he invaded the duchy in April 1196. Richard's campaign was short but brutal, designed to intimidate the Bretons into submission: burning down a church on Good Friday was just one of the tactics he used.

At this point the course of events becomes frustratingly unclear, but Richard may have negotiated a deal with the Breton magnates after his attack, as part of which he agreed to release Constance in August 1196 as long as she followed his advice in the government and affairs of Brittany. When the time came for Constance's release, however, Richard kept her captive (perhaps she had refused to go along with demands for her future good behaviour) and the leading Breton magnates met the nine-year-old Arthur at Saint-Malo de Beignon, about thirty miles west of Rennes. In return for their pledges of allegiance, Arthur promised them that he would not make peace with Richard without their consent. In August, Richard's troops entered Brittany again to put down what was becoming a full-scale uprising against Angevin authority. But resistance continued and Arthur was smuggled out of the duchy and placed in the safe custody of Philip II. Richard had misjudged the strength of Breton feeling in 1196 and overplayed his hand. Fairly or not, he was linked to Constance's abduction, and his display of military machismo in Brittany had achieved little. In 1197, mainly because there was little other option, he finally released Constance and pardoned the Breton barons who had fought against him. They formally confirmed their allegiance to the Angevins. But whilst this restored the situation of the early 1190s, the settlement was not deep-rooted. Mutual suspicions continued to simmer below the surface, and deals could soon be undone if circumstances changed.

Arthur stayed at the French court for over two years after leaving Brittany in 1196, becoming during that time friends with Louis, Philip II's son and the heir to the French throne. King Philip's public show of support for Arthur was telling. If Arthur could be persuaded to accept Philip's patronage and side with the French king against the Angevins, there might be a real prospect of driving a wedge between the northern and southern parts of Richard's French territories. It would be very surprising if, during his stay at Philip's court, Arthur had not been regularly reminded of the benefits of French overlordship and of the dangers Richard posed to Brittany. And in the longer term, the boy had a perfectly respectable claim to be his uncle's heir beyond Brittany. Richard had acknowledged this himself in Sicily in 1190. Six years later he was still childless and his brother John was his only viable successor apart from Arthur. Philip can only have relished the prospect of a compliant and dependant duke of Brittany succeeding to the rest of the Angevin lands in France. Arthur had returned to the Breton court by early 1199 and was soon playing an active role in the government of the duchy alongside his mother. By then, after more than two years in King Philip's company, and pumped full of French royal ideology, Arthur's sympathies were surely more Capetian than Angevin. If he wanted a protector in the future, he would look to Philip not Richard.

When Richard died in April 1199, the two men who would fight to succeed him were actually together: John was staying with Arthur in Brittany where news of Richard's death reached them both. It is possible that uncle and nephew had met to pool their grievances against Richard I and prepare the ground for some kind of joint action against him; one source says that John and Richard had quarrelled just before the latter's death, and Richard can hardly have been Arthur's favourite uncle after the events of the previous few years.[8] However, they were transformed from potential conspirators to determined arch-rivals by Richard's demise. John immediately rode with a few companions to Chinon, where the Angevin treasury was kept, and from there he made for Fontevraud where Richard's body had been taken for burial next to Henry II. Meanwhile, Constance of Brittany was active on behalf of her twelve-year-old son. He was at Angers where he was acclaimed count of Anjou on 18 April, and two days later he arrived at Tours where he was invested formally with the title. From there Arthur and Constance headed with an army to Le Mans, where they nearly cornered John on 20 April. And it was at Le Mans that Arthur met King Philip and performed homage to him for Anjou, Maine, Touraine and Brittany. As for John, having just managed to slip away from Le Mans in the nick of time, he made his way to Normandy where he was installed as duke at Rouen. Then, following his coronation at Westminster Abbey at the end of May, the war of the Angevin succession could properly begin.

John was back in Normandy within a few weeks of his coronation. His hold on the duchy was secure, despite the attack King Philip had made across the Seine into Norman territory straight after Richard's death. Meanwhile Queen Eleanor remained in control of Aquitaine in the south, buying support for her youngest son with lands and castles granted to the lords of Poitou. One of these, Aimeri de Thouars, was appointed by John as seneschal of Anjou in opposition to Arthur's nominee, William des Roches. And it was Aimeri who, in late May 1199, attacked Arthur at Tours, forcing King Philip to send troops to his rescue. Despite such pressure on the frontiers of Anjou from the Poitevin barons, however, and with his supporters controlling the strategically vital stretches of road and the river Loire that connected Angers and Tours, Arthur remained in a strong position and John

needed to weaken him quickly. Displaying the sort of political, diplomatic and military skills with which he is not normally credited, John
did this very successfully. In mid-August 1199 there was a meeting
between John and Philip, who by now had Arthur in protective custody.
John expressed his willingness to do homage to Philip, but the French
king demanded Anjou, Maine and Touraine, as well as Poitou, for
Arthur along with some of Normandy for himself. This was clearly too
much for John to concede and the talks stalled; but at least he was
parleying with Philip whilst Arthur himself was excluded from the
discussions. Moreover, by this point, John could feel confident about
rejecting Philip's demands. Earlier in August, John had managed to
re-establish the alliances that Richard had made with the counts of
Flanders and Boulogne. This gave him even more security in the north
and Philip something to think about on his own frontiers, and it freed
John to concentrate on an advance into enemy territory. As John made
his move south in September, Philip felt obliged to follow. But this was
not enough to reassure William des Roches (indeed, Philip antagonised
William when he destroyed the castle of Ballon in Maine, where
William claimed to have authority), who decided that his best interests
lay in negotiating a truce with the English king. John was happy to
grant William what he wanted, namely confirmation of his position as
seneschal of Anjou, even if this was at the expense of the incumbent,
Aimeri de Thouars. Arthur could not fight on without William's support
and, if Arthur was prepared to lay down his arms, there was no justification for Philip to carry on the struggle. At Le Mans on 22 September
1199, Arthur (no longer in Philip's custody) and Constance made peace
with John.

Events now took a confusing turn. At around the same time as the
meeting took place at Le Mans in September (it is not clear precisely
when), Constance of Brittany was married for the third time, this time
to Guy de Thouars, the younger brother of Aimeri. Her marriage to
Ranulf of Chester had ended (the reasons for this and the official
grounds for any annulment are not known) and Ranulf himself had
remarried by the end of 1199. The new marriage could be interpreted as
an attempt by John to compensate Aimeri de Thouars and his family for
the loss of the seneschalship of Anjou. Alternatively, however, it could

have been an act of defiance by Aimeri and his disgruntled kinsmen. And there are further signs that the peace deal did not end Constance and Arthur's distrust of John. According to Roger of Howden, immediately after the terms were agreed, Arthur and Constance, along with Aimeri de Thouars and many others, secretly left John's court, having been informed that Arthur was about to be arrested and imprisoned.[9] King Philip now returned to the action and Arthur was once more given his protection. He remained at the French court for the next two years.

Whatever Constance and Arthur were doing late in 1199, however, it was clear that the two main players in the ongoing political drama were still the kings, John and Philip. Early in 1200 they met to discuss the situation, and the terms they agreed were formally recorded in the Treaty of Le Goulet in May. Philip accepted John as Richard's heir in all the lands that Richard and Henry II had held in France, except for the county of Evreux, the whole Norman Vexin except Les Andelys, and the lordships of Issoudun, Graçay, and Bourges in Berry, which Philip had seized after Richard's death and still held. John also had to agree to abandon his allies in Flanders and Boulogne, pay Philip a relief of £13,333, and perform homage to the French king for his continental possessions. As for Arthur, he was acknowledged by all parties as the rightful heir to Brittany, but the ruler of Brittany was also confirmed as the vassal of the duke of Normandy (not the king of France) and, as such, was required to do homage to John for his duchy. Despite the concessions he had made in it, the Treaty of Le Goulet was a victory for John and a defeat for Arthur. Arthur's claims to the Angevin succession had been decisively rejected and even his status in Brittany was undermined by the newly precise definition of his duchy's relationship with Normandy. No wonder, then, that when Arthur met the bishop of Lincoln in Paris a few weeks after the treaty was agreed, he was unhappy and dejected: John and Philip, he might have felt, had feathered their own nests at his expense. Constance, too, seems to have lost the appetite for any further confrontation. She returned to Brittany and died there in September 1201. For his part, Arthur divided his time between the French and Breton courts, and he was invested as duke shortly after his mother's death. However, when John summoned him to Normandy to perform homage at Easter 1202, Arthur refused. By then the quarrel between John and King Philip had begun again and Arthur's hopes had revived.

The new crisis was entirely of John's making. His talent for alienating people may have been hinted at after the Treaty of Le Goulet by his treatment of Aimeri de Thouars and by his alleged plan to imprison Arthur. These were relatively insignificant, however, compared with John's inept and provocative behaviour in the year or so after the treaty was signed, when he bullied and victimised the Lusignans, one of the most important noble families in Poitou. In the process, John laid the foundation for the collapse of his continental empire and set the scene for Arthur's death.

In 1189, John had married Isabella of Gloucester. She was the daughter and heir of William, earl of Gloucester, and consequently one of the richest heiresses in England (her estates included Bristol and the marcher lordships of Glamorgan and Newport). John had been betrothed to her by Henry II in 1176, and the king had pressurised Earl William into recognising John as the heir to the Gloucester earldom at the same time. King Richard had then sanctioned the match in 1189 as part of the package of concessions he had made to John at the start of his reign in an effort to buy his good behaviour during the impending crusade. Isabella played little if any part in John's public life over the next few years, and husband and wife were probably estranged as early as 1193. Certainly, Isabella was not crowned with John in 1199, and she can have had little to do with him in private either – for one thing, they had no children. What is more, the legality of the marriage remained ambiguous. John and Isabella were cousins, albeit relatively remote ones, but the matrimonial law of the time led Archbishop Baldwin of Canterbury, on hearing that they were married, to forbid them to cohabit. John had to seek the intervention of a papal legate to overturn this sentence, but from the start the marriage remained conveniently fragile in strictly legal terms. Given Isabella's failure to produce children, it is really no surprise that John looked to end their marriage after he became king (his wife may have been just as relieved about this as he was), and after certain formalities had been observed, and some Norman and Aquitainian bishops had been persuaded to declare the marriage void, John was once again a single man, albeit one still in control of his former wife's lands. Until 1214, by which time she was in her mid-fifties, Isabella remained a royal ward!

By the spring of 1200, John had already decided on a new wife. On 24 August he married Isabelle, the daughter of Adhemar, count of Angoulême, one of the most important, and most troublesome, barons of Aquitaine. In October the newlyweds returned to England, and on 8 October they were crowned together at Westminster Abbey. The speed of these events is striking. Contemporary chroniclers were quick to suggest that John was bewitched by Isabelle's beauty and simply had to make her his regardless of the consequences. Roger of Wendover later described how, rather than fight Philip II who was overrunning his ancestral territories at the end of 1203, John preferred to stay in bed with his queen until dinner time.[10] But Isabelle was only twelve at the most in 1200 and may have been younger still, and such allegations tell us more about the writer's desire to moralise and provide a scurrilous context for John's political failures than anything else. In reality, there were hard-headed and perfectly sound political reasons for the match. Count Adhemar was fiercely proud and independently minded. As counts of Angoulême, he and his predecessors had traditionally performed homage for their lands to the king of France and not to the duke of Aquitaine. Richard, as duke, had had considerable trouble keeping Adhemar in line, and he had actually received the fatal wound to his shoulder during yet another phase of his ongoing quarrel with the count. Nevertheless, Adhemar's lands were in the heart of the duchy, where the roads connecting Poitou and Gascony met, and they were strategically vital. John's decision to marry Isabelle, therefore, was calculated in part to bring Adhemar and his family more comfortably into the Angevin fold and to stabilise central Aquitaine: she was her father's only surviving heir, and her husband would be the next count of Angoulême. The marriage also served another plainly political purpose. When she married John, Isabelle was already betrothed to another man, Hugh le Brun, lord of Lusignan. The Lusignans were Count Adhemar's neighbours and controlled the county of La Marche. If Hugh and Isabelle had been married, their families' lands would together have extended across most of central Aquitaine. Such a concentration of territorial power would have jeopardised the duke's overall control, and so John's marriage to Isabelle was also designed to stop the Angoulême–Lusignan alliance in its tracks.

Of course, John's approach was risky. The Lusignans would not take kindly to losing their alliance with Angoulême. John should have tried to buy them off, with money, land or another attractive marriage. But he didn't do anything like that. Indeed, his provocative conduct suggests that he planned to goad the family into doing something that would allow him to ruin them completely. Either this, or John miscalculated badly and turned a difficult but manageable diplomatic situation into a catastrophically disastrous one. Hugh de Lusignan's younger brother, Ralph, was also count of Eu in Normandy through marriage – his castle of Driencourt was seized on John's orders. Then, in March 1201, John instructed his officials to attack Ralph's lands after Easter and 'do him all the harm they could'; and a few days after this, in a clear challenge to the Lusignans' control of the county, he summoned all the leading men of La Marche to confirm their allegiance to him.[11] Ralph and Hugh responded promptly: the former, who, along with Hugh, had pledged his loyalty to John as recently as January 1200, formally renounced it, whilst his brother began raiding into Poitou. The Lusignans pursued other remedies too. Most importantly, they appealed about John's behaviour to King Philip, in his capacity as overlord of the duke of Aquitaine. John, meanwhile, was in England preparing an army. In June 1201 he landed in Normandy.

At this stage King Philip was keen to broker a peaceful settlement between the two sides. He persuaded the Lusignans to suspend their military activity, and he met John several times on the Norman frontier. John then went to Paris in June where he was entertained for the best part of a week in the royal palace, and he eventually agreed to hear the Lusignans' grievances in his court as duke of Aquitaine. This might have worked to resolve the situation, if John's conception of such a hearing had fitted with that of the Lusignans. They, of course, expected respectful treatment and justice; John, by contrast, was determined to humiliate them. Far from offering them a fair hearing when he summoned them to his court, he demanded that they should appear to answer charges of treason and prove their innocence through the ordeal of battle, in other words by fighting against trained duellists, hand-picked by John.

Not surprisingly, the Lusignans refused to come to John's court: there was every chance that they might lose any fight but, more importantly, they thought the method of trial John proposed demeaning and beneath their status. In other words, John was insulting them on several different levels at once and they felt compelled to appeal once more to King Philip. The French king at first persuaded John to agree to hold an appropriate trial, but when John finally fixed a day for it he refused to give the Lusignans safe conduct. Without this, once again they refused to attend. Over the next few months the process dragged on inconclusively, with John prevaricating at every opportunity. In the end, Philip's patience ran out and he summoned John to attend his own court in Paris at the end of April 1202 and answer for his conduct. It almost goes without saying that John failed to appear at the appointed place and time. As a result he was condemned by Philip and the assembled barons of his court as a disobedient vassal and his lands of Anjou, Aquitaine and Poitou were declared forfeit to the French Crown.

Arthur had rejoined the French court shortly after Easter 1202, almost as if in preparation for what was to follow. His importance was obvious to both sides. On 27 March, John had summoned his 'beloved nephew Arthur' to meet him at Argentan about fifteen miles south of Falaise in central Normandy a week after Easter, but the young prince had already decided that his best hopes lay with King Philip.[12] Before the end of April, Arthur was betrothed to Philip's six-year-old daughter, Marie, and following the sentence of forfeiture pronounced against John, he accompanied the French king's army on campaign in Normandy. At Gournay in July, Arthur was knighted by Philip and performed homage to him for all of John's confiscated lands. Near the end of July, while he concentrated on weakening the Norman frontier, Philip sent Arthur with a force of 200 French knights to join Hugh de Lusignan in an attack on Poitou. Arthur was keen to wait for the reinforcements he had called on from Brittany before committing himself to serious action, but his French and Poitevin allies pushed for an immediate attack on the castle of Mirebeau where Arthur's grandmother, Queen Eleanor, had taken refuge on hearing of their approach. Eleanor was old and increasingly frail, but she was still crucial to her son John's hopes of holding on to Anjou and Aquitaine. Her connections and standing counted for much, and if she could be captured, the main prop holding up John's support in the south would be removed. Eleanor, however, learnt of the proposed attack in time to send a letter to John urging him to come to her rescue. He was already on his way south when a messenger met him with Eleanor's news at Le Mans. In a remarkable forced march, John then covered the eighty miles and more between Le Mans and Mirebeau in forty-eight hours and arrived before the castle on 1 August. By then, Arthur and the Poitevins had already taken the outer ward and broken down all the gates except one. Eleanor was trapped in the keep. But when John's forces arrived, the attackers were taken by surprise and chaotically rushed out of the castle to meet him. John's men, with his seneschal of Anjou, William des Roches, prominent at the head of his troops, drove the besiegers back into the castle and soon the whole of the French and Poitevin army had been either killed or captured. Amongst those taken prisoner were Hugh and Geoffrey de Lusignan. According to one account, so unexpected was John's attack on Mirebeau that Geoffrey was still eating his breakfast of pigeons when he was seized.[13] The most important prize, however, was Arthur of Brittany.

John was triumphant. His victory at Mirebeau was as decisive and as total as any that his illustrious crusading brother had ever achieved. Most of his enemies had been dealt with at a single stroke, and King Philip was now left isolated and without allies. After a fruitless trek southwards from Normandy to assess the situation the French king retired to his own lands after furiously burning the city of Tours on the way. Meanwhile, John made his way back north with his prisoners. Most of them, including Arthur's sister Eleanor, were sent to England and imprisoned in castles, most notably Corfe in Dorset. The most important prisoners remained in Normandy, however: Hugh de Lusignan was locked up at Caen, whilst Geoffrey and Arthur were taken to Falaise. Everything seemed to be going John's way. Nevertheless, his dominant position was not deeply rooted and a sensible politician would have taken care to nurture it. John simply took it for granted. Most significantly, he soon lost the support of William des Roches. William had been instrumental in John's seizure of power in 1199 and at Mirebeau itself. His continued support was crucial if John wanted to focus on protecting Normandy without having to worry about his southern territories, and the English king's failure to appreciate William's importance is startling. William had supported John at Mirebeau when the latter had agreed to follow his advice concerning Arthur; he abandoned him when John took Arthur to Normandy, clearly signalling that William's opinions counted for nothing after all. Having deserted John, William took his neighbour Aimeri de Thouars with him and was prepared to fight to retain his hold over Anjou and Touraine (in October they captured Angers), thus introducing an unwelcome element of instability into the heart of John's territories.

It is not clear what William wanted John to do with Arthur, and it may be that, at this stage, the king had little idea of his own how to handle his nephew. According to one account, he was first swayed by a group of his advisers, who told him that Arthur had to be dealt with once and for all.[14] There was justification for this. Arthur was John's sworn vassal (the Treaty of Le Goulet had established this in 1200); he had rebelled against him and could expect to be punished, even with death. He was only fifteen or sixteen, but he was no innocent victim. However, the nature of the penalty they recommended was savage: if Arthur were blinded and castrated, they argued, he would not be fit to rule, if he survived at all. The Bretons would lose their figurehead and end their uprising. The chronicler who reports this story says that John consented to the plan and sent two men to Falaise to carry it out. However, Arthur's gaoler there, Hubert de Burgh, baulked when he was told of the idea of mutilating his prisoner and refused to allow it. But he was prepared to announce that Arthur was dead in the hope that this would knock the wind out of the Bretons' sails. Unfortunately, but not surprisingly, it had the opposite effect. The Bretons swore not to rest until they had avenged themselves on John, and Hubert was forced hastily to announce that Arthur was alive and unharmed. The damage had been done, though. Arthur may still have been alive, but this was not certain and the conspiracy theories about his murder developed quickly.

This account of what happened at Falaise may or may not be true, but its description of indecisive floundering at the top of John's government has an air of credibility about it. To be sure, Arthur was a problem and something had to be done. But with a botched plot to kill him followed by a botched attempt to fabricate his death, it is hard to imagine that he could have been more incompetently handled. Another story, though, suggests that John tried a different approach.[15] According to the monk Roger of Wendover, who wrote his account of these events at the abbey of St Alban's in the 1220s or 1230s, whilst John was at Falaise at the end of January 1203, he summoned Arthur to appear before him and tried to flatter him into submission. Addressing him 'with fair words', Wendover alleged, Arthur was promised great rewards if he agreed to pledge his loyalty to John and desert King Philip. But Arthur scornfully dismissed John's proposal and went even further: he was Richard's lawful heir, he claimed defiantly, and there would be no peace unless all the Angevin dominions, including England, were surrendered to him. Needless to say, John was never going to respond to such an ultimatum other than furiously, and soon after this exchange is alleged to have taken place, Arthur was taken to Rouen and never seen again. Wendover's account was not written until two or three decades after John's death, it is not corroborated elsewhere, and he gives no authority for it. Indeed, this is not the only episode from John's reign for which Wendover is the only evidence and his reliability has often been questioned. John was certainly at Falaise in January 1203, but this does not mean that Wendover was describing real events. More likely this is an account of what Wendover thought should have happened in the circumstances. He is highly critical of John throughout his account of the reign and may have used this fictitious encounter as a device to highlight John's careless disregard for honour and loyalty and Arthur's stirring but doomed sense of duty. To this extent, he would have seen it as a legitimate fabrication.

But whether this confrontation ever took place or not, Arthur did indeed disappear at around this time and the truth about what happened to him will never be known. That he was dead by the end of 1203, however, seems almost certain. He may have died a natural death after falling ill in prison; there is another suggestion that he was killed after falling during an attempt to escape.[16] But there is also good reason to believe that John was personally involved in Arthur's death. According to one account, written in about 1216, after trying unsuccessfully to get someone else to kill Arthur for him, John decided to take care of the matter himself. He took Arthur out alone in a boat with him on the river Seine. There the king killed his nephew with a sword, rowed three miles further with the body at his feet, and then threw it overboard.[17] The writer William the Breton does not say when this happened, and it is included in his great poem celebrating the achievements of Philip II. So it is right to treat his version of events with caution. Nevertheless, a second source goes some way to confirming the outline of what William said. It was indeed at Rouen, after dinner on Maundy Thursday (3 April) 1203, 'when he was drunk and possessed by the devil', that John killed Arthur with his own hands. He then weighted down the corpse with a heavy stone and threw it into the Seine. It was later caught up in a fisherman's net, recognised and buried secretly ('for fear of the tyrant', the source says) in the church of Notre Dame du Pré near Rouen.[18] There is some correspondence between these two accounts (rivers and boats, as well as John's central role, feature prominently in both), which may lend them a little more credibility. In addition, John was certainly at Rouen on 3 April. But the second account has more to recommend it than this. It was written at the Cistercian abbey of Margam in south Wales, probably some time in the 1220s. But the information it contains could have been given to the monks much earlier than this by one of the monastery's most important patrons, William de Briouze. There will be more about the Briouze family in the next chapter. It is enough to say here that William was ideally placed to know what had happened to Arthur and to tell the tale later to the monks of Margam. William was the man who had actually captured Arthur at Mirebeau. At the time of the alleged murder he was still one of John's favourites and he was almost certainly with the king at Rouen at Easter 1203. He was just the sort of man to know the details of a scandal involving the king.

If the Margam chronicle's account of Arthur's murder is to be believed, Good Friday 1203 at Rouen would have been significantly more sombre than usual. The king had slain his own nephew in a drunken rage and ugly rumours must have been circulating amongst the whispering courtiers, too fearful of John to voice them openly. The disasters that befell John in the following months may well have been seen as just punishment for his crime by those who knew anything about it. In truth, however, John was already in serious political and military difficulties before Arthur's disappearance. By the spring of 1203 he was facing problems all along the Norman frontier, from King Philip in the east, the leading lords of Maine and Anjou to the south, and from the Bretons in the west. John's victory at Mirebeau was still fresh in the memory, but he had failed to make the most of it. William des Roches had deserted John shortly after the battle and where he led others soon followed. In January 1203, Count Robert of Sées, who until this point had been solidly loyal to John, surrendered his castle of Alençon to the French, not principally in support of Arthur or Philip, but because he had no appetite for fighting against his southern neighbours. Then, in March, William des Roches, along with other leading magnates from the Loire provinces, formalised their positions and performed homage to King Philip in Paris. It was the loyalty of lords like this, with their lands close to the Norman border, that was crucial in this struggle. Without their support, there was a serious risk that John's continental lands would be divided in two, that Normandy would be cut off from Aquitaine, and that the duchy itself would be unable to withstand the threats from its other neighbours.

King Philip still had to take his chance, though. In April 1203, with the support of the Loire lords secured, he was able to sail unopposed down that great river into the heart of Anjou and take possession of Saumur in person. But the biggest prize, as ever, was Normandy, and Philip resumed his attack there as soon as he had returned from Anjou. When the castle of Vaudreuil surrendered to the French without a fight in June, John tried to convince his critics that the garrison had laid down its arms on his orders and that this was some kind of tactical retreat. In reality, his power in Normandy was crumbling. In the heart of the duchy, away from the unstable frontier regions, support for John and his family had always been strong, but there was now widespread discontent at the actions of John's mercenary troops, who were mistreating the local people and behaving, it was claimed, as if they were at war with them.[19] The ties of loyalty were being stretched to breaking point and Philip was giving a good impression to the waverers of being a credible alternative lord. But there was still work to do. Gaining control of the river Seine was essential to Philip's strategy, but barring his path to Rouen was the greatest of all the frontier castles, Château Gaillard. Built at enormous expense by Richard I on steep cliffs overlooking a huge bend in the Seine, the castle was reportedly impregnable. In addition, it was commanded by an English baron of unimpeachable loyalty and no little courage, Roger de Lacy. Undaunted, Philip began his siege in August 1203. This gave John a breathing space, which he used to attack his enemies in Brittany. Guy de Thouars, Arthur's stepfather, remained loyal to John until September 1203, and whilst that was the case the Breton-Norman frontier was kept relatively pacified. When Guy deserted, however, John's response was to raid into Brittany and sack Dol. Such activity did little to improve John's position and only antagonised the Bretons even more.

In December 1203, John travelled back to England to raise fresh funds to continue the war, but before he could return to Normandy, on 6 March 1204, the garrison of Château Gaillard surrendered. The defenders had bravely and staunchly withstood a five-month siege, and perhaps could have lasted out longer. But there were flaws in the castle's much-vaunted design, which became apparent as the siege went on and which the determined besiegers were eventually able to exploit. The way to Rouen was now open, but before he approached the city Philip wanted to make sure that it was isolated and cut off from any Norman reinforcements. So in May he headed west into central Normandy and in three weeks took Argentan, Falaise and Caen. He was met there by the Bretons, who had taken Mont St Michel and Avranches on their way, and the advance across country to Rouen began. After arriving outside the city at the start of June, Philip agreed to give the citizens thirty days to wait for help from their lord. But John did nothing in response to the urgent messages he was sent and the city gates were opened to Philip on 24 June.

Stranded in England, John could only wait for news of Rouen's inevitable capitulation. Normandy was lost, along with Anjou, Maine and Touraine. And in Aquitaine the tide had turned against John too. His mother, Queen Eleanor, had died on 31 March 1204, and the lords of Poitou who had been loyal to her were not prepared to put their faith in the son who had shown his true colours in his attack on the Lusignans in 1200. Having said that, there were many barons further south who also had their misgivings about King Philip, and although he visited Poitiers in August 1204, the rest of Aquitaine did not open its doors to him. Nevertheless, this was of no immediate comfort to John. In less than two years since the triumph at Mirebeau his continental empire had been comprehensively dismantled. This is what Arthur had wanted, of course, but he did not live to see his hopes fulfilled. And with his sister Eleanor still held captive by John, it was Arthur's half-sister Alix (the daughter of Guy de Thouars and Constance of Brittany) who was eventually acknowledged by the Breton nobility as the rightful heiress to the duchy. A new phase of Breton history now began: they had seen off the Angevins but would soon have to defend themselves once again, this time against the expansionist ambitions of the kings of France. Meanwhile, in England, a smarting king was already planning his counterattack.

CHAPTER EIGHT

THE FRIEND'S TALE
William de Briouze and the Tyranny of King John

WILLIAM DE BRIOUZE was a desperate man. His rise to the heights of influence and power had been rapid and spectacular. In less than ten years he had been transformed from an important but nevertheless provincial landholder into one of the greatest barons of his day. He had acquired lands in England, Normandy, Wales and Ireland, his daughters had married great magnates and his son had become a bishop. And he had King John to thank for all of this. John was William's patron and perhaps even his friend. But by this time, March 1208, the king had turned on Briouze and, with his back to the wall and in order to prove his loyalty and protect his family, William had agreed to hand over three of his own grandsons and four of his tenants' sons as hostages to the king. But when the king's men arrived to fetch the prisoners, Matilda de Briouze, William's wife, refused to surrender them. 'I will not deliver up my sons to your lord, King John,' she said ('with the sauciness of a woman,' commented Roger of Wendover, who told this tale), 'because he basely murdered his nephew Arthur, whom he ought to have kept in honourable custody.' Her husband was appalled by her unrestrained outburst and rushed to limit the damage. 'You have spoken like a stupid woman against our lord the king; for if I have offended him in any way I am ready to make amends without the security of hostages according to the judgement of my fellow barons in his court, if he will fix a time and a place for me to do so.'[1] William was right to be frightened, and keenly aware of how submissive he now needed to be. But he must have known as he spoke that his promise would count for little with a man like King John; at best it might buy him a little time. But it was already too late. And predictably, when the messengers told the king what Matilda had said he furiously ordered the arrest of William and his family. By then, however, the Briouzes had fled to Ireland. Their life on the run had begun and within three years William, Matilda and their eldest son were all dead, victims in one way or another of the king's vindictive rage.

* * * *

The fall of the Briouzes was spectacular and bewilderingly swift. And the events were all the more dramatic because William de Briouze had been one of King John's most powerful, influential and trusted barons. By the time of his death in 1211 he had become a hunted exile in France, and the sordid deaths of his wife and his eldest son were one of the scandals of the age. Like that of Henry II and Thomas Becket, this story is usually characterised as a relationship between a king and his friend that turned horribly sour. But, and like that story, too, it is conventional to argue that the quarrel between John and William de Briouze represented something much deeper and more profound. It laid bare just how much power and authority the English king retained in his own hands, and how flimsy, even non-existent, the mechanisms for restraining him were. It was a further demonstration, after the death of Arthur of Brittany, of how vulnerable and powerless even the mightiest families were at the hands of a malevolent and paranoid tyrant like King John. Their wealth and status counted for nothing, especially if they owed it all to a cruel and unpredictable king who could withdraw his favour on a whim and turn savagely against his former friends. As a result, the Briouze case has been seen as a turning point in John's reign and as a crucial landmark on the road to rebellion and Magna Carta. Once knowledge of the Briouzes' fate became known, no great man could be in any doubt that his family was at the mercy of this volatile and erratic king, or that John could decide to break him just because he wanted to. John had revealed his true character to his subjects and from this point he ruled through fear alone.

Now there are kernels of truth in all of this, but the story of the Briouzes' rise and fall is as much about pragmatic politics as it is about personalities. William was useful to John at the start of his reign but then, like Arthur before him, he turned into an overconfident and disobedient vassal who defied and disrespected the king's authority. William deserved to be punished, and the king needed to make an example of him to deter others from acting in the same way. What is more, in many ways, John's approach to his old friend, or at least to the context in which that approach evolved, suggests how able and effective, not how incompetent, a king he was. His treatment of Briouze was decisive and firm, and, more widely, their dispute was played out against the backdrop of John's strikingly successful efforts to expand his power beyond England and into Wales, Scotland and Ireland. So, pivotal though they have seemed both to contemporaries and historians looking back on these events, and important though they certainly were, they did not seal John's fate. Despite what had happened to the Briouzes, or more likely because of it, much still had to happen before John's barons turned against him in large numbers. If anything, by the end of 1211 John was stronger, not weaker, than he had ever been before, and at the unchallenged height of his power. His prospects looked good.

* * * *

The family's origins were Norman, and William de Briouze still held his ancestors' lands there when they were lost to King Philip in 1203–4. But the bulk of his power derived from his massive estates in England, Wales and Ireland. William the Conqueror had granted the castle and rape of Bramber in Sussex to William's great-grandfather, William (I) de Briouze, whose son Philip had taken the Welsh lordships of Radnor and Builth before the end of the eleventh century and acquired lands in Devon too. Philip's son, William (II) de Briouze, married Bertha, the daughter and co-heir of Miles of Gloucester, earl of Hereford, and through her added the lordships of Brecon and Abergavenny on the southern Welsh marches to his collection of lands. William (II) and his brother Philip accompanied Henry II to Ireland in 1171–2 and William served as sheriff of Herefordshire from 1173 to 1175. By the time he died in the early 1190s he had made his family into a significant force on the frontier between England and south Wales and helped to establish its connections across the Irish Sea.

By then, too, his eldest son, William (III), had already begun building his own career. William was clearly an able speculator with an eye for an opportunity and a readiness to take a chance. Even before his father's death, he had offered the enormous sum of £667 for the custody of the land and heir of Gilbert of Monmouth, who came of age in 1205. By 1194, William had also acquired the barony of Kington in Herefordshire and become lord of the barony of Barnstaple in Devon. But William's fortunes were ultimately based on his reputation as a tough and resilient fighter and on his role as a loyal and useful lieutenant for the Angevin kings. Like his father, William served as sheriff of Herefordshire almost continuously from 1191 until 1200 and also acted as a royal judge. He also served with King Richard in Normandy in 1194 and 1199. He was with the king at Châlus on 5 April 1199, the day before Richard received his fatal wound, and was probably with him when he died. Central to William's pre-eminence, though, were his achievements in Wales, where his main duty was to protect and strengthen England's frontier against the native Welsh, a job he performed with energy and ruthlessness. This was a pitiless and frequently savage environment, but William proved himself well suited to it. As early as 1175 he had masterminded the slaughter at Abergavenny of a minor Welsh chieftain, his family and followers, as vengeance for their part in the murder of William's uncle, Henry. And over the next thirty years he established himself as the greatest English baron in south Wales.

William de Briouze's achievement was all the more remarkable given the nature of the opposition he faced. In the second half of the twelfth century the dominant native Welsh ruler was Rhys ap Gruffudd ('the Lord Rhys'). By the time he died in 1197, Rhys had rebuilt the kingdom of Deheubarth in south-west Wales and done his utmost to increase his own power whilst keeping further English expansion into native Wales in check. He had done this in part through aggression, but after he submitted to Henry II in 1171, mainly by managing a largely peaceful relationship with the English king. As part of this policy, Rhys's eldest son Gruffudd had married William's third daughter, Matilda. But after King Henry's death in 1189, full-scale border warfare resumed. Between 1189 and 1196, Rhys and his sons campaigned relentlessly against the English lordships across south Wales. He had captured St Clears and

Kidwelly and was besieging Swansea by 1192. William de Briouze was the royal castellan of Carmarthen and Swansea and in due course Rhys's victories were reversed. Hostilities rumbled on, however. Williams's two castles, at Colwyn and Painscastle, which he had built to defend his lordships of Radnor and Builth, came under attack several times in the 1190s. Most famously, in 1195, Painscastle was defended against a Welsh attack by William's wife, Matilda. So impressive was her performance that the castle was always known to the English as 'Maud's Castle' after that. But her fierce resistance only provided a short respite. In his last great campaign, the Lord Rhys captured Painscastle in 1196 after burning Carmarthen.

Matilda de Briouze stood alongside her husband throughout his rise to prominence. She was the daughter of Bernard de St Valéry, lord of Beckley in Oxfordshire. The date of their marriage is lost (indeed, it is unclear when either William or Matilda was born), but they probably married sometime around 1170. Their children, or most of them (they had at least four sons and five daughters together, and some estimates have put the number of their children as high as sixteen), were already grown up by the 1190s. When their second son, Giles, was elected bishop of Hereford in 1200, he must have been at least twenty-eight, by then the minimum age for a bishop according to canon law. Later events were to show just how important Matilda was to her husband's career; and contemporaries were well aware of her abilities. Gerald of Wales described her in complimentary terms as 'prudent and chaste' and 'well equipped to rule her household, as highly skilled in preserving her property within doors as in increasing it out of doors'.[2] She was not just a domestic marvel, however, as the events at Painscastle in 1195 showed. Another writer, known to historians as the Anonymous of Béthune, who later described Matilda's death in graphic detail, claimed that she was 'a fair lady, very wise and accomplished and particularly energetic. She was never absent from any of her husband's councils. She carried on warfare against the Welsh in which she conquered a good deal.'[3]

Had Richard I lived, William de Briouze may simply have continued his career as a leading baron of the Welsh marches. However, the death of Richard and the accession of King John transformed his chances. William had no doubts about who should succeed Richard. He may well have been at Richard's deathbed himself and heard the dying king nominate his brother John as his successor; he might even have coaxed him to do so. Either way, William was a staunch supporter of John from the moment Richard died. According to the record of events made at the Cistercian abbey of Margam in south Wales, a monastery with which Briouze had close personal links, he was instrumental in getting John crowned in 1199.[4] Certainly, he was one of those barons, like William Marshal and William des Roches, whose support was crucial in enabling John to get the better of his nephew Arthur in 1199–1200. Once John was secure on the throne, moreover, William and his family soon began to reap their rewards for having backed the winning claimant. In 1200 the king granted William all the lands that he could conquer from his Welsh enemies to augment his barony of Radnor.[5] And it was in the same year that Giles de Briouze became bishop of Hereford. In 1202, William was granted custody of the Welsh marcher lordships of Glamorgan and Gower. Later, in July 1207, he took custody of the castle at Ludlow in Shropshire.[6] There were other acquisitions, too, in Devon and Surrey in particular, but the bulk of Briouze's estates were in the southern Welsh marches and there William continued to play an important role as a guarantor of royally sponsored power. And his network of influence spread there through more than acquisitions of territory. One of his daughters was married before the end of 1200 to Walter de Lacy. Lacy was the lord of Meath in Ireland, but he was also the Briouzes' neighbour on the Welsh frontier where his holdings included Ludlow in Shropshire. A younger daughter was married before 1210 to a son of Roger Mortimer, another baron of the Welsh march. And one of the Briouzes' other neighbours in that region had been the future king, then Count John of Mortain, who, through his first wife Isabella of Gloucester, was lord of Glamorgan. It seems likely that this is where the relationship between King John and William de Briouze was first established. And although it is hard to talk in terms of medieval rulers having 'friends' in the modern sense of the word, William came as close as anyone to filling this role for John. After having backed him energetically in 1199–1200, Briouze was frequently with the king and regularly witnessed his charters.

Having said that, William did not receive royal favours for free. In 1206 he secured the barony of Totnes in Devon through a lawsuit, but only after paying heavily for the judgment in his favour: he offered the king £100 to have the case heard before him, also a gift of 300 cows, thirty bulls and ten horses for speeding up the case, and £466 if he won it. Also in 1206, Briouze offered the king £533 together with a number of horses and hunting dogs for custody of the three Welsh castles at Grosmont, Skenfrith, and Whitecastle in Gwent.[7] So William was prepared to get into debt in order to further his family's fortunes. There was nothing unusual about this, though. Indeed, it was common for wealthy men to promise large sums of money to the king in order to secure their inheritances or in return for titles, offices or the custody of the estates of a rich heir or heiress. They might also pay for the king's intervention on their side in a legal dispute (as William de Briouze did over Totnes in 1206) or to recover the king's goodwill (his *benevolentia*) if for some reason they had lost it. They were prepared to do this because, typically, the promise remained just that and there was little if any expectation that the full amount offered would ever be demanded or collected by the king. The debt simply sat on the royal records from year to year and perhaps a small amount was paid off annually by prior agreement. Eventually, the debt might well be cancelled as further evidence of royal favour. Henry II imposed remarkably little financial pressure on his barons, particularly the richest ones, and whilst Richard I's spending on his crusade, his ransom to Duke Leopold of Austria and his wars against Philip II had been famously excessive, there was a hope at the start of John's reign, especially after the Treaty of Le Goulet in 1200 appeared to settle matters between John, Philip and Arthur, that such times were past and that the king's financial demands would now return to more tolerable levels. So when William de Briouze made all these offers to John, he probably thought that he was simply making a ritualised gesture; what is more, the king was his friend and would surely never expect these sums to be paid. In September 1202, John had cancelled all of the debts that William's father had owed to Henry II as well as those that William himself owed to Richard I. And in 1204 the king pardoned William the £925 that remained outstanding of the £1,000 he had offered in 1203 for the marriage of one of his sons to a wealthy widow.[8] Surely it was only a matter of time before the king forgave his other debts too.

Such thoughts may have been in William's mind when he began to develop his interests in Ireland. After his Irish expedition of 1171–2, Henry II had granted Philip de Briouze, William's uncle, the entire Irish kingdom of Limerick, but Philip had never done anything to secure possession of it. In January 1201, John granted the smaller honour of Limerick (in effect that part of northern Munster which was under English control) to William de Briouze; although the city of Limerick itself was retained by the king in his own hands. The price was £3,333 payable at £333 annually.[9] It is important to appreciate just how enormous these sums were. In the early thirteenth century an average baronial income was about £200 per year, and by the mid-thirteenth century most of the English earls had annual incomes of between £2,000 and £3,000. William de Briouze never became an earl, but at the peak of his career he was far richer than the average baron. His yearly income was substantial – over £800. The annual payment for Limerick (if it was ever made) would account for a large chunk of this, and there were all his other outgoings too. However, William was a royal favourite, and as long as his royal patron continued to favour him and allow his debts to lie dormant, William and his family were safe.

Unfortunately for them, the king's attitudes towards both his revenue and his barons were changing. John had lost his continental lands in 1203–4, but he had not abandoned them. His intention after the fall of Rouen was always to win them back and humble King Philip. What John envisaged, in effect, was an English conquest of France, something no English king had ever achieved. It is worth remembering that after 1066 further conquest was not usually the ambition of the English kings. True, William II had tried to take Normandy by force from his brother Robert Curthose, and Henry I had eventually succeeded in doing so. And after 1194, Richard I had fought to recover the relatively small amounts of territory Philip II had taken from him in the early 1190s. But usually, and as long as they had control of Normandy, the English kings fought to defend what they already had. William I, Henry I (after 1106) and Henry II campaigned extensively in France in order to protect their lands from external attack, not to expand them. And on the one occasion when Henry II had fought to gain new territory (the county of Toulouse in 1159), the campaign had been a disastrous failure. So John was proposing something new – an aggressive takeover on a quite unprecedented scale. And the longer he waited, the harder the task would become. As Philip strengthened his hold over and beyond the territories he had taken in 1204, he would establish fresh ties of loyalty and obedience, whilst getting richer and better able to pay for the defence of his new lands. If John waited too long, Philip's authority would be impossible to uproot. This lesson was brought home to the king in 1206 when John launched his first campaign to recover his losses. He landed at La Rochelle in Poitou and marched north to Angers. However, when Philip's army confronted John's, a truce was the only sensible option. Philip was left in control of all the territory north of the Loire, and Poitiers too, whilst a chastened John returned to England.

If he was to do better next time, then more than anything else John needed money – money to pay for troops, ships, supplies and equipment, money to bribe spies and informers, money to secure alliances. Richard I had all but exhausted the English treasury in 1194–9 and his aims had been significantly more limited than John's. Warfare was expensive and, as John made his plans, the costs were only going up. Henry II had paid eight pence a day for the services of a mercenary knight; John had to pay two shillings, three times as much. But over and above this general trend of rising prices in the decades either side of 1200, the first few years of the thirteenth century saw particularly rapid price inflation in England. Commodity prices doubled between 1200 and 1205. Bad weather and poor harvests were probably to blame more than anything else, but for John the consequences were serious, as everything he needed to launch his grand continental campaign started to cost more. At the same time, any extra financial burden he placed on his hard-pressed people was bound to cause more pain and resentment than it had before. The fact is that England's system of royal finance had evolved since the eleventh century to cater for the needs of an absentee king who needed money to defend his continental territories. By and large it had been successful; but Richard I's experiences had shown that, once the system was deployed for other purposes, to regain territory which had been lost, it struggled to cope with the pressure. John would need far more money than Richard had ever collected and this at a time of steeply rising prices and general war fatigue. So, if he was to get anything like what he needed from the existing structures of royal finance, he would have to exploit and abuse them for all they were worth. John would also need to think of new ways to raise money, and he could no longer afford to be as easygoing with his indebted barons as his predecessors had been.

On top of this, John was a man consumed by distrust, and with no small capacity for vindictive cruelty. His treatment of the Lusignans after 1200 had revealed him to be an untrustworthy and capricious lord, and his nephew Arthur had died a mysterious and probably violent death whilst in his care. John was certainly capable of turning against his supporters quickly, especially if he thought they were becoming too powerful or in any way a threat. And from the time he returned from France in 1206, it was William de Briouze who began to feel the king's friendship and support ebbing away. It is not at all clear why John turned against William and his family, but it probably had something to do with what was happening in Ireland.

Henry II had found it difficult to rule Ireland at a distance. The Treaty of Windsor of 1175 had tried to introduce some order into a confused situation by dividing Ireland between the English-controlled areas on the one hand (Dublin, Leinster, Meath and Munster from Waterford to Dungarvan) and the rest of Ireland which, Henry had hoped, would be brought under control by a cooperative native Irish leader, Rory O'Connor. But it had not worked: O'Connor was not strong enough to do his part, and the English settlers were not prepared to abandon their plans to conquer as much of Ireland for themselves as possible. The situation became even more unstable after the death of Strongbow in 1176 left a vacuum to be filled in Leinster. In 1177 new arrangements were made. King Henry kept the cities of Cork, Limerick and the kingdom of Leinster for himself (the latter during the minority of Strongbow's heir), while formal grants of the kingdoms of Cork and Limerick were made to Robert Fitz Stephen and Miles de Cogan (who were to share Cork) and Philip de Briouze respectively. Much would depend on how assertive these men were prepared to be and, as has been seen, Briouze had no great success with his award. More important in 1177, though, was King Henry's announcement that he intended to give Ireland to his son John whose kingdom it would be. John would bring

Ireland firmly within the Angevin network of territories, rule over the native Irish and the settler barons, and bring peace and stability across the Irish Sea. At least that was the plan. But John was only ten years old in 1177, and until he was old enough to claim the kingship in person, Irish politics would continue along their unpredictable and restless track.

John finally went to Ireland to claim his kingdom in 1185, although the peacock-feathered crown that Pope Urban III sent him for the occasion was yet to arrive. Gerald of Wales's description of the expedition paints it as a fiasco.[10] John was eighteen, but immature and feckless. On landing, he and his companions insulted the Irish leaders who came to meet them, laughing at their appearance and mocking their unkempt beards. John certainly seems to have made little if any effort to get the Irish lords on his side. He also failed to secure the support of the English settlers despite some attempts to do so by granting them lands. They, of course, had been doing all the hard work of establishing English power in Ireland since the late 1160s, and if they resented John's arrival and the prospect of him telling them all what to do, that is hardly surprising. Some of these men had been dramatically successful. In 1177, John de Courcy had begun his conquest of Ulster. According to Gerald of Wales, he was a natural warrior and adventurer, immensely strong, bold and impetuous.[11] By 1185 his progress was already startling, and he planned to rule the north of Ireland in his own way. Meanwhile, further south in Meath, Hugh de Lacy was establishing another effectively autonomous power base. Hugh had come to Ireland with Henry II in 1171. After that, he had taken control of Meath with royal approval, and during the next fifteen years he had extended his personal power whilst acting as one of the king's leading ministers across Ireland. Hugh's relationship with Henry II was not always straightforward, but by 1185 he was the most powerful man in southern Ireland (he was 'lord of the foreigners in Ireland', an Irish chronicler asserted), and John's expedition to Ireland was probably designed on one level to rein him in.[12] However, John also needed the support of men like de Courcy and de Lacy in 1185 if he was to get anywhere with his own claims to lordship over Ireland. But they were uncooperative at best. John was convinced that they had intervened to prevent the Irish leaders giving him tribute or hostages, but there was nothing he could do about it apart from complain to his father the king following his shamefaced return to England. He would not forget his bitterness about the way the settler barons had let him down.

By the time John became king in 1199, his status as lord of Ireland was verging on the notional. However, he did not mean for things to stay that way. He retained the title in the list he used in his official documents and on his seal, and he was clearly determined to bring Ireland more directly under his rule and, in the process, extract its resources. But by the start of the thirteenth century, the power of the settler barons was even more deeply entrenched than it had been in 1185. Hugh de Lacy had been killed in 1186, but his son Walter had succeeded him as lord of Meath and carried on where his father had left off; William de Burgh had flourished in Limerick where Philip de Briouze had failed; and William Marshal had acquired the lordship of Leinster when he married Strongbow's daughter Isabel in 1189. And as for John de Courcy, he was so powerful by 1200 that the English chronicler Roger of Howden described him as 'prince of the kingdom of Ulster in Ireland'; and elsewhere, at the end of a list of the rulers of the Christian world, Roger included 'John de Courcy in Ulster'.[13] Naturally suspicious of other powerful men at the best of times, the new king would certainly have remembered the way the settler barons had snubbed him in 1185. Moreover, de Courcy and Hugh de Lacy (Walter's younger brother) had been staunch supporters of King Richard during John's rebellion of 1193–4. John would have felt justified in wanting to make these men fall into line and defer to his newly acquired royal power.

There were various ways of doing this. First, John could back one English settler against another. This is what happened when the two erstwhile allies John de Courcy and Hugh de Lacy turned on each other. In 1203 de Courcy was defeated in battle by de Lacy, and in 1204 he was captured and then released by him. In 1205, Hugh was granted all of Ulster as earl to hold as de Courcy had held it on the day he had been captured; the great prince of northern Ireland, at whose power contemporaries had marvelled, lost everything. There can be no doubt that de Lacy had carried out this coup (indeed, had been able to carry it out) because the king had allowed it, tacitly or not. It seems that de Courcy had simply become too powerful for King John's liking. The other

English lords must have looked on, grateful that they had not been on the receiving end of the king's tyranny, but sure that on another occasion they might be. Another method John used was to send his own men into Ireland to challenge the vested interests. This is what he did with William de Briouze when he granted him the lordship of Limerick in 1201. Much of county Limerick was under the control of William de Burgh at the turn of the century; other settler lords had stakes there too. Even if John did not intend the grant to William de Briouze to upset the status quo, this was certainly its effect. And when John granted the city of Limerick itself to Briouze in 1203, which de Burgh had previously held, it must have been clear that the balance of power within Ireland had shifted decisively. William de Burgh was also checked in other ways. In the 1180s and 1190s he had been the leading figure in the conquest and organisation of northern Munster, and in the early 1200s he turned his attention to the seizure of the kingdom of Connacht. But in 1205, John lost interest in de Burgh and instead granted two-thirds of Connacht to the native Irish claimant Cathal Crovderg O'Connor.

Next to come into John's sights was the lord of Leinster, William Marshal. The Marshal's good relationship with John had first been jeopardised by the loss of Normandy in 1204. William had been determined to hang on to his own lands in the duchy, regardless of whether John or Philip ruled it. He performed homage to King Philip for his Norman lands in early 1205, but this meant that he was now obliged to fight for him when he was in France. This was bound to upset John, given his ambitions to return to France and regain his own lost lands by force. When the Marshal refused to accompany John on his campaign to Poitou in 1205, the king accused him of treason and demanded that the magnates present pass judgment on him. They refused to do so, but whilst John was unable at this stage to disgrace William publicly, he could withdraw his favour and close down the sources of royal support in other ways. John demanded William's eldest son as a hostage for his good behaviour, and it was clear that the king was backing the Marshal into a corner. In these circumstances, in the spring of 1207, William decided to retreat to his Irish estates, and John, initially at least, was happy to let him go. However, as he was about to leave, William was met by a royal messenger who required him either to stay in England or hand over his second son, Richard, as a hostage. William sent the messenger back to tell the king that he could have all his children as hostages if he desired, but he was going to Ireland and he sailed the next day. John clearly had misgivings about allowing a man as powerful and influential as the Marshal to do as he pleased in Ireland.

And King John had a willing assistant in Ireland, Meiler Fitz Henry. Meiler was one of the few survivors of the first wave of English settlement in Ireland – he had accompanied his uncle, Robert Fitz Stephen, on his first expedition to Ireland in 1169. In 1199, John appointed him justiciar, the king's principal representative there. But he was already by that time a tenant of the lords of Leinster (William Marshal) and Meath (the Lacys). Meiler was no diplomat. Indeed, his approach to the English barons in Ireland after 1199 seems to have been deliberately provocative. Behind the shield of royal authority he was able to pursue policies designed to destabilise the political situation there and, in the main, he did so with John's tacit backing. By the time the Marshal arrived in Ireland in 1207, Meiler was already in dispute with him and most of the other English lords, over a range of matters to do with estates, offices and custodies. During the spring and summer of 1207, there is evidence to suggest that something like a full-scale war broke out between Meiler on the one hand and a group of settler barons led by William Marshal on the other. In the end, both Meiler and the Marshal were recalled from Ireland to explain themselves before the king, and at the end of September 1207 a wary Marshal complied, leaving Leinster to be defended by his wife and a group of trusted followers. His caution was well placed. Meiler came back to England too, but not before having instructed his men to attack the Marshal's lands as soon as he was gone. When the king met both men at Woodstock in October, it was Meiler who received the warm royal welcome whilst William was greeted coldly.

But the Marshal could look after himself. Whilst he was detained in England, his wife and supporters in Ireland did not flinch, even when they were ordered by John to return to England or lose any lands they held there. By the spring of 1208, Meiler had been captured by the Marshal's men, forced to submit and give his own son as hostage. John had no choice but to make terms with the Marshal: Leinster was re-granted to him and the Marshal returned to Ireland where he was to stay for the next five years. As for Meiler, he had lost his position as justiciar of Ireland by the end of 1209.

John had found it impossible to break William Marshal. His support was too deeply entrenched and his influence too great. This must have rankled with the naturally jealous and resentful king. And it may be that it was his failure decisively to deal with the Marshal that prompted John to look elsewhere for a victim. He found one in William de Briouze. There was more to Briouze's fall than injured royal pride, however, or a desire to make an example of someone, whoever it was. And here, Arthur of Brittany may have continued to plague John from his grave. Briouze had had custody of Arthur after he was captured at Mirebeau in August 1202, but he had given him up by the end of the year. According to William the Breton, who wrote Philip II's biography a decade and a half or so later, Briouze handed over Arthur because he was worried about what John intended to do with him; he wanted to distance himself from the boy's fate.[14] Such an observation may be full of hindsight, of course, and Briouze was probably with John at Rouen at the time of Arthur's disappearance in early April 1203. He may even have encouraged John to have the boy killed. Either way, whether complicit in the alleged murder or not, William de Briouze almost certainly knew what had happened to Arthur, and by 1208, John may have felt that anyone in possession of such sensitive information was by definition a threat to be eliminated. What is more, John had a deadly weapon to use against his former friend because William had paid the king only £468 of the £3,333 he had promised for the honour of Limerick in 1201.[15] John could break him publicly and with the law on his side.

Having said this, John's attitude to William de Briouze may have changed less suddenly than this, and there are several hints that William had already started to lose John's favour before 1208. During 1206 the king had instructed Meiler Fitz Henry to establish the precise boundary between the honours of Limerick and Cork. This was potentially a threat to some of the lands that William had acquired in 1201. And in the same year he also came off second best in a series of lawsuits heard in the royal courts concerning some of his lands in Wales and England. None of these reversals was particularly serious in itself, but taken together they might suggest that the tide had started to turn against William de Briouze. His fate was not settled yet, though. At the start of 1207, Meiler Fitz Henry had seized some of William's Irish lands, but when William complained to the king about the justiciar's behaviour, they had been returned. Later in the year, however, when he came to England with William Marshal, Meiler was able to spread the rumour that Briouze was not only too friendly with the Marshal, but he was also plotting with the Lacys and the Welsh against the king. And, to be sure, it may be that Briouze had been drawn into the hostilities between Meiler and the Marshal during 1207–8: his seneschal of Limerick, Geoffrey de Marisco, was amongst those recalled to see the king in September 1207, and whether the king still trusted Briouze by then must be in doubt.[16] One English source claims that John suspected Briouze of plotting against him, and that the king's suspicions were confirmed when William refused to attend John's court to explain himself.[17] If true, this would have given John ample excuse for taking punitive action against him. But it remains unclear quite how deeply implicated or directly involved William really was in the resistance to Meiler's attempts to extend royal power in Ireland. Nevertheless, even whispers against him cannot have helped, and once the Marshal's dispute with the king was over, it was Briouze's unpaid debt for Limerick that gave John the excuse to turn on him. By the time the king granted part of Briouze's honour of Limerick to another settler baron, Walter de Lacy, in December 1208, William's time in royal favour was already over.[18]

The course of the years 1208–9 is relatively well documented, but all of the relevant accounts of what happened are tainted in some way or other. Roger of Wendover described the fate of the Briouzes with hindsight and a moraliser's concern to show John in as unfavourable a light as possible. The biographer of William Marshal had his own hero's reputation to consider more than anything else. But perhaps most remarkable is the account given of this part of the Briouze affair by the king himself. In the summer of 1210, John published his own version of what happened.[19] It is a long and detailed account, full of information not found elsewhere, and it seeks to show that William de Briouze and his family were treated patiently and fairly by the king, that they were pursued 'according to the customs of the realm and the law of the exchequer', and that they were, more than anything else, the authors of their own downfall through the actions they took and the promises they broke. It is of course a highly partisan account, but it was witnessed by thirteen men including seven earls, some of whom were reportedly involved directly in the events themselves. The fact that John published this account at all suggests that he was under significant pressure by 1210 to explain his treatment of the Briouzes. Nevertheless, it is hard to dismiss it simply as special pleading. There is certainly no reason to doubt that, as far as the king at least was concerned, his memory of events was accurate and his conduct had been entirely proper.

John's description begins with the events of spring 1208 when he ordered the confiscation of William's Welsh lands because of his unpaid debts. William's wife, Matilda, his nephew William de Ferrers, earl of Derby, and Adam de Port, his sister's husband (both of these men later witnessed the documents of 1212), then met the king at Gloucester and persuaded him to see William de Briouze. At Hereford, William promised to pay his debts within a specified time, offered his Welsh castles of Hay, Radnor and Brecon as surety, and three of his grandsons and four of his tenants' sons as hostages. It was at this point that the encounter between the king's officers and Matilda de Briouze, as later described by Roger of Wendover, was supposed to have taken place, when she refused to surrender the hostages because of what she believed had happened to Arthur of Brittany. Whether this confrontation did actually occur is uncertain, of course, but there is reason to believe that the king was as furious with Matilda as he was with her husband. When William de Briouze later offered the enormous sum, just over £26,650, to recover the king's goodwill, John refused whilst Matilda was still at liberty. And the king was taking much more aggressive action against William at around this time too. The king later claimed that, after his meeting with Briouze at Hereford and once his castles were in royal hands, William and two of his sons attempted to retake them by force. They failed and so burned the town of Leominster instead. In April 1208, perhaps in response to this, a large force (500 infantry and 25 mounted sergeants) under the command of the sheriffs of Gloucestershire and Shropshire was sent against William de Briouze, and at the end of the month

William was given four days to pay the £666 the expedition had cost. Later, in the summer of 1208, William was summoned to appear at court, but pleaded sickness and failed to attend. He must have feared that he would not be safe in John's company and by the end of 1208 he and his family had fled to their lands in Ireland.

At this point the biographer of William Marshal also takes up the story.[20] After a rough three-day crossing of the Irish Sea, the Briouzes landed at Wicklow and were given shelter for three weeks by William Marshal. Their conversations over dinner must have been interesting. The Marshal knew what it meant to lose royal favour, although he was always better placed to weather such a storm than William de Briouze. He may have reminded Briouze of his warning in 1206 when John had accused the Marshal of treason (at least this is what the Marshal's biographer records him as having said then): 'Be on your alert against the King: what he thinks to do with me, he will do to each and every one of you, or even more, if he gets the upper hand over you.'[21] When news of the Briouzes' presence in Ireland reached the king's new justiciar, the bishop of Norwich, John de Gray, he demanded that the Marshal surrender 'the king's traitors' to him. The Marshal refused; he claimed to be ignorant of the quarrel between Briouze and the king and that he was only providing hospitality to a man he described rather oddly as 'his lord'. The Briouzes were then sent on their way to their new refuge under the protection of their son-in-law, Walter de Lacy.[22] Of course, events such as this can only have hardened John's conviction that the English lords in Ireland were conspiring against him. It is easy to imagine how furious their defiance made him, and he began making plans for a military expedition to rein them in. Before it left, however, Walter and the Marshal managed to arrange a meeting between Briouze and the king back in Wales. When the two men finally met at Pembroke in 1210, according to the king's account of what happened, John refused William's offer of £26,667 and the king commented pointedly on William's position: 'We told him we knew well that he was not in his own power at all, but in that of his wife, who was in Ireland.'[23] And that was where the king was heading too.

Leaving William de Briouze behind in Wales, John set sail and landed near Waterford in the middle of June 1210. The king's plan,

officially at least, was to apprehend Matilda de Briouze and the traitorous lords who had protected her and her family. In reality his ambitions were wider than this. John's army of at least 1,000 infantry and 800
knights was probably the largest ever seen in Ireland. This expedition
was designed to succeed where the one of 1185 had failed, in firmly and
decisively putting the settler barons in their place. It would crush their
resistance and establish John's authority over Ireland once and for all. By
this point in his reign, John was raising money on a huge scale to fund
his planned continental campaigns. He wanted to subject Ireland to an
English-style administration so that he could get his hands on Irish
revenue too. By the end of June 1210, John had reached Dublin and
begun his march into Meath. Ahead of him, Matilda de Briouze, her
two sons William and Reginald, and Walter de Lacy had fled north into
Ulster. John followed, but before he could catch up with them they had
fled from their refuge in Carrickfergus Castle and escaped across the
Irish Sea into Galloway, where they were soon joined by Hugh de Lacy.
The king's frustration did not last long. He described how he soon
received news that Matilda had been captured in Scotland along with
one of her daughters, her eldest son William, his wife and two of their
children. Her younger son Reginald and the Lacys remained on the
loose. The king then sent John de Courcy (the former lord of Ulster,
now back in royal favour and keen to revenge himself on the Lacys) to
collect the hostages. When they appeared before him, Matilda offered
the surrender of all her husband's castles and lands and a payment of
£26,667. John later claimed that he accepted these terms, only for
Matilda to go back on them a few days later. Either way, the king kept
his prisoners with him as he travelled south to finish his expedition.[24]

By this point the great lordships of Meath, Ulster and Limerick had
all been subjugated by John, and the process of imposing systems of
English government, administration and law on the country was well
under way. The Irish chieftains had still not been reconciled to English
rule, and to this extent John's expedition was not a complete success. But
of the effectively autonomous English territories in Ireland, only
Leinster under William Marshal remained by the end of 1210. When
he returned to Dublin in August, John summoned the Marshal to
appear before him. He accused him of harbouring traitors and the

Marshal, his biographer recorded, responded with characteristic defiance, challenging anyone who would like to back up such an accusation by force. Nobody did, of course, and John had to be content once again with hostages and promises of future loyalty from the Marshal.[25] As for Matilda de Briouze, the king described how she made a second offer of £26,667 as well as an additional £6,667 because of her failure to stick to the first agreement.[26] John accepted these terms, but it was also agreed that Matilda and those of her family captured with her should remain in royal custody until the fines had been paid. They were brought back to England on John's return ('loaded down with chains', according to Roger of Wendover) and imprisoned at Windsor.[27] Matilda asked the king whether she could see her husband, and the fugitive William de Briouze, his safety guaranteed for the occasion, arrived to speak with her privately. He then met the king and accepted the arrangement his wife had made. It was hopelessly unrealistic, however: the sums involved were simply too large for even the richest baron to pay. William fled again, this time to France, leaving his wife to admit that she had no way of paying the fine. All she had to offer were twenty-four silver marks, twenty-four gold coins and fifteen ounces of gold. Her husband was declared an outlaw and she was left to the mercy of the king.[28]

What happened next is murky and unclear. However, most of the contemporary chroniclers mention it and they knew it was shocking.[29] Opinions differ as to where Matilda was finally imprisoned; it may have been at Corfe Castle in Dorset, but it was probably at Windsor. There is also no unanimity about who was imprisoned with her (there are reports that she had more than one child with her, and even some of their wives), although for various reasons it seems most likely that Matilda was confined with just her eldest son William for company. All that is known with any certainty at all is that the two of them died in their prison. Some of the chroniclers leave it at that, but others go into more detail. She and her son died of hunger or were starved to death, it was alleged; they were kept in darkness for a long time, one writer said, and died miserably of neglect.[30] The most graphic account comes from the Anonymous of Béthune, who had extolled Matilda in such complimentary terms earlier in his work. He describes how mother and son were both discovered dead on the eleventh day of their imprisonment.

William was propped up against a wall with Matilda sitting between his legs and leaning on his chest. Matilda had presumably died after her son, because hunger had driven her to eat some of the flesh from his cheeks.[31] This account was written shortly after John's death in 1216 and almost certainly before 1220. And, it is fair to say, whilst the author was prepared to compliment John on his capacity for lavish hospitality, he was also a fierce critic of the king's policies and morals.[32] However, the Anonymous was no fan of John's opponents either, so on this level his vivid and dramatic treatment may at least be even-handed. But it has also been suggested that the author's patron was a prominent courtier of the count of Aumale, Matilda de Briouze's nephew. The chronicler's precise and detailed account of Matilda's death may therefore have come from the count's circle or even ultimately from the count himself, although whether that makes it more reliable is open to question.

Hostages did not fare well in King John's custody. There was Arthur, of course, and in 1212, John hanged the twenty-eight hostages, one a boy of just seven, whom he had taken from the Welsh princes in the previous year. So the deaths of Matilda and her son, whilst still outrageous, cannot have been a complete surprise. When the news crossed the Channel and reached William de Briouze himself, however, is unclear. But he probably knew what had happened by the time he died, a beaten man, at Corbeil outside Paris on 4 September 1211. He was buried in the abbey of St Victoire at Paris by his son Giles, the exiled bishop of Hereford. Stephen Langton, the exiled archbishop of Canterbury and another victim of John's anger, is also said to have assisted at the funeral. Had Langton looked across to England at this point, the king would have appeared untouchable. John dominated his barons: he had brought Wales, Scotland and Ireland under direct control from England more than any previous king, and his coffers were overflowing with cash. Far from weakening him, John's treatment of the Briouzes had enabled him to become stronger still. Within four years of William de Briouze's funeral, however, John's power had collapsed once again and Langton had taken centre stage.

CHAPTER NINE

THE EXILE'S TALE

Stephen Langton and the Road to
Magna Carta

THE ARCHBISHOP HAD been back in England since the end of July.
After seven years of Stephen Langton's exile, King John had finally
relented and allowed him to enter the kingdom. John had gone further
too: he had ended his long quarrel with the pope, he had agreed to right
all the wrongs he had done to the Church, and he had been absolved
of his sins by Langton himself at Winchester Cathedral. England now
belonged to the papacy and King John was answerable in all things to
his new overlord, Pope Innocent III. Three weeks or so after his return,
on 25 August 1213, Langton preached a sermon at St Paul's. His text
was taken from Psalm 27: 'My heart has hoped in God and I am helped;
my flesh blooms again; of my own will I confess to him.'[1] The message
for England was clear: the time of renewal and redemption had come.
When he had finished preaching, Langton met his bishops and abbots,
other leading churchmen and the barons assembled there for the service.
For the first time since 1207, he announced, church services could be
held in some English churches again. But, at this early stage, they should
be celebrated quietly, in low voices. Soon, couples would be able to
marry in church again, communion could be given at last, confessions
heard, and the dead buried in consecrated ground. For six years the
English faithful had been denied these sacraments because of the obsti-
nacy and belligerence of their king. But this was not Langton's only
business. He called some of the nobles aside and spoke privately with
them. 'Did you hear,' he said 'how, when I absolved the king at

Winchester, I made him swear that he would do away with unjust laws, and would recall good laws, such as those of King Edward, and cause them to be observed by all in the kingdom?' Some would have nodded and listened eagerly for what was coming next; others, nervous about where the archbishop was taking them, would have shuffled their feet uneasily, or glanced over their shoulders to see who might have been eavesdropping. 'A charter of Henry the first king of England has just now been found,' Langton went on, 'by which you may, if you wish it, recall your long-lost rights and your former condition.' And placing a piece of parchment in the midst of them, he ordered it to be read aloud for all to hear. When the document had been read out and its meaning understood by the barons who heard it, they were pleased, and all of them, in the archbishop's presence, swore that when the time was right, they would stand up for their rights, and die for them if necessary. The archbishop, too, faithfully promised them his assistance as far as lay in his power. Having entered into this pact, they all went their separate ways.[2] A year later, the barons met once more, this time at Bury St Edmund's. The same charter of Henry I, the one that they had been shown by the archbishop at St Paul's, was again produced, and they swore together on the altar of the abbey that if the king refused to accept their demands, they would go to war against him.[3]

So the story goes, and with its whispered plotting, its sworn alliances, and its depiction of a resolute leader bent on reforming the realm with the support of a group of brave and principled barons, it is certainly a dramatic one. But whether these events actually occurred in anything like this form is another matter entirely. A second chronicler, the Barnwell annalist, records that John's critics attempted to use the coronation charter of Henry I as a basis for discussion with the king at the end of 1214, only for John to stall and prevaricate. And there are yet more who mention the charter and who knew it was important.[4] But only one writer, the famously unreliable Roger of Wendover, describes what happened at St Paul's on 25 August 1213, and even he is cautious enough about his account to stress that it was based on rumour. He may simply have made it up, because, writing more than a decade later, knowing what happened after Stephen Langton's return to England, he thought this was the sort of thing that should have happened, even if it had not.

* * * *

Two years after these events are supposed to have taken place, another royal charter was dominating English politics. There is no more famous document in English history than Magna Carta. Eight centuries have passed since its creation, and over that time its status as the venerated foundation stone of the English constitution, as a guarantor of individual freedom and as a bulwark against tyranny, has become assured and entrenched. However, it is probably fair to say that not many people know what Magna Carta actually says, and that few could explain whether or why it deserves its almost sanctified reputation. Fewer still could probably explain in more than the most general terms how it came to be created at all. It is rarely mentioned, too, that the charter issued by King John in 1215 was a wretched failure, and that it was only the revised versions of that document, produced in the following decade under very different circumstances from the first and during the reign of Henry III, which gave the charter its final and definitive form.

It is also worth emphasising that hardly any of the charter still remains in force, and so an understanding of its history after its creation is essential to anyone seeking to grasp its wider importance. Whilst the charter retained its political importance through the thirteenth and fourteenth centuries, it was not until the seventeenth century that Magna Carta began to acquire its fabled significance. The lawyers and parliamentarians of the English Civil War, in their struggle against the arbitrary rule of Charles I, resurrected and rebranded the charter as a key part of England's mythical 'ancient constitution', an essentially imaginary set of laws and customs stretching back to pre-Roman Britain that protected the 'liberties' of all English people. It safeguarded inalienable rights, such as *habeas corpus* and trial by jury, they argued, and confirmed the need for consent to taxation and the principle of a limited monarchy. By the nineteenth century, although many of Magna Carta's outdated and defunct sections had been repealed by Parliament itself, the events of 1215 were seen as a major staging post along the route towards parliamentary democracy. And even today, political debates and media commentary about British freedoms and British values regularly mention Magna Carta and summon it in aid of all manner of positions.

So the charter has acquired a symbolic and almost timeless importance, one not necessarily justified by what it actually says. Because the charter was very much a product of its time and its main concerns are narrow, local and specific; often they are obscure and highly technical. Magna Carta was designed first and foremost to restrict King John's ability to raise money and to prevent him acting arbitrarily against his leading barons. It was designed to protect the resources and privileges of England's ruling elite. Having said that, it was by no means an exclusively 'baronial' document. It was a grant by the king to 'all the free men of our kingdom', and it reached out to other groups in society beyond the landed aristocracy, even to women and peasants at times.[5] The barons agreed to treat their own tenants as well as the king agreed to treat his, a concession that at once increased the number of those with a stake in politics and acknowledged the emergence of a new political class, the knights of the shire, who eventually became the commons in Parliament. And, whether this was intended or not, the charter, albeit falteringly, enunciated embryonic notions that later grew into fundamental principles, such as the need for consent to taxation, the imperative for government to be truly representative, and, most importantly, that the king was subject to the law – he had to rule within limits and not just according to his will. If he tried to do otherwise, 'the commune of all the land' (a fascinatingly undefined phrase in the charter) could move against him.[6] Magna Carta was not supposed to embody a comprehensive programme of constitutional reform; nor did it do so. But it did mark a turning point in the relationship between the English king and his people.

Given its status and the meanings which have been imposed upon it, it is not surprising that the charter's authorship has also been a matter of debate. Surely such a historic text cannot have been created by accident: there must have been some genius presiding over it, a clear-sighted visionary who saw in the charter a chance to point the way towards the future development of England's hallowed constitution. If so, the most obvious candidate for this role was Stephen Langton, archbishop of Canterbury. He certainly had the intellectual ability (Langton was one of the great scholars of his day), and he suffered enough at John's hands to appreciate the need for change. Roger of Wendover's description of the meeting at St Paul's in 1213 emphasised Langton's pre-eminence among the reformers, and there were clear echoes of Henry I's Coronation Charter in its great descendant of 1215. Unfortunately, however, such a romantic scenario is too simplistic. Just as Magna Carta has no single meaning, so it had no single author, and whilst Langton was heavily involved in the events and negotiations that created it, so were many others. Nevertheless, it is possible to recognise his finger-prints on parts of the charter, and no one else's tale provides a better backdrop to these momentous affairs.

* * * *

Stephen Langton lived more than half of his life in brilliant obscurity. A Lincolnshire boy, born around 1150, he was one of three sons of Henry Langton, a knight and minor landowner in Langton by Wragby, Lincolnshire. He may have been the eldest of the brothers, but even if he was, there was never going to be much to inherit from his father. So his prospects were limited from the start, and from his early years he was destined for a career in the Church. It is quite possible that he received his early education in the cathedral school at Lincoln, about fifteen miles from his home, but nothing is really known for certain about his upbringing. But as it had been for Herbert of Bosham thirty years before, Paris was the young man's chosen destination. By the 1160s, the fame of the city's schools and their teachers had grown, and, more so than ever before, it was a place where the able and the dedicated could flourish, especially if they had the funds to maintain themselves. It was the intellectual centre of western Europe and one of the few environments in which a clever lad from a relatively humble background could hope to climb the otherwise vertical and unconquerable rock face that passed for a social structure in the twelfth century. Stephen and his brother Simon were only two amongst many young Englishmen who set out for Paris at about this time. However, few if any of them became as famous as Stephen Langton.

Stephen was probably in Paris by the time he was fifteen, sometime around 1165. That was the year the future King Philip II was born there, and, like Gerald of Wales who was also in Paris then, Stephen may have heard the bells ringing in celebration of the new prince's birth on 21 August of that year.[7] For perhaps a decade and a half after that he would have learnt his scholarly trade alongside students from all over Europe. Paris in the late twelfth century was a cosmopolitan place – dynamic, energetic and diverse. The organisation of the schools there was still relatively informal. The teaching masters were mostly based on the Île de la Cité, alongside the royal palace and the great cathedral of Notre Dame, which was still being constructed in the 1180s and 1190s. They were not yet in any sense members of a corporate body; there were no academic departments or faculties, and the institutionalised 'university' did not really start to develop its recognised form until the thirteenth century. Until it did each master, licensed to teach by the bishop of Paris, fended for himself. Before that, though, they had to earn the right to call themselves 'master'. This process was long and demanding. The student would spend several years on the seven so-called liberal arts, grouped together into the *trivium* (grammar, rhetoric and logic) and the *quadrivium* (arithmetic, geometry, music and astronomy). Many of those who lasted through this gruelling training (and plenty did not) would end their studies at this point, in the hope of getting a place in the household of a great lord or bishop, or even in the royal administration in England, France or Germany. But some stayed on to study the higher subjects, law, medicine and, most important of all, theology. This is what aspiring leaders of the Church came increasingly to do during this period: the goal for many would be a bishopric later in life. An aspiring teacher would do the same and, once his studies were complete, he might stay on in Paris and open a school of his own. Such a place was probably no more than a rented room in a house, and the master would have relied on his reputation to attract pupils who would pay to be taught by him.

By the 1180s, Stephen Langton ran a school like this in Paris. He would probably have lectured on the Bible in the mornings and disputed theological points and issues arising from his commentary in the afternoons. He also gave sermons to popular and clerical audiences alike, and several hundred of these survive in various forms. Some of the surviving manuscripts describe Langton as 'Thunder-Tongued' ('de Lingua-Tonante'), which suggests that he must have had a vigorous and rousing preaching style.[8] But it is on his biblical scholarship that his reputation as a theologian rests. In the early twelfth century, scholars had put together the so-called *Glossa Ordinaria*, a huge collection of texts from Church Fathers like St Augustine and St Jerome, as well as more recent passages commenting on all parts of the Bible, on their literal meaning in a historical sense, as well as their wider symbolic, moral and spiritual significance. Langton built further on this and wrote his own commentaries on more or less all of the Old and New Testaments, and in the process developed the method of dividing them into books and chapters that is still in general use today.

As Langton's study of the Bible deepened, he inevitably had to grapple with questions about the nature of earthly power, and about the relationship between secular and ecclesiastical authority. Where do secular rulers get their power from? What if a Christian is required to sin in order to obey the instructions of a ruler? Can the ruler be opposed or his orders defied? The starting point was St Paul's assertion in Romans 13: 'Let every soul be subject to the higher powers for there is no power except from God, and those that exist have been ordained by God.' In other words, political power was a divine gift and, as such, subjects owed their rulers obedience. There were circumstances, though, in which disobedience was permissible. The power of a ruler to kill his subject, like all his other powers, had been given to him by God, and the subject should not resist or flee from such a sentence if the ruler's decision arose out of the lawful exercise of his power: in Langton's words, a subject cannot be disobedient 'to those things that directly pertain to the ordinance of God, such as paying taxes and the like'. 'But if,' he continued, 'someone abuses the power that is given to him by God and if I know that this bad use would constitute a mortal sin for me, I ought not to obey him, lest I resist the ordinance of God.'[9] That is to say, disobedience is legitimate if a ruler commands a subject to commit a mortal sin. Elsewhere, though, the dilemmas are framed differently and the solutions are more ambiguous. If a ruler wages war unjustly and the injustice is plain, his people are still obliged to obey him if the matter was adjudicated in a court, and even if that court was biased towards the ruler. Similarly, a knight summoned by a ruler to fight in an unjust war is required to serve even if, in doing so, he would sin. The solution Langton proposes is for the knight to follow the ruler as summoned, 'but when it comes to taking up arms, either I retire, or I remain without taking up arms'.[10] Such an approach would have been laughed at on the battlefield of course, and the real world was much more complex and challenging than solutions like this allowed. But it is as well to remember that, in the rarefied scholarly atmosphere of Paris in the 1180s, such problems were highly theoretical ones meant purely for dispute and intellectual argument.

Nevertheless, certain themes do emerge from Langton's treatment of political power: its divinely ordained legitimacy gave a ruler almost unlimited authority and imposed on his subjects a general duty to obey. However, the importance of court judgments in legitimising the exercise of that power was also central: if a ruler acted on his own will, without a judgment, it might be possible for his subjects to disobey him. It is hard to believe that such arguments did not contribute significantly to the way Langton approached the practical and all too worldly political problems he faced in later life. Although, having said that, the ideas themselves were not original. Another Englishman schooled in Paris, John of Salisbury, had drawn a clear distinction in his work *Policraticus*, written by about 1159, between a tyrant, who rules according to his will ('per voluntatem') and a just ruler, who rules according to law ('per legem'). John even justified the killing of a tyrannical ruler.[11] And notions of due legal process (in particular, the importance of judgments arrived at by a court) were central to many of the legal procedures concerning the recovery of land instituted by King Henry II in England in the 1170s and 1180s. In addition, nor were Langton's views radical. They are pervaded by a deep respect for secular power, and his conclusions on the nature and exercise of political authority are notably cautious and conservative. He was no revolutionary.

Paris was Langton's home for the best part of forty years. As well as a teacher in the schools, he also became a canon of Notre Dame, which entitled him to a house, an income and a stall in the cathedral. His life would have been comfortable and, there is no reason to doubt, contented. But he was not a complete stranger to England either. It is quite likely that he crossed the Channel in the 1170s or 1180s, perhaps to visit Thomas Becket's new shrine at Canterbury, perhaps to visit his family in Lincolnshire. And some time between 1191 and 1205, Langton was definitely in York. He held a prebend in the diocese (in other words, he received the income from a specified ecclesiastical estate there), and much later, in 1226, he referred warmly to his Yorkshire links. But when he finally left Paris for good, in 1206, it was not to return to England. He was summoned to Rome where high ecclesiastical office awaited him.

This was the pope's idea. By the start of 1206, Innocent III had been pope for eight years. He was a remarkable man. Born in 1160 or 1161, Lothar de Segni belonged to the Roman landholding aristocracy, and he was brought up and educated in Rome until he went to Paris, where he stayed until 1187. Lothar also studied canon law at Bologna for a short time after leaving Paris, but his talents had already been spotted by the Church hierarchy and in 1189 he was made a cardinal. At that time, the cardinals were in effect the parish clergy of Rome. Each one was permanently resident in the city and had his own church there, but much of the cardinals' time was spent working within the papal admin- istration. Lothar clearly distinguished himself in this role, and he enhanced his reputation further during the 1190s with his theological writings. In January 1198, on the death of Pope Celestine III, he was chosen as pope and took the name Innocent III. He was only thirty- seven and probably the youngest man who has ever been elected to the position. His youth was no bar to his ambition, however. Pope Innocent had an exalted idea of the pope's status and role in the world. He was interested in reforming the Church, launching a crusade and eradicating heresy. He held strongly to the view that it was the pope's universal responsibility to preserve peace and good government. Such a view gave him the scope to intervene where he saw fit in secular affairs across Europe and inevitably gave rise to a series of conflicts with lay rulers, not least in France and Germany. Another such dispute was with King John, and Stephen Langton was at the heart of it.

The future pope had almost certainly encountered Langton in Paris, just at the time when the Englishman's fame as a biblical scholar was growing. They were roughly the same age, too, and shared an admira- tion for Thomas Becket, whose shrine at Canterbury the pope had visited, and whose image tellingly appeared later on Langton's archi- episcopal seal. When Innocent summoned Langton to Rome in 1206, therefore, they had perhaps known each other for twenty years. Langton was brought to Rome to be made a cardinal, just as Lothar de Segni had been in 1189. More precisely, Langton became cardinal-priest of St Chrysogonus, and the signs were that, his successful teaching career having been brought to an abrupt end, a new one in the papal administration was about to begin. At this point, however, events in England began to take over.

Archbishop Hubert Walter of Canterbury had died on 13 July 1205. King John's reaction was one of relief, it seems, rather than sorrow: 'Now for the first time I am King of England', he is reported to have declared.[12] The death of any bishop mattered to the king as much as it mattered to the Church. Bishops were great landholders and owed military service to the king; but he also needed their support to set the seal on his legitimacy and his rule. It had long been the practice across the western Church for bishops to be chosen by the lay ruler: he wanted loyal, reliable men he could trust in these positions of authority. However, since the middle of the eleventh century, reformers within the Church had been trying to establish the principle that Church appointments should be free from secular interference – they were a matter for the clergy only, it was claimed. So when a bishop died, they argued, his successor should be chosen by the free vote of the cathedral clergy, and their choice should be subject to confirmation by the pope, who would also settle any disputes about the election. Such an approach would take the appointment of bishops entirely out of the hands of local lay rulers, and these ideas had certainly gained some ground by the end of the twelfth century. Unsurprisingly, however, the kings, dukes and counts who had been accustomed to controlling such appointments for centuries were reluctant to surrender their control entirely. As a result, in most parts of Europe by 1200, a compromise had been reached whereby, on the death of a bishop, the clergy of the church in question (the monks or canons of the cathedral) would ask their ruler for permission to choose a replacement. This would be granted, but it might also be made clear by the ruler who his own preferred candidate was. The cathedral clergy would then proceed to elect the man of their choice, who was invariably the one supported by the secular power. Sometimes the latter had to be a little more forceful in making his wishes known. So, for example, in

1172, Henry II allegedly wrote to the monks of Winchester after the death of their bishop: 'We order you to hold a free election, but nevertheless forbid you to elect anyone except Richard [of Ilchester] my clerk'.[13] But usually, the election would be managed more quietly. In this way, the clergy's cherished notion of 'freedom of election' was observed whilst the secular leader usually got his man.

However, the importance of the English king getting his way was even greater when it came to the archbishopric of Canterbury. The archbishop was the leader of the English Church, but he was also *ex officio* the king's chief counsellor. For John, as it had been for his predecessors, this was not just a chance to assert his own power over ecclesiastical matters: it was vital that a candidate pleasing to him was appointed. So, after he had taken in the news of Archbishop Hubert's death, John went straight to Canterbury and spent nearly a week there discussing the impending election with the monks. There were some procedural problems to address. Uniquely, the bishops of the Canterbury province claimed the right to take part in the election along with the monks, and so when the king left Canterbury (taking with him a valuable collection of silver plate Hubert had bequeathed to the monks), the situation remained unresolved. Meanwhile, the monks and the bishops could put their respective claims to the pope, whose authority in such matters was regarded as conclusive by the early thirteenth century. The bishops' right to be involved in the election had long been disputed by the Canterbury monks, and this was a chance to deal with the arguments once and for all. However, rumours soon reached the monks that the king's men were already at Rome, charged with the task of getting papal support for John's preferred candidate, the current bishop of Norwich and former royal clerk, John de Gray. There was a clear risk that sticking to the king's timetable would work against the monks: the pope might support the bishops' claim to take part in the election, and they might be stuck with an archbishop they didn't want. So a group within the monastic chapter decided to take matters into their own hands and seize the opportunity to nullify the bishops' case and break free once and for all from royal control. Ignoring the king's instructions, they secretly elected one of their own colleagues, their sub-prior Reginald, as their new archbishop and sent him immediately to Rome to obtain the pope's confirmation of his appointment. If the pope allowed it, they thought, there would be nothing the king or the bishops could do about it.

Reginald had to act promptly, but also secretly. Unfortunately, he could not contain himself once he had left England: no sooner was he across the Channel than he began proclaiming himself archbishop-elect, and by the time he arrived at Rome, King John, his bishops and the pope were all well aware of the monks' scheme. The monks and the bishops prepared themselves for long and exhaustive arguments in the papal court. A more pressing problem for the Canterbury chapter in England, though, was the fury of the king, who felt he had been roundly insulted by Reginald's election. The anxious monks were sensible enough to seek out the king before he got to them and, without mentioning Reginald at all, they asked John for permission to elect a new archbishop. John graciously gave his consent, but at the same time he pointed out to the monks that John de Gray would be an excellent choice. When the monks returned to Canterbury, they were accompanied by some of the king's own clerks, and, with them watching on, John de Gray was unanimously elected. On 6 December 1205 the monks and the bishops withdrew their appeals to Rome, and five days later John de Gray was enthroned at Canterbury in the king's presence. The monks' plan to assert their independence had backfired disastrously and the king's control over the English Church looked as strong as ever. All that was needed now was papal confirmation of the election, and on 18 December, John sent a messenger to Rome to collect the rubber stamp he surely expected.

Pope Innocent, however, saw things differently. Probably exasperated by the claims and counter-claims before him, and almost certainly dismayed by the instability he saw at the heart of the English Church, Innocent decided to take matters into his own hands. First he rejected the bishops' claim to have a share in the election. Then he declared that the elections of Prior Reginald and John de Gray had both been irregular and unlawful, and by the end of March 1206 he had quashed them. Next Innocent ordered the delegation from Canterbury to hold another election there and then in his presence. The pope must have bit his tongue when the voters split evenly between the two candidates, but he was ready with a solution to end the deadlock. He proposed a candidate of his own: Stephen Langton, cardinal-priest of St Chrysogonus. The nomination was eventually accepted unanimously by the Canterbury monks in December 1206, although it is hard to see why they took so long or what else they could have done in the circumstances, far from home and with the pope himself staring hard at them as they considered their options. As for King John, he was far less susceptible to papal influence. After the pope had written to the king telling him of Langton's election, John sent a furious reply.[14] Langton was quite unacceptable, John said: the king did not know him, and he had spent too much time in France, in the heart of his enemy's lands. The issue was not so much Langton's personal qualifications, rather that, for John, there were much bigger principles at stake. The new archbishop had been chosen in a way that completely ignored the king's wishes and his traditional rights over such appointments; generations of practice had simply been cast aside at a stroke. Under threat was the notion that the king was supreme within his own kingdom and the idea that no external power should be allowed to interfere so tellingly in a matter of such domestic importance. None of John's predecessors would have accepted Langton's appointment, and it would have been deeply damaging for the king to accept an archbishop whom he did not want after his own choice had been rejected.

A stand-off between king and pope now began. Innocent wrote back to John in May 1207 dismissing his complaints and accusing him of insolence and impudence. Langton's credentials were impeccable, he said, and, anyway, he had been elected in the pope's presence and so there was no need for royal approval; this was only sought as a courtesy, not as a matter of right.[15] In other words, the pope was making his claim to supremacy in all such matters. For him, as for John, the issues of principle could not have been more serious. Six months later, it had become clear that neither side would be giving way any time soon. So Innocent announced that he would consecrate Langton without John's consent, and the ceremony took place at Viterbo on 17 June 1207. Langton clearly thought he had no choice but to go along with the pope's plan. When he wrote an open letter to the English people soon after his consecration, he made it clear that the pope was his superior and so had to be obeyed. He was also starting to identify himself strongly with

Thomas Becket by this time. The latter's courage and endurance for the sake of the Church were an example to all churchmen, but Langton may have felt that their shared status as exiles from England and victims of an oppressive king gave them something special in common. It was certainly no coincidence that Langton chose to put a depiction of Becket's murder on one side of his archiepiscopal seal. His predecessor's struggle had been doomed but necessary; Langton's own might well go along a similar path.[16]

Pope and king had taken up their seemingly irreconcilable positions. Anything but intimidated by Innocent's actions, John's response was decisive and uncompromising. He expelled the monks of Canterbury, drove them into exile and confiscated their lands. Langton was forbidden entry into England, and John declared that anyone who referred to him as archbishop should be treated as the king's enemy.[17] There were attempts to negotiate over the coming months, but no meaningful progress was made and such evidence as survives suggests that John was able to rely on a large measure of popular support from within England for his stance. As he dragged out the discussions and collected the income from the Canterbury estates, there was little pressure on him to settle the dispute, and so the pope decided to resort to other measures. In March 1208 a papal sentence of interdict was imposed on England. In official terms this meant that no church services were to be performed in England except the baptism of infants and the confession and absolution of the dying. In practice, it meant that the English Church more or less shut down until the pope said otherwise: no masses, no communion, no confession, no marriages in church and no burials in consecrated ground. Of course, it was ordinary loyal sons and daughters of the Church who would suffer as a result of this; but that was the point. Starved of their usual spiritual solace and comfort, they would blame their king and force him to back down for the sake of his people's souls. However, if that was the plan, there is little sign that it worked. John simply became even more determined not to give in. He ordered that all the parish clergy's mistresses should be arrested and ransomed, for example.[18] This was embarrassing for the Church authorities, of course, as churchmen were supposed to be celibate. And it may reveal more about the king's irreverent sense of humour and his confidence in the face of the papal sentence than it does about any desire on his part to attack the Church. Much more significant, in fact, was John's order to confiscate the property of any church, monastery or individual that complied with the pope's ban. Royal officials were sent in to bishoprics and abbeys whilst others were appointed to assess the parish clergy's revenue and allocate them an allowance. Soon enough, though, John had tempered his hard line (this may have been the plan from the start, as the interdict had long been anticipated by the king and his supporters). Churches were allowed to recover their lands, as long as they paid to do so, and John managed to turn a doom-laden papal sanction into a lucrative scam. It has been estimated that John collected over £60,000 in extra revenue from the Church during the six years the interdict was in force.

There was no sign by the end of 1208 that John was about to crack under the strain of the interdict. If anything, he was profiting from it. In January 1209, Pope Innocent warned John that stiffer measures could be taken against him personally.[19] By August, though, negotiations were making some progress. It seems that the king was finally prepared to accept Langton as archbishop and make good any losses suffered by the Church during the interdict. In return, John wanted a guarantee that Innocent's interference in the Canterbury election would not be treated as a precedent for similar papal action, and that his own traditional rights over episcopal appointments would be respected. The diplomatic atmosphere was tense and uncertain, however, and in October, when Langton himself sailed to Dover to take part in the discussions, the king refused to see him and the archbishop returned disappointed to France. The distrust on both sides persisted and, on 8 November 1209, John was excommunicated. Innocent's hope was that the excommunication would drive a wedge between John and his people. The king was now officially excluded from the Christian community and his subjects were not bound to follow his orders. At the very least this should have made it difficult for John to govern, at worst it might have imperilled whole areas of domestic and foreign policy. To be sure, most of the English bishops, compromised by their divided loyalties, left the kingdom after John's excommunication and went into self-imposed exile. Beyond this, however, like the interdict, the excommunication appears to have had little effect on England. And if John was worried about his soul as he entered the second decade of his reign, it did not show.

Meanwhile, Stephen Langton had settled in northern France. He spent most of his time at the Cistercian monastery of Pontigny, where Thomas Becket had also passed part of his exile. When Langton conducted the funeral of William de Briouze at the abbey of St Victor in Paris in 1211, it must have been clear to those who were paying attention that the archbishop was publicly identifying himself with those who had suffered at John's hands. At that point, however, there was little to suggest that things would change in the immediate future. Langton, now in his early sixties, could have been forgiven for thinking that his life would end in unfulfilled exile. In fact, that life was just about to enter its most important and controversial phase.

By 1212, King John was at the height of his power and his authority appeared unshakeable. In England, he had bullied and coerced his magnates into submission. All of them, especially those who owed him money, feared the loss of the king's favour and none of them wanted to be the next William de Briouze. John had also carried out his successful campaigns in Scotland, Ireland and Wales between 1209 and 1211, and brought the rest of the British Isles to heel like no previous English king. The king's paramount aim, however, remained the recovery of his lost French territories. Everything he had done since the catastrophic events of 1204 had been in some way related to this, most of all his fund-raising. Of course, John's use of debt had an important disciplinary dimension, too, particularly when it came to keeping his barons in line and obedient; but in the end the money was intended to fund the most ambitious military operation any English king had ever undertaken. By 1212, John felt ready. His war chest was full of silver and his foreign alliances were in place. However, John's position suddenly appeared much more fragile in August 1212 when the king was told of a plot against him: he would either be murdered or his death would be engineered on his impending campaign in Wales. These were not just ugly rumours. John's critics had tired of his abrasive and extortionate methods. As well as exploiting their financial difficulties, it was alleged that John had taken far too keen an interest in the wives and daughters of his leading subjects.[20] Meanwhile a charismatic hermit, Peter of Wakefield, was travelling around northern

England predicting that John's reign would come to an end by the following Ascension Day, 23 May 1213. He could not say whether John would die, abdicate or be driven out of the land. But he claimed to have had a vision which foretold that, once the king had reigned for fourteen years, he and his heirs would rule no more. The king took Peter's conduct seriously enough to have him brought to court. When Peter was questioned in the king's presence and had the temerity to repeat his dire warnings ('Know for sure,' he said, 'that on the day I have named, you will be king no more'), he was taken away and imprisoned at Corfe Castle which only increased his notoriety and made John's regime look brittle and insecure.[21] The king was clearly nervous, and in response to the mounting pressure, he offered to make concessions, to rein in his financial demands and investigate the misconduct of his officials. This was not enough, though, and the tide was quickly turning against him. By the spring of 1213, King Philip of France was preparing a great invasion fleet. It would sail to England under the command of his son Louis. This was opportunistic, to be sure, but Philip was encouraged by the extent of the discontent that was rapidly coming to light in England and by Innocent III's hints that he was considering declaring John formally deposed.

Suddenly, after this dramatic change in the political weather, it had become essential for John to settle his quarrel with the pope. On 13 May 1213 he agreed to accept Langton as archbishop and allow him into the kingdom, and to pay compensation to the English Church for the damage it had suffered during the interdict. These terms were not very different from those that had been mooted several times before. However, something was new: two days later, John surrendered England and Ireland to the papacy and received them back as a vassal of the pope. In a way, and as at least one chronicler noted, Peter of Wakefield's prophecy had come true. By submitting to the pope, the king had lost supreme power in his kingdom.[22] But John's surrender of authority was largely theoretical, and in practice he continued to rule as before. Once Ascension Day had passed with John still king, for instance, Peter of Wakefield himself was dragged from his prison cell and hanged. This was spiteful and cruel, but John was now regaining his confidence. For as well as being his feudal overlord, the pope was now John's ally not his enemy; Innocent was now John's protector and anyone who attacked the English king would also have to deal with the pope. This was no abject surrender. It was a clever move, and if John's opponents had thought they had him on the run, he in turn had outmanoeuvred them. When John's ships caught the French invasion fleet at anchor in the Flemish port of Damme and destroyed it on 30 May, it must have seemed that the king's authority had been endorsed with divine favour. This impression was reinforced on 20 July in a ceremony at Winchester Cathedral, when the newly returned Archbishop Stephen Langton absolved the king from excommunication. John swore on the Gospels that he would love and defend the Church, revive the good laws of his ancestors and abolish bad laws, judge all men justly and give every man his rights. In reality, of course, whilst John had been at pains to make a new image for himself, his political and military aims had not changed. He was still set on his invasion of France.

Langton's priorities were somewhat different. There were thorny issues to settle. How much compensation would the king pay to the Church? How would episcopal elections be conducted in the future? But in all of this, Langton was hampered by his unfamiliarity with England and by the ill-defined nature of his role. He had spent next to no time in the kingdom since he had left for Paris as a boy in the 1160s. He was a stranger to its traditions and practices, its systems of government and methods of administration. And as for the bishops and barons with whom he now dealt, they may have deferred to his title, but they had little reason yet to have confidence in him as a man. Above all, Langton's relationship with the king was fraught with potential difficulties. John was interested in his own rights and his own plans, and he would do what he thought necessary to protect them. And of course the king had Innocent III to turn to if Langton got in his way. Now that John had submitted to the pope and become his vassal, Innocent was concerned to see that no further disputes soured his relationship with England. The pope's own envoys were already in England when Langton returned in July 1213, and they remained there, active on Innocent's behalf in secular and ecclesiastical affairs, for the rest of John's reign and beyond.

Quite where Langton was supposed to fit into all of this is unclear. The English must have been wary of him, the king must have tolerated him at best, and the pope didn't want any trouble. And it is in this context that Roger of Wendover's story about Langton's 'discovery' of Henry I's coronation charter must be put. This charter certainly played an important role in the conflicts to come, and it is easy to see why. It guaranteed the freedom of the Church and it bound the king to general promises of good government.[23] But its attempt to regulate the king's relationship with his barons in more specific ways would have struck a chord with John's leading men. In particulars, it appeared to set out the principle that the king should exercise his financial rights over his vassals' inheritances and their families justly and reasonably, not, as John was accused of doing, arbitrarily and vindictively. It was the closest thing to a guarantee against tyranny that John's critics had. And it is also quite possible that Langton knew about the charter (there is a copy of it in the Canterbury archives), even though he had only been back in the kingdom for just over a month when the meeting at St Paul's is supposed to have taken place. However, Langton's own fundamentally conservative beliefs on the nature of royal authority make such a scene highly unlikely. And even if he had wanted to play such a role, he was in no position in August 1213 to take sides and act as the radical leader of the English bishops and nobles against their king. Langton may have been back at the centre of affairs by then, but he also remained an outsider. Caught between king and pope and eyed uncertainly by bishops and barons, it is unlikely that he was trusted by any of them.

In the short term, however, this mattered little. And now that John's quarrel with the papacy was over, the king could revive his plans to invade France. After years of planning, diplomacy and fund-raising, his forces set sail for Poitou in February 1214. The plan was simple but grand. John's allies, his nephew Emperor Otto IV and the counts of Boulogne and Flanders, would strike against King Philip in the north, while John's troops would push up through southern France. To meet this two-pronged assault, the theory went, Philip would have no choice but to divide and so weaken his forces, leaving them at the mercy of either or both of the attacking armies. Unfortunately, the strategy failed in almost all respects. John found it much harder than expected to break out of his southern enclave; he had got as far as Angers by June but was then forced by a large French army to fall back to La Rochelle. Then, decisively, on 27 July 1214, John's allies were crushed by King Philip at the Battle of Bouvines in Flanders and John was left stranded and unable to respond. He eventually returned to England in October, having spent all of his money and with his reputation in shreds. This was the chance John's opponents had been waiting for, and they now started to challenge him openly.

The signs were already there before the disastrous French expedition had set sail. Many of John's barons had refused to accompany him to Poitou, arguing that, although they held land from him, they were not required to go on campaign with him overseas. Many had also refused to pay the tax that John had tried to impose on them in place of military service. John could disregard all this whilst his French campaign was under way, but by the end of 1214 the king was poor, defeated, and unable to ignore his critics. Influential men now felt able to pool the long-festering financial and personal grievances they had against the king and give collective voice to their demands for redress. In January 1215 the king met them at London; ominously, they came armed. Another meeting was fixed for Northampton at the end of April, and the king promised to reply there to the demands he had received for reform and confirmation of the charter of Henry I. This was probably no more than a stalling tactic, however. John was borrowing money to recruit mercenaries and on 4 March he took a vow to go on crusade, a move that prompted Innocent III to describe those who resisted the king as 'worse than Saracens'.[24] The Northampton meeting never took place and on 5 May the king's opponents formally renounced their fealty to him. When the city of London, with its vast resources and strong walls, opened its gates to the rebels on 17 May, it was clear that power was slipping away from John fast. He still had his supporters amongst the baronage, he had his mercenaries, and he still held castles throughout England. Nevertheless, if full-scale civil war was to be avoided, he would have to negotiate and do so seriously this time.

As the political situation deteriorated, Langton's task of preserving the peace and protecting the Church became ever more difficult. Frustratingly, though, it also becomes harder to get a sense of what he was actually doing as the arguments between John and the barons intensified. It has been traditional to see him as sympathetic to the rebels and, as time went on, as an increasingly dogged opponent of the king. He was a man of principle, the argument goes, a central figure in the negotiations and instrumental in formulating the barons' written demands. After all, as has been seen, the idea that a ruler should act according to law and proper judgement was covered by his teaching in Paris. However, it has also been argued that Langton's role during this period was limited. Far from being the barons' champion and the architect of their views, he was at best a mediator between the two sides and even, perhaps, no more than an intermediary carrying demands and counter-proposals back and forth. Having said this, Langton was certainly keen to reduce the scope for open conflict. Late in 1213, when the scale of baronial reluctance to accompany John to Poitou had become apparent, the archbishop had talked the king out of punishing his disobedient vassals without a formal judgment against them. But such conduct only got Langton into trouble with the pope. After John had taken his crusading vow in March 1215, Innocent criticised Langton for favouring the king's opponents and clearly the view in Rome was that the archbishop was becoming a problem. This was unfair, and at a distance of nearly a thousand miles and several weeks' travel, and with the reports of his own envoys and John's superficially impeccable conduct distorting the picture he was getting, Innocent's understanding of Langton's actions was anything but objective.

Ten days after the submission of London to the rebels in the middle of May 1215, representatives of the royal and baronial sides finally sat down to negotiate an end to their quarrel. Over the next two weeks, as the meetings continued in the great meadow beside the Thames at Windsor called Runnymede, the list of baronial demands became longer and more detailed and the outline of a settlement was beaten out. By 10 June, the final discussions were ready to begin and five days later the king was prepared to accept what was on the table in front of him. He quickly issued a charter, later called Magna Carta, which set out at great length and in unprecedented depth precisely what he was conceding. However, the conflict only came formally to an end four days later when the barons who had assembled for the negotiations also agreed to accept the deal.

Now there is no reason to doubt that Langton was busily involved in the events which culminated in the issue of Magna Carta. But this is not the same as saying that he was active in shaping the barons' demands. Various attempts have been made to link Langton directly with some of the documents which were prepared during these negotiations, and which served as preliminary drafts along the way to a final written settlement. However, none of these attempts has been really convincing. Indeed, it seems likely that Langton was involved in the negotiations reluctantly at best and that he had serious misgivings of his own about the legitimacy of the course the barons seemed intent upon pursuing. John had granted a charter to the English Church in November 1214 guaranteeing free elections in the future.[25] The king may just have been playing for time, and he did not surrender all his rights over such matters, but it was a step in the right direction as far as the ecclesiastical authorities were concerned. Either side of that concession, John had become a vassal of the papacy and a crusader. The idea of rebelling against such a man, even one as fickle and as untrustworthy as John, must have given a conservative like Langton pause for thought.

He may also have had qualms about the contents of the charter itself. For there is no doubt that the sixty-three separate clauses (or 'chapters', as historians call them) of Magna Carta amounted to the most radical, detailed and far-reaching attempt yet made to restrain and permanently limit royal power. The early clauses of the charter set out to regulate the king's relationship with his barons, particularly the ways in which he could use the lands they held from him to take their money and control their family affairs. For the first time, clear limits were set on the amounts the king could charge when the heir of such a baron (or 'tenant-in-chief') wanted to succeed to his predecessor's lands – £100 for succession to an earldom or a barony, £20 for a knight's fee (chapter 2). The charter also stipulated how far the king could go in exploiting the minorities and marriages of his barons' children (chapters 4 and 5), and it expressly prohibited the king from forcing the widows of his tenants-in-chief to re-marry against their will (chapters 6 and 8). In addition, it was also made clear that the king could raise certain kinds of taxation in the future only if he obtained the consent of 'the common counsel of our kingdom', later defined as an assembly made up of the king's lay and ecclesiastical tenants-in-chief (chapters 12 and 14). There were also sections of the charter that attempted to order the operations of the

judicial system and make royal justice more available and more equit-
able. Most famously, the king undertook to deny, sell or delay right and
justice 'to no one' (chapter 40) and 'no free man' was to lose his property,
be arrested, imprisoned or exiled, save 'by lawful judgement of his peers
or the law of the land' (chapter 39). It was in these parts of the charter
that later generations were to see the origins of parliamentary democracy and the rule of law. And finally (in chapter 61), in an attempt to
make John keep the promises he had made, a committee of twenty-five
barons was appointed to supervise the king's observance of the charter.
Of all the charter's provisions this was perhaps the most radical, because
it created a layer of political authority above the king. If the twenty-five
agreed that John had breached any provision of the charter, they 'with
the commune of all the land' had the power to seize his castles, lands
and possessions, and do whatever else they thought necessary 'until it is
redressed, according to their judgement'.[26]

Of course, if Langton had his doubts about the legitimacy of the
charter, he might have stepped aside entirely, leaving the king and his
opponents to thrash out a deal for themselves. However, he had to be
sure that, as the discussions drew to a close, the position of the Church
was safeguarded and its rights preserved. It was essential that, whatever
else it did or did not do, the king's charter dealt explicitly and clearly
with the one issue that meant more to him than any other, namely the
freedom of the Church. And that is exactly what it does right at the
start in its first substantive chapter. 'We have granted,' John said,

> ... to God and by this our present charter have confirmed, for us
> and for our heirs in perpetuity, that the English church is to be
> free, and is to have its rights in whole and its liberties unharmed, and
> we wish it to be observed; which is manifest from this, namely that
> the liberty of elections, which is deemed to be of the greatest impor-
> tance and most necessary for the English church, by our free and
> spontaneous will, before the discord moved between us and our
> barons, we granted and confirmed by our charter, and obtained its
> confirmation from the lord pope, Innocent the third, which we shall
> both observe and wish to be observed by our heirs in perpetuity in
> good faith.[27]

Here was more than just a formulaic, conventional opening to a royal charter of this kind. This concession, unlike all the ones that followed it in the charter, and unlike any similar clause in the charters of previous kings, was made directly and exclusively to God, not to the king's free subjects. The implication of this was that, if John's deal with his barons broke down, his concession to the Church was irrevocable and would still stand. Moreover, the careful wording of the clause and its reference to the charter of November 1214 made it clear that the king's desire to guarantee the freedom of the Church pre-dated the start of 'the discord moved between us and our barons'. In other words, at no point in the future would the king be able to argue that this part of the charter had been extracted from him by force or under threat of rebellion. At the same time, the very existence of the clause gave the Church a stake in the survival of the charter more generally and in the maintenance of the good government that it sought to promote. So somehow, despite the difficult position he found himself in and his own reservations about what was happening, Langton had managed to follow the orders the pope had given him on his return to England in 1213 to 'do all that you believe helpful to the salvation and peace of the king and kingdom, not forgetting the honour and advantage of the Apostolic See and the English church'.[28]

In the end, however, Langton's efforts proved futile. The opening clause of the charter may have purported to protect the freedom of the Church come what may, but, in the real world, the political peace needed to hold if any of the charter was to last. Soon enough it became clear that this was not going to happen. King and barons continued to doubt each other's good faith, and whilst John was prepared to pay lip service to the charter and make gestures towards the implementation of some of its clauses, he also sent his account of events to Rome and asked the pope to annul the offensive document. Meanwhile, whilst the king's more moderate opponents were determined to make him abide strictly by all of his written promises, the irreconcilable hardliners were arming themselves for a fight. It was only a matter of time before conflict resumed, and all of Langton's efforts to prevent this failed. He and the bishops, for example, tried unsuccessfully to bring the parties together at Oxford on 16 August and at Staines on the 28th. Meanwhile the archbishop had also become entangled in a dispute with the king over the control of Rochester Castle. Rochester was a royal castle, but Henry I had made the archbishops of Canterbury its custodians. The king nevertheless retained the power to appoint and dismiss Rochester's constables when he saw fit, and by the summer of 1215, with war imminent, John was keen to bring this strategically vital fortress, which controlled the main road from Dover and Canterbury to London, firmly under his control. So on 9 August he wrote to Langton and ordered him to hand over Rochester Castle to Peter des Roches, bishop of Winchester and one of John's staunchest supporters.[29] For some reason this transfer never took place. Perhaps Langton was worried that his position as mediator between the king and his opponents would be compromised if he complied with a request so obviously designed to strengthen the king's military position. In the event, two months later, the castle was seized by a group of rebels and the king himself only regained control of it after a bitter seven-week siege. John, triumphant but furious, immediately denounced Langton as a 'notorious and barefaced traitor to us, since he did not render up our castle of Rochester to us in our so great need'.[30]

By then, Langton had left England. His position had been weakened further when a letter from Pope Innocent arrived in the kingdom shortly after the king had requested the surrender of Rochester Castle.[31] The pope's letter was dated 7 July 1215, and it had been written in response to the complaints John had made to Innocent about the situation he faced in England at the end of May, so before the charter was even close to being issued. However, Innocent's fury at the way John's opponents had behaved is clear. The pope criticised the English bishops, too, not least Langton himself, for their failure to give adequate help to John against his enemies: their inaction had imperilled Innocent's plans for a crusade and John's participation in it. The pope proceeded to excommunicate 'all such disturbers of the king and the kingdom, together with their accomplices and supporters', he imposed an interdict on their lands, and he ordered Langton and the bishops to publish his sentences immediately. Of course, the pope's letter was unfair to Langton, who had done his best to bring about a settlement and protect the Church. But, more importantly, it was hopelessly out of date and events had overtaken it almost before it was written. If the papal sentences were implemented, an already tense situation would be made much worse. As a result, Langton refused to carry out the pope's orders without consulting him first, and so at the start of September he was suspended by the bishop of Winchester, Peter des Roches, the first addressee of the papal letter and the man whom the king had wanted to put in charge at Rochester.

Any small amount of trust that king and archbishop might have had in each other was definitely gone by September 1215. John had out-manoeuvred Langton, whilst the pope had failed to grasp both the extent and the subtlety of Langton's efforts on behalf of the Church. As he set out for Rome at the end of September to put his case to Innocent personally, the archbishop could have been forgiven for thinking that the last ten years had all been for nothing. This feeling can only have been compounded on 4 November 1215 when Pope Innocent III, the man who had chosen Langton as archbishop, consecrated him, and insisted so stridently on his acceptance by John, confirmed his suspension from office. By then, another letter from Innocent, this one condemning and annulling Magna Carta, had arrived in England and the civil war was under way.

CHAPTER TEN

THE MATRON'S TALE
Nicola de la Haye and the Defence of England

AFTER HER HUSBAND died, it was Nicola de la Haye who held the castle for the king both in war and in peace. But when King John came to visit Lincoln in 1216, she went to meet him, leaving the castle by the eastern postern gate with its keys in her hand. She offered them to John, her lord, humbly protesting that she was an old woman, looking after the castle was hard work, and it caused her much anxiety. She could not do the job any longer, she went on, and anyway she had no right or claim to the position she held. John replied sweetly and softly, 'My dear Nicola, it is my desire that you continue to keep the castle, until I order otherwise.' England was in turmoil, civil war was shaking the kingdom, and John calmly put his trust in a woman to hold one of the most important castles in England. Reluctantly, perhaps, Nicola did as she was instructed until the king was dead, and long after that too.[1]

This story was the stuff of local legend. It was not recorded until nearly sixty years after it was supposed to have happened, when King John's grandson, Edward I, carried out a great inquiry across England to investigate abuses in local government and the extent to which royal rights had been lost during another civil war, this time in the 1260s. This inquiry is known to historians as the Hundred Rolls, because evidence was given to the royal investigators by juries of local people from each hundred in each county, and that evidence was recorded on great parchment rolls. However, testimony was also given by juries from larger villages and towns, and one of those was the jury from Lincoln, which recounted the tale of Nicola de la Haye's meeting with King John in 1216. How accurately the jurors recalled the details of the meeting is unclear. It provides a rare example of John being pleasant, but that doesn't necessarily make it unreliable. In any event, by 1216, John and Nicola had experiences in common stretching back over twenty-five years; it is quite possible that they liked each other. Nicola died in 1230, so some of those Lincoln jurors from the 1270s may have known her in her final years; perhaps they had even heard this story from her own lips, or from someone who had been there with her. It is hard to believe, though, given what else is known about Nicola's career, that she would ever have been so meek and submissive, even before a king, as the jurors' account suggests, or that she would ever have thought of giving up any fight she was in because she was too old or too tired to keep going. Her tenacity and determination were shown clearly a year after John's visit, in 1217, when the earl of Salisbury, who was the uncle of the new boy king, Henry III, tried to take Lincoln Castle from her. Nicola's furious response was to make straight for the royal court where she reminded her audience of all the faithful service she had given to King John and his infant son, and she obtained an order restoring the castle to her. It remained in her custody until 1226 when she retired on her own terms.

* * * *

It is commonly said that England has resisted invasion successfully ever since 1066. This is not quite true. Henry IV, Henry VII and William III all overthrew a reigning monarch after arriving in England with an army. However, there have been unsuccessful attempts to invade too. Probably the most famous of these were in 1588 and 1940, two years which, in their own way, have done much to forge notions of, first, English and, later, British national identity. But another such failure, which arguably came closer than either the Spanish Armada or Operation Sea Lion to conquering England, is less well known. It took place in 1216–17, after the peace agreed at Runnymede in the summer of 1215 had collapsed, and when King John's opponents at home had taken up arms against him and been joined by supporters from across the Channel led by the son of the French king. So when John came to Lincoln and commanded Nicola de la Haye to stay at her post, it was a time of grave peril for him, his dynasty and his kingdom. Exactly 150 years had passed since William of Normandy had landed at Pevensey Bay, and England was once again teetering on the edge of conquest by a French prince.

The events that took place at Lincoln during the next eighteen months were crucial to the eventual fate of that invasion. And that a woman was at the heart of everything that happened makes them more remarkable still. Nicola's tale provides an almost unique example from this period of a woman carrying out what were universally perceived as a man's traditional duties. Other women performed military roles at this time: both Joan of Sicily and Matilda de Briouze did so, as has been seen. But their experiences were singular and exceptional, untypical of their lives more generally. Nicola, by contrast, was heavily involved throughout her adult life at the highest levels of politics, government and society, where she successfully combined the roles of landholder, royal official and military leader. And she did so, what is more, at a time of acute national danger. Contemporaries struggled to find the language to describe her, so unaccustomed were they to what she did: for one she was a 'noble woman' who behaved 'manfully'.[2] But this story is not just about the way Nicola successfully challenged conventional views of femininity. Nor was this short period just about resolute defence and derring-do. Because this invasion was defeated politically as well as militarily. Of course, the English armies had their conventional arms and they used them well, not least in the streets of Lincoln itself. But they developed and deployed another weapon with great skill, too, namely Magna Carta. This was a new kind of propaganda war, a war 'for hearts and minds', as modern commentators might say. To undermine his opponents, John's heir, his young son Henry III, was promoted to his people in a new and extraordinary way. The charter was used by the embattled English government to promise a fresh and hopeful start; royal rule, yes, but not arbitrary or fickle like John's had been. There would be clear limits to what a king could do in the future as well as defined norms of royal conduct and behaviour. It was during these months that the charter so grudgingly given by King John, which had looked irrelevant and even meaningless in the summer of 1215, was revived by his successor's regime, took its place at the heart of English politics and government, and became a permanent feature of the constitutional landscape. And as this happened, a new relationship between ruler and ruled began to take shape.

* * * *

In 1215, Magna Carta was a failure. More than that, it seemed, it was a failure without a future. But whilst the charter had certainly not brought peace to England, this was probably inevitable. King John was never going to do what his more moderate opponents wanted and stick to the letter of his promises. He made some concessions and dealt with a few grievances in the weeks after Runnymede. But these were only gestures and the king had also written secretly to the pope asking for the charter to be annulled. Eventually, in the autumn, Innocent III's response was made public in England: the settlement forced upon the king in June was 'not only shameful and base but also illegal and unjust'. The pope condemned it outright and threatened to excommunicate anyone who tried to put its terms into practice.[3] Meanwhile, there were still plenty of hard-line rebels in England in the summer of 1215 who thought the charter had not been radical enough in its attempt to restrict the king's power. They were determined to get rid of him whatever he did. Like the Treaty of Versailles seven centuries later, Magna Carta was a compromise that satisfied no one and which only led to war.

By September 1215, King John was on the Kent coast waiting for his mercenaries to arrive from Flanders. Meanwhile his opponents had marched on the archbishop of Canterbury's great castle at Rochester in the hope of taking it and cutting off John's approach to London, which was still in rebel hands. The keeper of the castle, Reginald of Cornhill, until this time a loyal servant of the royal regime, offered no resistance and Rochester surrendered meekly. John was forced to besiege the castle himself and only took it back after a determined and intensive seven-week effort. 'Living memory does not recall a siege so fiercely pressed or so staunchly resisted,' claimed the anonymous thirteenth-century monk known as the Barnwell chronicler.[4] Meanwhile, the rebel leaders based in London knew that they needed help. Their cause was strongest in the northern and eastern parts of England, but even within those areas the king's supporters controlled dozens of castles. John's mercenaries were now arriving in large numbers from Flanders, too, and the rebels desperately needed an army of their own. To find one, they looked across the English Channel; more specifically, they offered the crown to Louis, the son of Philip II, if he would come to England and help depose John. King Philip, concerned not to antagonise the pope, distanced himself from the rebel cause, but Louis was keener to consider the appeal and he sent a contingent of his knights to London in November 1215. Unless and until Louis himself arrived in England with a sizeable army, however, the military initiative would remain with John.

This was clearly demonstrated between December 1215 and March 1216 when John and his army undertook an expedition first to the north of his kingdom and then back to the south. By the middle of January he was at Berwick having seen off attempts by Alexander, king of Scots, to take advantage of the unrest in England and stake a claim to Northumbria. But by the middle of March he was at Colchester receiving the surrender of the rebel garrison there. This was an impressively dominant, albeit largely unopposed, demonstration of military force, and whilst John refilled his treasure chests with the money his terrified subjects offered him not to devastate their lands, his mercenaries took the chance to feed off the countryside as they intimidated and in some cases butchered the opposition they met. By the spring of 1216, John had reasserted his control over the north and east of England and only London still held out against him. It was at this point, however, with John seemingly on the point of winning the war, that Prince Louis decided to invade England.

Whilst John had been on his three-month trek around the kingdom, Louis had been sending reinforcements to London. On 21 May 1216 the prince himself landed at Thanet with 1,200 knights, only days after the fleet John had gathered to resist the invasion had been destroyed by storms. Louis tried hard to justify his attempt to seize power. He made a claim to the throne through his wife, Blanche, Henry II's granddaughter. He also argued that John had never been the rightful king of England, since he had been judged a traitor by Richard I's court in the 1190s. And even if John had succeeded Richard legally in 1199, he had been condemned by the French court and effectively deposed after murdering Arthur of Brittany. More important than any of these theories, though, was the fact that Louis had been invited by the rebellious English barons to take power; for them, Louis was not John (for one thing the French prince had a reputation for piety, chastity and loyalty, in stark contrast to his adversary), and that was enough. And with Louis' arrival in England, the course of the civil war changed dramatically. Suddenly John was vulnerable again as his opponents, who had been forced to submit to him earlier in the year, found in Louis a renewed focus for their resistance. Influential men, the earls of Arundel, Surrey and York, for example, came out into the open and sided with Louis, as did John's own half-brother, William, earl of Salisbury. John fought on, of course, and retained influential support of his own: William Marshal and Earl Ranulf of Chester were still loyal, the crucial stronghold of Dover was held for John by his justiciar Hubert de Burgh, and John's men in the north of England were standing firm against the ever-opportunistic king of Scots.

England was divided and, perhaps unsurprisingly, by the summer of 1216 the war had reached stalemate. John had decided not to challenge the invaders head on. Instead he withdrew to the west of his kingdom and left his men to defend their strongpoints as best they could. The strategy worked and Louis failed to fulfil his early promise of a quick victory. What is more, although the prince attracted a considerable amount of support after his arrival in England (London was still in rebel hands and perhaps two-thirds of the English barons were on Louis' side by this point), that support was fragile. There are indications that tension had been quick to grow between his French supporters, eager for English lands, and the English rebels who, of course, wanted to keep and extend theirs. The earls of Salisbury and York abandoned Louis and returned to John, and 'day by day', in the words of the Dunstable annalist, 'the adherents of the Frenchmen dwindled'.[5] This was John's chance, and he acted decisively. The king left his base in the Cotswolds in mid-September 1216 and headed east. His objective was Lincoln Castle, a royalist bastion under rebel siege. Holding the line there was the castellan, Nicola de la Haye.

For a woman to be in charge of any castle at all, let alone an old woman and a castle that was perhaps the most important strategic and military site in eastern England, was certainly extraordinary. But then

Nicola de la Haye was an extraordinary woman. She was the eldest of the three daughters of Richard de la Haye who, like his father before him, had been appointed castellan of Lincoln by royal grant. When Richard died in about 1169, he left no sons to succeed him, so his lands were divided between Nicola and her sisters as co-heiresses. For her part, Nicola inherited the barony of Brattleby just to the north of Lincoln, but she also inherited a claim to be castellan of Lincoln itself. So if she was not a particularly wealthy heiress, her unusual inheritance gave any husband she might have a means to establish or extend his power and influence within Lincolnshire and in royal service. Her first marriage, to a man called William Fitz Erneis, cannot have lasted long. He was dead by the end of the 1170s, and unfortunately next to nothing is known about him or his life with Nicola, except that they had a daughter, Matilda. We can only speculate, too, about how old Nicola was when she became a widow, but she was probably about thirty by the time of her second marriage, which had taken place by 1185. Nicola's new husband, Gerard de Canville, was well connected and ambitious. His father had been a loyal supporter of King Stephen, but he then served Henry II until his death in 1176 when his eldest son, Gerard, succeeded him in most of his lands. Gerard himself was also known at the court of Henry II where he appeared, regularly if not frequently, as a witness to the king's charters in the 1170s and 1180s. His younger brother, Richard, was later a commander of Richard I's crusading fleet in 1190; he was appointed governor of Cyprus in 1191 but died that year during the siege of Acre. Royal connections such as these probably led to Gerard's marriage to Nicola, and in August 1189 the couple travelled all the way to Normandy for a royal charter confirming their inheritance in both England and Normandy from the new king, Richard I. This grant, which cost the couple just over £450, included Lincoln Castle as it had been held by Nicola's father and grandfather, and the shrievalty of the county of Lincoln was probably also included in the grant.[6]

Gerard's record of royal service was not unblemished, however. Whilst his brother was on crusade with Richard I, back in England Gerard became entangled in the dispute between the king's chancellor, Bishop William de Longchamp of Ely, and the king's brother, John.

Longchamp was supposed to have accompanied Richard on crusade, but in April 1190 the king sent him back to England to take charge of the royal government. In June he was also named papal legate for England by Pope Clement III. Longchamp was neither slow nor reluctant to assert his authority. He presided over ecclesiastical councils at Gloucester in August and at Westminster in October 1190. And he excluded the bishop of Durham, Hugh du Puiset, whom Richard had appointed justiciar for the north of England, from any role in central government. By the end of the year he had launched an expedition against Rhys ap Gruffudd, the most powerful prince in south Wales. Along the way he made a concerted effort to raise as much money as possible for the king whilst managing to make two of his brothers sheriffs. All of this activity caused resentment amongst the members of the established English baronage. Perceived by them as a low-born foreign upstart, Longchamp's financial exactions, his preference for officials of his own, and the extravagance of his entourage were bound to provoke. His high-handed manner only made things worse and he became an obvious target for the ambitions of the king's brother, John, count of Mortain. John was keen to expand his authority over the kingdom whilst Richard was away and he was adept at exploiting the baronial opposition to Longchamp's authoritarian rule.

One of the barons who took John's side in this quarrel was Gerard de Canville, by this time, of course, sheriff of Lincolnshire and, through his wife Nicola, keeper of Lincoln Castle. The chronicler Richard of Devizes picks up the story after Gerard ('a factious man, prodigal of his allegiance', Richard called him) had repudiated Longchamp's authority and performed homage to John.[7] The conflict turned on the custody of castles. Whoever controlled the most important of these would almost certainly win out. On hearing of Gerard's desertion, Longchamp dismissed him as sheriff and ordered the surrender of Lincoln Castle. Undeterred, Gerard and John set out together to besiege the castle at Nottingham and the one at Tickhill in south Yorkshire. Both were vital strategic points on the north-south route through England and both surrendered, Richard of Devizes says, 'solely through fear'. As for the castle at Lincoln, crucial in its own way to the control of eastern England, it was left under the command of Nicola de la Haye. According to our chronicler, Gerard's faith in his wife's abilities was justified. 'Putting aside all her womanly instincts,' Richard admiringly records, 'she defended the castle like a man.' And this was no easy task. Longchamp himself brought troops, many of whom were professional mercenaries, up to the walls of Lincoln and laid siege to it for over a month. But the garrison under Nicola's leadership never surrendered, and the siege was only lifted when John and Longchamp were persuaded to negotiate a truce. One of the terms agreed in July 1191 was that Gerard de Canville should be allowed to remain in possession of Lincoln Castle.

Nicola and Gerard had been rewarded for their loyalty to John, and Gerard remained his committed supporter in 1193 when John tried to seize power in England after Richard's capture on his way home from crusade. But such success was short-lived. When Richard I finally returned to England in 1194, he was quick to punish those who had sided with John in his absence. Gerard lost the custody of Lincoln Castle and his position as sheriff of Lincolnshire. He also had to offer the enormous sum, just over £1,330, in order to keep his lands and, as the royal records put it, the king's 'goodwill'. As for Nicola, she made her own offer to the king of £200 to safeguard her right to arrange her daughter's marriage to anyone except an enemy of the king.[8] She and Gerard were now effectively on probation; suspect, perhaps even traitorous, in the eyes of the royal government. The rest of Richard's reign must have been difficult for them, deprived as they were of their accustomed status and influence. If nothing else, they had lost their splendid castle. John did not forget his old friend, though. When he became king in 1199, Gerard was reappointed as custodian of Lincoln Castle, and he also became sheriff of Lincolnshire once again. This time he held the post until 1205. In 1208 he re-surfaces in the records working hard for the king supervising the administration of the revenues of the diocese of Lincoln during the interdict, and in 1208–9 he served as a royal justice in Lincolnshire and Cambridgeshire.

Meanwhile, Nicola remained in the shadows. There are occasional references to her in the royal financial records, usually concerning the debt she had contracted in 1194 to keep control of her daughter's marriage. In 1200 she renegotiated the amount with King John, but in 1201 she still owed £40 and one palfrey.[9] She had two sons with Gerard too, Richard, who married in 1200, and Thomas. But it was not until after her husband's death that Nicola began to play a prominent part of her own in public life once again. Gerard de Canville died shortly before January 1215, when his eldest son succeeded to his lands. But as an unmarried widow, no longer legally subordinated to a husband who could exercise her rights during their marriage, Nicola was now able to take personal control of the inheritance she had received from her father over forty-five years ago. Part of this, of course, was the position of castellan of Lincoln.

Perhaps because he remembered how successful Nicola had been on his behalf in defending Lincoln Castle in 1191, John was happy to have her there at another particularly difficult time. The king's continental plans had been destroyed on the battlefield at Bouvines in July 1214, and by early 1215 baronial opposition was growing. London fell to the rebels in May and Magna Carta was forced out of the king in June. By early 1216, the civil war was raging and control of Lincolnshire was crucial if John's cause was to hold up in eastern England. He went to Lincoln twice in 1216, in February and September, and it was on one of these occasions, so the story goes, that he rejected Nicola's offer to resign her position as castellan. She had already proved her worth by the time of John's second visit. During August 1216 the city had been attacked by a force under Gilbert de Gant, who had been recognised as earl of Lincoln by Prince Louis. Gilbert took the city but he failed to capture the castle and Nicola was able to buy a truce. One writer, the anonymous Barnwell chronicler, wrote in admiring and complimentary terms about the 'matrona' called Nicola, who kept Lincoln Castle out of rebel hands.[10] The use of this Latin word to describe her reflected Nicola's age, certainly, but it suggests much more than this too, with its connotations of maturity, wisdom and experience.

John still had need of Nicola's loyal and effective service and, as if to make this clear, on 18 October 1216, only hours before his death that very night, he appointed her sheriff of Lincolnshire alongside another loyalist, Philip Mark.[11] This was unprecedented: there is no record of a woman serving as the sheriff of any English county before Nicola. Even in peaceful times, as the king's chief official in the shire, the sheriff had a range of onerous fiscal, judicial and military duties to perform. In wartime, however, the sheriffs' importance was enhanced significantly, and it was their job to control their counties and keep them pacified and loyal. The sheriff was expected to exercise huge influence over the leading figures and families of the shire, and Nicola's appointment was a striking testament to her standing in the county, and to John's faith in her abilities. What is more, her gender was clearly no bar to her doing the job. To be sure, she was not the only sheriff of Lincolnshire named on John's deathbed, but Philip Mark was already sheriff of the neighbouring county of Nottinghamshire and presumably he had to spend time there. In fact, there is little to suggest that he played much of a role in Lincolnshire affairs after his appointment, and in January 1217 another man, Geoffrey de Serland, was appointed to serve as sheriff of Lincolnshire, but this time expressly 'under our beloved lady Nicola de la Haye'.[12]

There is no reason to think that Nicola's appointment was simply an empty gesture or that she was just a figurehead. At a time of national crisis, she was the woman the king and his successors relied on to keep this vital part of eastern England in line, and by early 1217 she was exerting her authority as sheriff by supervising the transfer of hostages and confiscating the lands of local rebels. But England remained at war and Nicola's principal duty was still military. By now, of course, King John was dead, and the resistance to Prince Louis was being carried on in the name of the new king, John's nine-year-old son, Henry III, by a regency government led by the papal legate, Guala, and William Marshal, earl of Pembroke. The situation looked bleak. At the end of 1216, Louis controlled London and nearly all of the eastern half of England; the rulers of Scotland and north Wales were his allies and, within England itself, two-thirds of the greatest barons were on his side. Nevertheless, the ecclesiastical establishment backed Henry III (no English bishop supported Louis, so he could not have had himself crowned even if he wanted to!), in western England the young king's support was also solid and, even in rebel territory, there were pockets of staunch loyalist resistance. At Dover, Corfe, Newark and Newcastle, and at other strongholds across the kingdom, not least at Nottingham under Philip Mark and at Lincoln under Nicola de la Haye, the king's adherents were dug in, well supplied, and ready for a long war. Louis knew, as did the Barnwell chronicler, that 'the royal castles were many and well-fortified'.[13] What is more, Henry III's greatest asset was that he was not his father. It would be hard for those rebels with personal grievances against John to make the same criticisms of his infant son, especially if there now appeared to be a realistic prospect of those grievances being addressed. So when Guala and the Marshal issued a revised version of Magna Carta in November 1216 in the name of the new king, it was designed to weaken and fracture the opposition by holding out to them the promise of a new approach to government.[14]

Despite the apparent strength of Louis' position at the end of 1216, the onus was on him to act quickly if he was to retain his advantage. This was easier said than done, and although he managed to tighten his hold on East Anglia and besiege a few royal castles, by January 1217 he was forced to agree to a three-month truce. The fact was that he needed more troops and he had to return to France to raise them. Whilst he was away, his support within England began to show signs of strain and in March the Marshal's eldest son, also called William, and Henry III's uncle, the earl of Salisbury, deserted his cause and returned to the royalist side. Numbers of lesser men defected, too, unsure whether Louis would ever return. Before the prince left, though, he had travelled to Lincoln. By February 1217 the city had been taken once more by Gilbert de Gant. But when Louis arrived there, according to a chronicler who was with the French army during the war, he found the castle still firmly under Nicola de la Haye's control and 'she kept the guard very loyally'.[15] The siege continued after Louis' departure; if anything it intensified as reinforcements arrived to strengthen the attack. One English chronicler, as has been seen, was keen to record the progress of the siege 'in which a noble woman, by the name of Nicola, manfully defended herself', whilst another also applauded her for behaving 'manfully'.[16] The use of such language is certainly striking: clearly, no greater compliment could be paid to a woman than to say she was acting like a man! In the end, recognising the significance of the events unfolding at Lincoln, the royal government ordered its supporters to gather at Newark in Nottinghamshire in May. They would march east from there to relieve the siege. Half of Louis' army, and the prince himself, who had returned to England at the end of April, were still besieging Dover. If

the royalists could defeat the other half at Lincoln, they might well deal
a mortal blow to Louis' cause in England.

The royal army took shape at Newark on 17–18 May. It takes about
half an hour today to drive the eighteen miles or so from Newark to
Lincoln along the A46. In 1217 it was a tolerable day's march for a force
made up, according to the biographer of William Marshal, of 405
knights and 317 crossbowmen (he makes no mention of the infantry),
and by the early morning of 20 May the regent's troops were drawn up
along the north-western wall of the city.[17] The Marshal's plan appears
initially to have depended on Louis' supporters, under the command of
the count of Perche, leaving the safety of the city in order to fight on the
open plain outside the walls. There was no guarantee of success even if
this happened: the Marshal's biographer estimated that there were 611
French knights and about a thousand infantry at Lincoln, 'not counting
the English with them'.[18] But, and more pertinently, the Anglo-French
army was safe and secure where it was, and there was no compelling
reason why it should venture out and risk all in a pitched battle. It made
military sense to reject the royalist challenge, and the count of Perche
decided to keep his troops where they were until Louis himself arrived
with reinforcements. The pressure was now on the Marshal to come up
with a different strategy before this happened and he must have been
grateful indeed for the intelligence he received at this point from the
bishop of Winchester, Peter des Roches. At great personal risk, Bishop
Peter had managed to get into the castle through an entrance that
formed part of the western wall of the city, and from there onto the city
streets. There he had discovered a disused, blocked-up gate further
along the western wall of the city to the north of the castle. He was sure
it could be opened and used as the royalists' point of entry. The Marshal's
biographer describes how, during his daring mission, Peter met Nicola
in one of the towers of the castle and reassured her that the siege would
shortly be raised. She was reportedly 'full of joy' to see him and hear the
news.[19] Meanwhile the Anglo-French army had to be distracted whilst
work to unblock the gate got under way. So the earl of Chester threw
himself and his troops at the city's north gate whilst a second royalist
force entered the castle and took up its positions. As the royalist cross-
bowmen began to fire down into the city from the castle ramparts, the

foot soldiers burst out of the castle's main entrance and into the
surrounding streets. The castle and cathedral at Lincoln face each other
across a gap of about 200 yards and the first hand-to-hand fighting of
the battle must have taken place here. But it soon moved down the steep
hill connecting the upper and lower parts of the city, and the confused
Anglo-French army, having been forced to pull back, lost any chance of
responding to what was happening at the now unblocked western gate
to the north of the castle. It had been opened easily and the royalist
troops were now pouring through. So keen was the seventy-year-old
Marshal to take the lead that he would have rushed his horse into the
city without his helmet on had his squire not pulled him back. But once
properly armoured, he charged deep into the mêlée ('over a distance
greater than three spears' length', his biographer claimed) outside the
cathedral.[20] There the count of Perche was fatally wounded when a
spear went through his visor. Nevertheless, before he fell from his horse,
he was able to aim three great blows at the Marshal and dent the helmet
that the regent had almost left behind.

The Anglo-French army had been completely surprised by the
sudden boldness of the royalist attack. The Marshal and his men had
secured the upper part of the city and when their opponents' attempt to
regroup and fight their way back up the hill towards the castle failed,
the battle was effectively over. Those supporters of Louis who did not
manage to escape through the southern gate at the river end of the city
were captured and held for ransom later. The earls of Winchester,
Hereford and Hertford were taken along with numerous other high-
profile partisans of the French prince, including Nicola's long-time rival
Gilbert de Gant. Her unshakeable defence of Lincoln Castle had lasted
well over a year and it was vital to the outcome of the battle and for
the future of England. Without access to the castle and, through it, to
the city, it is hard to see how the Marshal's army could have forced a
victory. The regent would have been left stranded outside Lincoln and,
if Louis had moved quickly, he might have been able to crush the life
out of the Henrician cause against the walls of the city. The Battle of
Lincoln on 20 May 1217 did not at one stroke end Prince Louis'
campaign in England. However, later events were to show how it had
turned the tide of the war decisively against him. The young Henry III,

who was at Nottingham when he heard about the victory, owed Nicola a great debt. So did William Marshal, who had staked England's political destiny on success at Lincoln. It is no wonder that William's biographer referred to Nicola as 'that worthy lady (may God protect her in body and soul!)'.[21]

Louis was still at Dover when news was brought to him on 25 May of the disastrous events at Lincoln. He promptly lifted the siege he had been conducting since July of the previous year, made for London and sued for peace. Three weeks later, the outlines of a workable agreement were in place: Louis would release his English supporters from their oaths of loyalty to him and they would be allowed to recover the lands they had held at the beginning of the war; he would return the lands he had seized; prisoners on both sides would be released. Unfortunately, however, the negotiations foundered on points of detail and, once they had stalled, Louis' supporters began to submit to the regency government in large numbers. Between May 1217 and the middle of August, over 150 men formally abandoned his cause, and Louis' attempt to conquer England finally came to an end on 24 August when the ships carrying his reinforcements from France were routed just off Sandwich by an English fleet under the command of Hubert de Burgh, the defender of Dover Castle. This was a remarkable victory by all accounts, as the French fleet was far larger than the English one. But the decisive moment came when the French flagship was seized. Its captain was Eustace the Monk, whose career up until this point had been colourful to say the least. Before taking his monastic vows, he is reputed to have studied black magic in Spain. Later, his career in the cloister presumably having proved unsatisfying, he became an outlaw in the forests near Boulogne, only then to take up piracy, preying on shipping in the English Channel. He was employed occasionally by King John as a kind of privateer in his struggle with Philip II, but in 1212 he switched sides to serve the French king. He commanded the fleet that brought Louis to England in 1216, but his luck ran out a year later. Weighted down with a great missile-launching trebuchet, thirty-six knights, their retinues and their horses, as well as treasure, his ship was low in the water, slow, and an easy target. Quickly surrounded, it was boarded after the English threw pots of powdered lime down on to its deck from high up in the rigging of one of their own ships that had drawn up alongside. Blinded and confused, Eustace's men could do nothing to prevent their attackers coming aboard. Eustace himself was eventually found hiding deep below in the bilges. He tried to buy his freedom with an offer of £6,667, but the English sailors, many of whom had suffered at Eustace's piratical hands in the past, only gave him one choice: would he have his head cut off on the side of the ship or on the great trebuchet which he was carrying to England?

Louis learned of his forces' defeat in the Channel two days later, on 26 August 1217. With the Marshal about to begin his blockade of London, the prince had no choice but to make as good a peace deal as he could. In September, first at a meeting on an island in the Thames near Kingston, and then at a larger assembly at Lambeth, Louis renounced his claim to the English throne whilst managing to retain for his lay supporters that provision from the June negotiations which allowed them to keep the lands they had held before the war. On 23 September he sailed back to France. Six weeks later the government of King Henry III issued Magna Carta once again, bringing it a step closer to its final and definitive form. And it was from this point, too, that it started being referred to as 'Magna' Carta, to distinguish it from a second, smaller, document issued in 1217, which dealt exclusively with the law of the royal forest.[22] In 1215 the charter had caused war and taken England into a chaotic and uncertain future; in 1217 it announced that war was over and that Henry III was the undisputed king. During these two turbulent years, its life as the cornerstone of the English constitution had begun.

And what of Nicola de la Haye? Despite all her efforts on behalf of the ruling dynasty, her own struggles were not yet at an end, and she had to fight hard to keep her position after the civil war. In doing so she showed once again all the toughness that had characterised her career so far. Only four days after the Battle of Lincoln, on 24 May 1217, she was removed from her post of sheriff of Lincolnshire and replaced by Henry III's uncle, the earl of Salisbury. For good measure, the earl seized Lincoln Castle as well, and it was this outrage that prompted Nicola to travel to the royal court to get her castle back. Salisbury was ordered to return to her the castle, the city and the county; but even this victory was fleeting. In December 1217, Nicola was ordered to stand down as sheriff once again in favour of the earl, although she kept control of Lincoln and its castle.

Salisbury's hostility towards Nicola requires some explaining. After Nicola's husband Gerard de Canville had died in 1215, their son Richard was left as his heir. But Richard died early in 1217, leaving a daughter, Idonea, to inherit both the Canville lands and probably, in due course, Nicola's estates and offices too. Now it just so happened that Idonea was betrothed to the son of the earl of Salisbury. When it had been arranged prior to Gerard de Canville's death, this marriage was clearly prestigious and a sign of the esteem in which Nicola's family was held at court. However, with Gerard and Richard dead, only Nicola stood in the way of a significant transfer of assets and wealth into the hands of Salisbury's family. Salisbury claimed that he had a right to take control of Idonea's inheritance because his son (her fiancé) was still a minor; but, whatever the merits of this argument, his attitude towards Nicola after 1217 suggests that he was trying to force the issue. Earl William was no ordinary rival either. He had sided with Prince Louis after the latter had landed in England in 1216, but later in the war he had returned to the royalist side. After that he had played a conspicuous role in the royalist victory at Lincoln (it was probably as a reward for his actions there that he was made sheriff of Lincolnshire), in the sea battle off Sandwich, and in the negotiations at Lambeth that brought Louis' invasion to an end. After 1217, in other words, he was one of the most powerful men in the kingdom and not to be challenged lightly. Nicola refused to be intimidated, though, even in 1219 when the earl went so far as to attack her in Lincoln Castle, and force her to defend her walls once again. In the end a royal army came to her relief and in August the earl was ordered in stern terms to respect 'our beloved and faithful Nicola de la Haye'.[23] But this only prompted him to change tactics. Early in 1220 news reached the king that the earl had been trying to get into Lincoln Castle again, this time by offering his son and nephew as hostages. This approach failed too, and for the next six years Nicola held the castle with little incident. It may be no coincidence that she finally gave up its custody only in June 1226, three months after Salisbury's death. Her last battle had been won, and Nicola retired to her estates. She died peacefully at her manor of Swaton in southern Lincolnshire in 1230.

Dreams and Fortune

THE DREAM COULD not have been more vivid. The procession carried
the king's corpse into the church after nightfall and placed it in the
left-hand aisle. But the unexpected activity and the lights below had
disturbed the sleeping rooks, crows and jackdaws roosting in the beams
above and they took flight, knocking all the hanging, fiery torches to the
floor. As they fell the flames went out and the torches were smashed
into pieces as they hit the ground. Meanwhile, the startled birds had
flown down low into the church and knocked over the two large candles
standing either side of the dead king's feet. At the same time, the other
two candles, one placed on either side of his head, spontaneously came
out of their holders and clattered to the ground before anyone could
steady them. All the lights had now gone out, and with the church in
complete darkness, the terrified and confused company fled frantically
out of the building. The king's body was left alone 'completely devoid of
human solace, as if it were haunted by unclean things'.[1]

Just as this book started with a fantastic account by Gerald of Wales
describing the mythical origins of the Angevin dynasty, so it ends with
another of his fabulous stories, this time about the Angevins' demise.
For the corpse at the centre of this dream (Gerald's own dream, he tells
us) was Henry II's, and the candles that surrounded him only to be
prematurely snuffed out represented his four sons: the two at his feet
knocked over by the birds stood for young Henry and Geoffrey of
Brittany, who both predeceased their father, whilst the two at his head,

which fell unassisted onto the cold stone floor, represented Richard and John, who both brought about their own downfalls after Henry's death. There is plenty of other symbolism in the account too. Of course the events took place at night when bad things invariably happen. Henry's corpse was placed on the left, or unlucky, side of the church (the Latin for left is 'sinister'). The birds themselves, all black, were ominous and threatening. Perhaps they embodied demons or evil spirits; but their frenzied flight around the church and through the crowd, unsettling enough in itself as an idea, evoked a world of chaos and disorder. And the extinguishing of all the lights needs little interpretation. The Angevin realm, riven by disorder, instability and anarchy, had been pitched into darkness. Only an abandoned, hollow cadaver remained – carrion for predators.

Now it is only right to say that Gerald of Wales was hardly a neutral observer when it came to the Angevins. He finished the work called *On the Instruction of a Prince*, from which this account of his dream (as well as the story of Mélusine) is taken, just after King John's death. By then, Gerald was a bitter and disenchanted man. Between 1184 and 1196, as a younger, more optimistic Gerald was celebrating the achievements of his pioneering relatives in *The Conquest of Ireland*, he was also actively involved in royal service and so intimately acquainted with the Angevins' ruling style and methods, as well as the turbulence of court life and the resentments and rivalries it created. But Gerald was above all else an ambitious clergyman, and the great disappointment of his life was his failure to become a bishop. For this he blamed the Angevin kings, who had refused to promote him to the see of St David's in Wales, first in 1176 and again, this time much more acrimoniously, after 1198. On the second occasion, Gerald was even elected bishop by the canons of St David's, but neither King John nor Archbishop Hubert Walter would accept his appointment: in Gerald's view, this was because he was too Welsh! Whether this was the real reason or not, Gerald's feelings of rejection were profound and he never stopped seeing himself as a wronged man who had suffered great injustice at the hands of sinful tyrants. In 1216–17, the time when Gerald was completing *On the Instruction of a Prince*, he was a keen supporter of Louis of France's invasion of England (he even wrote a poem in praise of the French prince) and he enthusiastically anticipated a Capetian takeover of the kingdom and all the good things that would surely, in his view, follow from that.

Louis' triumph never materialised, of course, and Gerald's hopes of a French victory were dashed. Nevertheless, and despite its extravagant sermonising and prevailing sense of personal injustice, there is something worth emphasising in Gerald's view of the Angevins. He rightly saw their story as one of rise and fall. Until roughly 1185, Gerald argued, Henry II faced challenges, mainly from his own family and the French kings. But he overcame them all and he even survived the shame of his involvement in Becket's death to be largely successful in everything he did. Crude though it is, this analysis is not too dissimilar from what actually happened. Then, in the last part of his reign, things started to go wrong for Henry and he had a miserable end, pursued and humiliated by his sons and their resurgent ally Philip II. Again, there is more than a little truth in this view of Henry's final years. Gerald attributed all of this to Henry's failure to acknowledge the divine role in his success: he was not grateful enough to God and so he was punished. But Gerald also widens the context: to be sure, Henry II was the main character in this particular story, but the Angevins were tainted stock and so bound to fail sooner or later. They were greedy tyrants who overstretched themselves and paid the price for their ambition, pride and selfishness. Now no modern historian would support interpretations based on this kind of moralising. The strengths and weaknesses of individual rulers, as well as major social, economic and political trends, all played a part in these developments, and historians can weigh up the relative contributions of different factors in ways that contemporaries could not. But the fact remains that Angevin power, so quick to rise and seemingly supreme by the mid-1180s, had collapsed within thirty years of Henry II's death. The dynasty survived, of course, but only just and at a great cost.

Meanwhile, as the remnants of Louis' defeated invasion fleet retreated back to France in 1217, nearly all those whose tales have featured in this book were already dead. Only Nicola de la Haye and Archbishop Stephen Langton were still alive. Both had more work to do: Nicola would keep her obstinate hold on Lincoln Castle until 1226 (she died four years later), whilst Langton, after his return to England from Rome in 1218, would play a full role in the minority regime of Henry III until

his retirement from court in 1227 (he died the next year). In their
different ways, both Nicola and Stephen contributed significantly to the
defence and the preservation of Angevin power; but in the end neither
of them could stop its decline. Some who have been featured here,
William Atheling and Hugh Bigod perhaps, would have been amazed
at how great that power became; others, Arthur of Brittany certainly,
and maybe Herbert of Bosham, Strongbow and even William de
Briouze, might have celebrated its destruction; and as for the Young
King and his sister Joan, they would have been dismayed at what
happened to their inheritances. However different their views might
have been, though, they had all known success and failure, triumph and
disaster at the hands of the Angevin kings, and all had played their part
in an extraordinary drama of continental scope. So whatever their own
opinions about Henry II, Richard I and John might have been, these
princes, princesses and priests would all have agreed with Gerald of
Wales on one thing: 'Fortune's favour is fickle,' he said, 'and her wheel is
always turning. There are few young people, and hardly any old ones,
who have not experienced this.'[2]

Abbreviations

I have tried to keep the number of endnotes to a minimum throughout and have given a reference only when quoting directly from, or referring directly to, the contents of a source. The list below is of the sources I have used most often. Full citations for those sources less frequently used are given in the notes themselves.

Ann. Mon.	*Annales Monastici*, ed. H.R. Luard, 5 vols, Rolls Series (London, 1864–9).
ASC	*The Anglo-Saxon Chronicle: A Revised Translation*, ed. D. Whitelock, D.C. Douglas and S.I. Tucker (London, 1961).
Carpenter, *Magna Carta*	*Magna Carta*, with a New Commentary by David Carpenter (London, 2015).
Crouch, 'Complaint'	David Crouch, 'The Complaint of King John against William de Briouze (c. September 1210): The Black Book of the Exchequer Text', in *Magna Carta and the England of King John*, ed. Janet S. Loengard (Woodbridge, 2010), pp. 168–79.

CTB	*The Correspondence of Thomas Becket, Archbishop of Canterbury, 1162–1170*, ed. and trans. Anne J. Duggan, 2 vols (Oxford, 2000).
EHD II	*English Historical Documents*, vol. II, 1042–1189, ed. D.C. Douglas and G.W. Greenaway, 2nd edn (London, 1981).
EHD III	*English Historical Documents*, vol. III, 1189–1327, ed. Harry Rothwell (London, 1975).
EHR	*English Historical Review.*
Gerald of Wales, *Expugnatio*	*Expugnatio Hibernica: The Conquest of Ireland by Giraldus Cambrensis*, ed. and trans. A.B. Scott and F.X. Martin (Dublin, 1978).
Gerald of Wales, *Opera*	*Giraldus Cambrensis: Opera*, ed. J.S. Brewer, J.F. Dimock and G.F. Warner, 8 vols, Rolls Series (London, 1861–91).
Gesta Stephani	*Gesta Stephani*, ed. K.R. Potter and R.H.C. Davis, rev. edn (London, 1976).
Henry of Huntingdon, *Historia Anglorum*	Henry of Huntingdon, *Historia Anglorum*, ed. and trans. D. Greenaway (Oxford, 1996).
Histoire des ducs	*Histoire des ducs de Normandie et des rois d'Angleterre*, ed. F. Michel (Paris, 1840).
History of Saladin	*The Rare and Excellent History of Saladin, by Baha al-Din Ibn Shaddad*, trans. D.S. Richards (Aldershot, 2001).
HWM	*History of William Marshal*, ed. A.J. Holden, trans. S. Gregory, with historical notes by D. Crouch, 3 vols (London, 2002–6).

Innocent III, *Letters*

Selected Letters of Pope Innocent III concerning England (1198–1216), ed. C.R. Cheney and W.H. Semple (London, 1953).

John of Salisbury, *Historia Pontificalis*

The Historia Pontificalis of John of Salisbury, ed. and trans. Marjorie Chibnall (London, 1956).

John of Worcester, *Chronicle*

The Chronicle of John of Worcester, vol. II, ed. R.R. Darlington and P. McGurk, vol. III, ed. P. McGurk (Oxford, 1995, 1998).

Matthew Paris, *Chronica Majora*

Matthaei Parisiensis, Monachi Sancti Albani, Chronica Majora, ed. H.R. Luard, 7 vols, Rolls Series (London, 1872–83). Down to 1235 this is Roger of Wendover's chronicle with additions by Matthew Paris.

Matthew Paris, *Historia Anglorum*

Matthaei Parisiensis, Historia Anglorum, sive, ut vulgo dicitur, historia minor. Item, eiusdem abbreviatio chronicorum Angliae, ed. F. Madden, 3 vols, Rolls Series (London, 1866–9).

Memoriale

Memoriale fratris Walteri de Coventria, ed. W. Stubbs, 2 vols, Rolls Series (London, 1872–3). All references are to vol. II, which contains the so-called Barnwell Chronicle.

MTB

Materials for the History of Thomas Becket, Archbishop of Canterbury, ed. J.C. Robertson, 7 vols, Rolls Series (London, 1875–85).

Orderic Vitalis, *Ecclesiastical History*

The Ecclesiastical History of Orderic Vitalis, ed. M. Chibnall, 6 vols (Oxford, 1969–80).

Peter of Blois, *Letters*	*Patrologia cursus completus, series Latina*, ed. J. –P. Migne, 221 vols (Paris, 1844–64), vol. 207, cols 1–463.
PR	Pipe Roll. Citations to the pipe rolls are to the volumes published by the Pipe Roll Society. A reference, for example, to *PR 6 John* is to the pipe roll for the sixth year of John's reign.
Ralph of Coggeshall, *Chronicon*	*Radulphi de Coggeshall Chronicon Anglicanum*, ed. J. Stevenson, Rolls Series (London, 1875).
Recueil	*Recueil des Actes de Henri II, roi d'Angleterre et duc de Normandie, concernant les provinces françaises et les affaires de France*, ed. L. Delisle and E. Berger, 4 vols (Paris, 1906–27).
RLC	*Rotuli Litterarum Clausarum in Turri Londinensi asservati*, ed. T. Duffus Hardy, 2 vols (Record Commission, 1833–4).
RLP	*Rotuli Litterarum Patentium in Turri Londinensi asservati*, ed. T. Duffus Hardy, 2 vols (Record Commission, 1835).
Roger of Howden, *Chronica*	Roger of Howden, *Chronica*, ed. W. Stubbs, 4 vols, Rolls Series (London, 1868–71).
Roger of Howden, *Gesta Henrici*	Roger of Howden, *Gesta Henrici Secundi Benedicti Abbatis*, ed. W. Stubbs, 2 vols, Rolls Series (London, 1867).
Roger of Wendover, *Flores*	*Rogeri de Wendover, liber qui dicitur flores historiarum*, ed. H.G. Hewlett, 3 vols, Rolls Series (London, 1886–9).
Rot. Chart.	*Rotuli Chartarum in Turri Londinensi asservati*, ed. T. Duffus Hardy, 2 vols (Record Commission, 1837).

Rot. Oblat.	*Rotuli de Oblatis et Finibus in Turri Londinensi asservati*, ed. T. Duffus Hardy, 2 vols (Record Commission, 1835).
RRAN II	*Regesta Regum Anglo-Normannorum 1066–1154. Vol. II, Regesta Henrici Primi, 1100–1135*, ed. C. Johnson and H.A. Cronne (Oxford, 1956).
Song	*The Deeds of the Normans in Ireland. La Geste des Engleis En Yrlande: A New edition of the chronicle formerly known as The Song of Dermot and the Earl*, ed. Evelyn Mullally (Dublin, 2002).
Staunton, *Lives*	*The Lives of Thomas Becket*, ed. and trans. Michael Staunton (Manchester, 2001).
William of Malmesbury, *Gesta Regum*	William of Malmesbury, *Gesta Regum*, vol. I, ed. R.A.B. Mynors, R.M. Thomson and M. Winterbottom (Oxford, 1998).
William of Malmesbury, *Historia Novella*	William of Malmesbury, *Historia Novella*, ed. E. King and trans. K.R. Potter (Oxford, 1998).
William of Newburgh, *Historia Rerum Anglicarum*	William of Newburgh, *Historia Rerum Anglicarum*, in *Chronicles of the Reigns of Stephen, Henry II and Richard I*, ed. R. Howlett, 4 vols, Rolls Series (London, 1884–9).

Notes

Prologue

1. *On the Instruction of a Prince* (*De Principis Instructione*) in Gerald of Wales, *Opera*, vol. VIII, pp. 301–2.
2. Ibid.

Chapter 1 The Prince's Tale

1. William of Malmesbury, *Gesta Regum*, pp. 760–1.
2. Orderic Vitalis, *Ecclesiastical History*, vol. VI, pp. 298–9.
3. Ibid., pp. 306–7.
4. *ASC* E, s.a. 1100.
5. Orderic Vitalis, *Ecclesiastical History*, vol. VI, pp. 224, 240, 300–1.
6. Henry of Huntingdon, *Historia Anglorum*, pp. 466–7.
7. Orderic Vitalis, *Ecclesiastical History*, vol. VI, pp. 200–1, 212–15.
8. Suger, *The Deeds of Louis the Fat*, trans. with introduction and notes by Richard Cusimano and John Moorhead (Washington DC, 1992), p. 114.
9. *Liber Monasterii de Hyda*, ed. E. Edwards, Rolls Series (London, 1886), pp. 312–13.
10. *PR 31 Henry I*, p. 113.
11. *RRAN*, vol. II, no. 1204.
12. Henry of Huntingdon, *Historia Anglorum*, p. 464; Orderic Vitalis, *Ecclesiastical History*, vol. VI, p. 238; Suger, *The Deeds of Louis the Fat*, p. 117.
13. Ibid.
14. Orderic Vitalis, *Ecclesiastical History*, vol. VI, pp. 240–1.
15. William of Malmesbury, *Gesta Regum*, pp. 758–9.
16. Ibid.

Chapter 2 The Earl's Tale

1. William of Malmesbury, *Historia Novella*, pp. 24–5; *Gesta Stephani*, pp. 10–13; John of Salisbury, *Historia Pontificalis*, p. 85.
2. *Liber Eliensis: A History of the Isle of Ely, from the Seventh Century to the Twelfth, Compiled by a Monk of Ely in the Twelfth Century*, trans. Janet Fairweather (Woodbridge, 2005), p. 348.
3. *The Historical Works of Gervase of Canterbury*, ed. W. Stubbs, 2 vols, Rolls Series (London, 1879–80), vol. I, p. 94.
4. William of Malmesbury, *Historia Novella*, pp. 26–7, 29–30; Orderic Vitalis, *Ecclesiastical History*, vol. VI, pp. 448–51; Henry of Huntingdon, *Historia Anglorum*, pp. 702–5.
5. Henry of Huntingdon, *Historia Anglorum*, p. 702.

6. John of Salisbury, *Historia Pontificalis*, pp. 83–6.
7. William of Malmesbury, *Historia Novella*, pp. 6–7.
8. *RRAN II*, no. 1427.
9. Ibid., no. 1448.
10. William of Malmesbury, *Historia Novella*, pp. 8–9; John of Worcester, *Chronicle*, vol. III, pp. 178–9.
11. Ibid., vol. III, pp. 180–1.
12. *ASC* E, s.a. 1127.
13. John of Worcester, *Chronicle*, vol. III, pp. 176–9; William of Malmesbury, *Historia Novella*, pp. 6–7; John of Hexham in *Symeonis monachis opera omnia*, ed. T. Arnold, 2 vols, Rolls Series (London, 1882–5), vol. II, pp. 281–2.
14. *RRAN II*, no. 1687.
15. John of Worcester, *Chronicle*, vol. III, pp. 202–3.
16. John of Hexham in *Symeonis monachis opera omnia*, vol. II, p. 283.
17. *RRAN II*, no. 1715; Henry of Huntingdon, *Historia Anglorum*, pp. 486–9; William of Malmesbury, *Historia Novella*, pp. 18–21.
18. *ASC* E, s.a. 1135; John of Worcester, *Chronicle*, vol. III, pp. 208–11; William of Malmesbury, *Historia Novella*, pp. 22–3.
19. *RRAN II*, no. 1902.
20. Orderic Vitalis, *Ecclesiastical History*, vol. VI, pp. 446–7.
21. Henry of Huntingdon, *Historia Anglorum*, pp. 706–7.
22. *Ann. Mon.*, vol. II, p. 228.
23. Henry of Huntingdon, *Historia Anglorum*, pp. 736–7, where Hugh is also described as an earl; Orderic Vitalis, *Ecclesiastical History*, vol. VI, pp. 542–3.
24. William of Malmesbury, *Historia Novella*, pp. 92–3.
25. *Gesta Stephani*, pp. 118–19.
26. *ASC* E, s.a. 1137.
27. Ibid.
28. *Gesta Stephani*, pp. 164–5.
29. Ibid., pp. 166–7.
30. Ibid., pp. 174–5.
31. Ibid., pp. 222–3.
32. Ibid., pp. 236–7.
33. *EHD II*, no. 22.
34. Ibid., no. 23.
35. *Recueil*, vol. I, no. 234 (p. 380); *PR 12 Henry II*, p. 19, *PR 13 Henry II*, p. 19, *PR 22 Henry II*, p. 62.

Chapter 3 The Disciple's Tale

1. Staunton, *Lives*, p. 143.
2. Ibid., pp. 142–3; *The Letters of John of Salisbury*, ed. W.J. Millor, H.E. Butler and C.N.L. Brooke, 2 vols (Oxford, 1955, 1979), vol. II, pp. 98–9.
3. Staunton, *Lives*, pp. 143–4.
4. *MTB*, vol. III, p. 29.
5. Staunton, *Lives*, p. 48; *EHD II*, no. 119 (p. 752).
6. Staunton, *Lives*, p. 53.
7. Ibid., p. 49.
8. Ibid., pp. 49–50.
9. Ibid., p. 55.
10. Ibid., p. 56.
11. Ibid.
12. Ibid., p. 50.
13. Ibid., p. 62.

14. Ibid., p. 60; *EHD II*, no. 120 (pp. 755–6).
15. Staunton, *Lives*, p. 62.
16. *MTB*, vol. IV, p. 85; Staunton, *Lives*, p. 63 n. 70.
17. Ibid., p. 63.
18. Ibid., p. 65.
19. Ibid., pp. 64, 66–7.
20. Ibid., pp. 91–6; *EHD II*, no. 126.
21. Staunton, *Lives*, pp. 97–9.
22. Ibid., pp. 127–8.
23. Ibid., pp. 136–7.
24. Ibid., p. 138.
25. *EHD II*, no. 137.
26. Staunton, *Lives*, p. 151.
27. Ibid., pp. 158, 82; *EHD II*, no. 124 (pp. 763–4).
28. Staunton, *Lives*, p. 157.
29. Ibid., p. 161.
30. Ibid., pp. 169–72; *EHD II*, no. 144.
31. Staunton, *Lives*, pp. 170–1; *EHD II*, no. 144 (pp. 802–3).
32. Staunton, *Lives*, p. 172; *EHD II*, no. 144 (p. 803).
33. Staunton, *Lives*, p. 177 n. 42; *EHD II*, no. 146.
34. *CTB*, vol. II, no. 311.
35. *MTB*, vol. III, pp. 473–6.
36. Staunton, *Lives*, pp. 183–4; *EHD II*, no. 149.
37. Staunton, *Lives*, p. 187; *EHD II*, no. 149 (p. 808).
38. Staunton, *Lives*, p. 189.
39. Ibid., pp. 192–4.
40. Ibid., pp. 193–4; *EHD II*, no. 151.
41. Staunton, *Lives*, p. 194; *EHD II*, no. 151 (p. 811).
42. *MTB*, vol. III, pp. 539–51.
43. Staunton, *Lives*, p. 194; *EHD II*, no. 151 (p. 811) translates the same phrase as 'partner in pain'.

Chapter 4 The Warrior's Tale

1. *Song*, l. 1,819.
2. Ibid., ll. 1,847–74.
3. Gerald of Wales, *Expugnatio*, pp. 80–1.
4. *Song*, ll. 1,879–82.
5. Ibid., ll. 1,921–6.
6. Ibid., ll. 1,939–42.
7. Gerald of Wales, *Expugnatio*, pp. 82–3; *Song*, ll. 1,751–2.
8. Ibid., ll. 1,953–6.
9. Gerald of Wales, *Expugnatio*, pp. 86–9.
10. *EHD II*, no. 22.
11. Gerald of Wales, *Expugnatio*, pp. 54–5; William of Newburgh, *Historia Rerum Anglicarum*, vol. I, p. 167.
12. *Gerald of Wales, The History and Topography of Ireland*, trans. John J. O'Meara, revised edn (London, 1982), pp. 101, 103–4.
13. Ibid., p. 102.
14. *The Annals of Clonmacnoise, Being The Annals of Ireland from the Earliest Period to AD 1408*, trans. Conell Mageoghagan, ed. Denis Murphy (Dublin, 1896; repr. Llanerch, 1993), pp. 199–200.
15. Gerald of Wales, *Expugnatio*, pp. 24–5.
16. Ibid., pp. 26–7.

17. *Song*, ll. 228–37.
18. Gerald of Wales, *Expugnatio*, pp. 142–7; *EHD II*, no. 159.
19. *Ioannis Saresberiensis Metalogicon*, ed. J.B. Hall (Turnhout, 1991), p. 183.
20. Roger of Howden, *Chronica*, vol. II, pp. 306–7; idem, *Gesta Henrici*, vol. I, p. 339.
21. Gerald of Wales, *Expugnatio*, pp. 30–3.
22. Ibid., pp. 36–7.
23. Ibid., pp. 54–5.
24. Ibid., pp. 56–7; William of Newburgh, *Historia Rerum Anglicarum*, vol. I, p. 168.
25. For example, *PR 16 Henry II*, pp. 75, 105.
26. Gerald of Wales, *Expugnatio*, pp. 64–5; *Song*, ll. 1,500–3.
27. William of Newburgh, *Historia Rerum Anglicarum*, vol. I, p. 169.
28. Gerald of Wales, *Expugnatio*, pp. 70–1.
29. Ibid., pp. 80–1.
30. Ibid., pp. 82–3; *Song*, ll. 1,750–1.
31. Gerald of Wales, *Expugnatio*, pp. 92–3; *Song*, ll. 2,585–6, 2,593–5; Roger of Howden, *Gesta Henrici*, vol. I, p. 25.
32. Gerald of Wales, *Expugnatio*, pp. 96–7.
33. Ibid.
34. *The Historical Works of Gervase of Canterbury*, ed. W. Stubbs, 2 vols, Rolls Series (London, 1879–80), vol. I, pp. 234–5.
35. *Irish Historical Documents, 1172–1922*, ed. Edmund Curtis and R.B. McDowell (London, 1943; repr. 1968), pp. 19–22.
36. Gerald of Wales, *Expugnatio*, pp. 96–7.
37. Ibid., pp. 98–9.
38. Ibid., pp. 104–5.
39. *EHD II*, nos 160–2.
40. Gerald of Wales, *Expugnatio*, pp. 134–5.
41. *Song*, l. 2,849.
42. Gerald of Wales, *Expugnatio*, pp. 140–1; *Song*, ll. 3,000–1.
43. Gerald of Wales, *Expugnatio*, pp. 140–1.
44. Ibid.
45. Roger of Howden, *Gesta Henrici*, vol. I, pp. 102–3; idem, *Chronica*, vol. II, pp. 84–5; Marie Therese Flanagan, *Irish Society, Anglo-Norman Settlers, Angevin Kingship: Interactions in Ireland in the Late 12th Century* (Oxford, 1989), pp. 312–13.
46. *Song*, ll. 3,340–51.
47. Gerald of Wales, *Expugnatio*, pp. 160–1.
48. Ibid., pp. 164–5.
49. Ibid.; *Annals of Ulster*, ed. B. MacCarthy, 4 vols (Dublin, 1887–1901), vol. II, pp. 184–5; *Miscellaneous Irish Annals (AD 1114–1437)*, ed. S. Ó hInnse (Dublin, 1947), p. 63.
50. *The Annals of Loch Cé: A Chronicle of Irish Affairs from AD 1014 to AD 1590*, ed. William M. Hennessy, 2 vols (London, 1871), vol. I, pp. 172–3.
51. Gerald of Wales, *Expugnatio*, pp. 164–5.

Chapter 5 The Young King's Tale

1. *HWM*, vol. I, pp. 242–3 (l. 4,768).
2. Roger of Howden, *Chronica*, vol. I, p. 218.
3. Ibid.
4. *MTB*, vol. VI, pp. 206–7.
5. Staunton, *Lives*, p. 62.
6. Ibid., pp. 50–1.
7. Ibid., p. 96; *EHD II*, no. 126 (p. 770).
8. *CTB*, vol. II, nos 296 (pp. 1,246–7), 297 (pp. 1,252–3).
9. Roger of Howden, *Gesta Henrici*, vol. I, p. 6.

10. R.J. Smith, 'Henry II's Heir: The *Acta* and Seal of Henry the Young King, 1170–83', *EHR*, 116 (2001), pp. 297–326, at p. 305.
11. Roger of Howden, *Gesta Henrici*, vol. I, p. 34.
12. Ibid., p. 41.
13. Roger of Howden, *Chronica*, vol. II, p. 46.
14. Ibid.
15. William of Newburgh, *Historia Rerum Anglicarum*, vol. I, p. 170.
16. *Radulfi de Diceto, Decani Lundoniensis, Opera Historica*, ed. W. Stubbs, 2 vols, Rolls Series (London, 1876), vol. I, p. 371.
17. Roger of Howden, *Gesta Henrici*, vol. I, p. 77; idem, *Chronica*, vol. II, p. 67.
18. Ibid., vol. II, p. 69.
19. Peter of Blois, *Letters*, no. 2 (col. 7).
20. Roger of Howden, *Gesta Henrici*, vol. I, p. 122.
21. *Radulfi de Diceto*, ed. Stubbs, vol. I, p. 428.
22. *HWM*, vol. I, pp. 122–3 (ll. 2,402, 2,412–18).
23. Peter of Blois, *Letters*, no. 14 (cols 42–51).
24. *HWM*, vol. I, pp. 258–9 (ll. 5,073–85).
25. Walter Map, *De Nugis Curialum*, ed. M.R. James, C.N.L. Brooke and R.A. Mynors (Oxford, 1983), pp. 278–9.
26. Roger of Howden, *Chronica*, vol. II, p. 266.
27. Roger of Howden, *Gesta Henrici*, vol. I, p. 292; idem, *Chronica*, vol. II, p. 274.
28. 'Chronica Gaufredi Coenobitae Monasterii S. Martialis Lemovicensis ac Priori Vosciensis coenobii', ed. P. Labbe, in *Nova Bibliotheca Manuscriptorum* (Paris, 1657), vol. II, p. 336.
29. *HWM*, vol. I, pp. 100–1, 186–7 (ll. 1,956–8, 3,644–8); Gervase of Tilbury, *Otia Imperialia*, ed. and trans. S.E. Banks and J.W. Binns (Oxford, 2002), p. 486.
30. Walter Map, *De Nugis Curialum*, ed. James, Brooke and Mynors, pp. 280–3.

Chapter 6 The Princess's Tale

1. *History of Saladin*, p. 188.
2. Ibid.
3. Anna Komnene, *The Alexiad*, trans. E.R.A. Sewter (London, 1969; revised edn ed. Peter Frankopan, London, 2009), pp. 177–9.
4. *History of Saladin*, p. 188.
5. Ibid., p. 196.
6. Ibid.
7. Ibid.
8. *The Lais of Marie de France*, trans. Glyn S. Burgess and Keith Busby, 2nd edn (London, 1999), p. 41.
9. *The Travels of Ibn Jubayr*, trans. Roland Broadhurst (London, 1952; repr. New Delhi, 2013), p. 339.
10. *PR 22, 23, 24 Henry II*, passim.
11. Roger of Howden, *Chronica*, vol. II, p. 95.
12. *CTB*, vol. II, no. 216 (pp. 944–5).
13. Roger of Howden, *Chronica*, vol. II, p. 48; idem, *Gesta Henrici*, vol. I, p. 55.
14. Ibid., vol. I, pp. 169–72.
15. *The Travels of Ibn Jubayr*, trans. Broadhurst, pp. 340–1.
16. Ibid., p. 340.
17. Ibid., p. 341.
18. Ibid., pp. 349–50.
19. *The Crusades: Idea and Reality, 1095–1274*, ed. Louise and Jonathan Riley-Smith (London, 1981), pp. 63–7.
20. *The Chronicle of Richard of Devizes of the Time of King Richard the First*, ed. John T. Appleby (London, 1963), p. 17; Roger of Howden, *Gesta Henrici*, vol. II, pp. 132–3.

21. *The Chronicle of Richard of Devizes*, ed. Appleby, p. 17.
22. Roger of Howden, *Gesta Henrici*, vol. II, p. 126.
23. Ibid., pp. 160–1.
24. *History of Saladin*, p. 150.
25. Ibid., pp. 185–6.
26. Ibid., p. 154; Imad al-Din, *Conquête de la Syrie et de la Palestine par Saladin*, trans. H. Massé (Paris, 1972), pp. 350–1.
27. *The History of the Holy War: Ambroise's Estoire de la Guerre Sainte*, ed. Marianne Ailes and Malcolm Barber, 2 vols (Woodbridge, 2003), vol. I, ll. 11,314–15 (p. 183), vol. II, p. 182.
28. *Calendar of Documents Preserved in France, Illustrative of the History of Great Britain and Ireland. Volume I, AD 918–1206*, ed. J. Horace Round (London, 1899), no. 278.
29. Ibid., no. 1,105.
30. Roger of Howden, *Chronica*, vol. IV, pp. 83–4; *Ann. Mon.*, vol. II, pp. 64, 71.
31. *Calendar of Documents Preserved in France*, ed. Round, no. 1,090 and p. 387 n. 4.
32. C. De Vic and J. Vaissète, *Histoire Générale de Languedoc*, 16 vols (Toulouse, 1872–1904; repr. Osnabrück, 1973), vol. IV, pp. 189–90.
33. *Calendar of Documents Preserved in France*, ed. Round, no. 1,104.

Chapter 7 The Nephew's Tale

1. *HWM*, vol. II, pp. 94–7 (ll. 11,866–908).
2. Gerald of Wales, *Description of Wales*, in *Gerald of Wales, The Journey through Wales and the Description of Wales*, trans. Lewis Thorpe (London, 1978), pp. 211–74, at p. 231.
3. *The Lais of Marie de France*, trans. Glyn S. Burgess and Keith Busby, 2nd edn (London, 1999), no. XII.
4. William of Malmesbury, *Gesta Regum*, pp. 728–9.
5. Roger of Howden, *Gesta Henrici*, vol. I, p. 350; Gerald of Wales, *Opera*, vol. VIII, pp. 176–7.
6. William of Newburgh, *Historia Rerum Anglicarum*, vol. I, p. 235, vol. II, p. 463.
7. Ibid., vol. I, pp. 335–6.
8. Ralph of Coggeshall, *Chronicon*, p. 99.
9. Roger of Howden, *Chronica*, vol. IV, pp. 96–7.
10. Roger of Wendover, *Flores*, vol. I, p. 317.
11. *Rot. Chart.*, p. 102.
12. *RLP*, vol. I, p. 7b.
13. *Histoire des ducs*, pp. 94–5; Ralph of Coggeshall, *Chronicon*, pp. 137–8.
14. Ralph of Coggeshall, *Chronicon*, pp. 139–41.
15. Roger of Wendover, *Flores*, vol. I, pp. 315–16.
16. Matthew Paris, *Historia Anglorum*, vol. II, p. 95.
17. William the Breton, *Philippidos*, in H. François Delaborde, *Oeuvres de Rigord et Guillaume le Breton: Historiens de Philippe-Auguste*, 2 vols (Paris, 1882–5), vol. II, pp. 170–1, 173–4 (ll. 471–90, 552–66).
18. *Ann. Mon.*, vol. I, p. 27.
19. *HWM*, vol. II, pp. 130–1 (ll. 12,595–602).

Chapter 8 The Friend's Tale

1. Roger of Wendover, *Flores*, vol. II, pp. 48–9; Matthew Paris, *Chronica Majora*, vol. II, pp. 523–4.
2. Gerald of Wales, *The Journey through Wales*, in *Gerald of Wales, The Journey through Wales and the Description of Wales*, trans. Lewis Thorpe (London, 1978), pp. 63–209, at p. 83.
3. *Histoire des ducs*, p. 111.
4. *Ann. Mon.*, vol. I, p. 24.
5. *Rot. Chart.*, pp. 66b–7.
6. *RLP*, vol. I, pp. 19b, 74.

7. Ibid., p. 57; *RLC*, vol. I, p. 63; *Rot. Oblat.*, pp. 46, 232; *PR 7 John*, p. 277.
8. *RLP*, vol. I, p. 18b; *PR 5 John*, p. 197; *PR 6 John*, p. 101.
9. *Rot. Chart.*, p. 84b; *Rot. Oblat.*, p. 99; *PR 4 John*, p. 141.
10. Gerald of Wales, *Expugnatio*, pp. 226–9, 236–45.
11. Ibid., pp. 178–81.
12. *Miscellaneous Irish Annals (AD 1114–1437)*, ed. S. Ó hInnse (Dublin, 1947), p. 73.
13. Roger of Howden, *Chronica*, vol. IV, pp. 25, 162.
14. William the Breton, *Philippidos*, vol. II, pp. 170–1 (ll. 477–92).
15. The outstanding debt of £2,865 6s 8d appears unreduced on successive pipe rolls: *PR 8 John*, p. 60; *PR 9 John*, p. 38; *PR 10 John*, p. 70; *PR 11 John*, p. 1; *PR 12 John*, p. 84.
16. *RLP*, vol. I, p. 77.
17. *Ann. Mon.*, vol. II, p. 396.
18. *RLC*, vol. I, p. 98.
19. Crouch, 'Complaint', pp. 168–79.
20. *HWM*, vol. II, pp. 208–11 (ll. 14,161–98).
21. Ibid., pp. 158–9 (ll. 13,171–4).
22. Ibid., pp. 210–13 (ll. 14,199–232).
23. Crouch, 'Complaint', pp. 176–7.
24. Ibid., pp. 177–9.
25. *HWM*, vol. II, pp. 214–19 (ll. 14,286–372).
26. Crouch, 'Complaint', p. 178.
27. Matthew Paris, *Chronica Majora*, vol. II, p. 530.
28. Crouch, 'Complaint', pp. 178–9.
29. Ralph of Coggeshall, *Chronicon*, p. 164; Matthew Paris, *Chronica Majora*, vol. II, p. 531; Roger of Wendover, *Flores*, vol. II, p. 57; *Brut y Tywysogion or The Chronicle of the Princes. Penarth MS.20 Version*, ed. Thomas Jones (Cardiff, 1952), p. 84; *Memoriale*, vol. II, p. 202; *Ann. Mon.*, vol. I, pp. 30, 59, vol. II, pp. 81, 265, vol. III, p. 32, vol. IV, pp. 54, 399.
30. *Ann. Mon.*, vol. II, p. 265.
31. *Histoire des ducs*, pp. 114–15.
32. Ibid., p. 105.

Chapter 9 The Exile's Tale

1. *Ann. Mon.*, vol. II, p. 277.
2. Roger of Wendover, *Flores*, vol. II, p. 84; Matthew Paris, *Chronica Majora*, vol. II, p. 552.
3. Roger of Wendover, *Flores*, vol. II, pp. 111–12; Matthew Paris, *Chronica Majora*, vol. II, pp. 582–3.
4. *Memoriale*, vol. II, p. 218; Ralph of Coggeshall, *Chronicon*, p. 170; *Histoire des ducs*, pp. 145–6.
5. Carpenter, *Magna Carta*, pp. 38–9 (Magna Carta 1215, ch. 1).
6. Ibid., pp. 64–5 (Magna Carta 1215, ch. 61).
7. Gerald of Wales, *Opera*, vol. VIII, pp. 292–3.
8. Quoted in Christopher Holdsworth, 'Langton, Stephen (c. 1150–1228)', *Oxford Dictionary of National Biography*, ed. Colin Matthew, Brian Harrison, Lawrence Goldman and David Cannadine (Oxford, 1992–) [http://www.oxforddnb.com/view/article/16044].
9. Quoted and translated in J.W. Baldwin, 'Master Stephen Langton, Future Archbishop of Canterbury: The Paris Schools and Magna Carta', *EHR*, 123 (2008), pp. 811–46, at p. 815 and n.16.
10. Ibid., p. 818 and n 27.
11. John of Salisbury. *Policraticus. Of the Frivolities of Courtiers and the Footprints of Philosophers*, ed. and trans. Cary J. Nederman (Cambridge, 1990). See, for example, Book IV, ch. 1, Book VIII, chs 17, 18, 20.
12. Matthew Paris, *Historia Anglorum*, vol. II, p. 104.
13. *Recueil*, vol. I, p. 587.

14. Innocent III, *Letters*, no. 29.
15. Ibid.
16. *Acta Stephani Langton, Cantuariensis Archiepiscopi, AD 1207–1227*, ed. Kathleen Major (Oxford, 1950), no. 3.
17. *Memoriale*, vol. II, pp. 198–9; Roger of Wendover, *Flores*, vol. II, pp. 47–8.
18. *Ann. Mon.*, vol. II, p. 261.
19. Innocent III, *Letters*, no. 39.
20. William of Newburgh, *Historia Rerum Anglicarum*, vol. II, p. 521; *Monasticon Anglicanum*, ed. W. Dugdale, revised edn J. Caley, H. Ellis and B. Bandniel, 8 vols (London, 1817–30), vol. VI, part I, p. 147; *Histoire des ducs*, pp. 105, 115–25.
21. Matthew Paris, *Chronica Majora*, vol. II, p. 535.
22. Roger of Wendover, *Flores*, vol. II, pp. 76–7.
23. *EHD II*, no. 19.
24. Innocent III, *Letters*, no. 80.
25. W. Stubbs, *Select Charters*, 9th edn (Oxford, 1913), pp. 282–4.
26. Carpenter, *Magna Carta*, pp. 36–69 *passim*.
27. Ibid., pp. 38–9 (Magna Carta 1215, clause 1).
28. Innocent III, *Letters*, no. 56.
29. *RLP*, p. 181b.
30. V.H. Galbraith, *Studies in the Public Records* (London, 1948), pp. 136–7, 161–2.
31. Innocent III, *Letters*, no. 80.

Chapter 10 The Matron's Tale

1. *Rotuli Hundredorum*, 2 vols (London, 1812–18), vol. I, p. 309.
2. *Ann. Mon.*, vol. III, p. 49.
3. Innocent III, *Letters*, no. 82; *EHD III*, no. 21.
4. *Memoriale*, vol. II, p. 227.
5. *Ann. Mon.*, vol. III, p. 47.
6. *Ancient Charters, royal and private, prior to AD 1200*, ed. J.H. Round, Pipe Roll Society, 10 (London, 1888), no. 55; *PR 2 Richard I*, p. 89.
7. *The Chronicle of Richard of Devizes of the time of King Richard the First*, ed. J.T. Appleby (London, 1963), pp. 30–1.
8. *PR 6 Richard I*, pp. 118–19.
9. *PR 2 John*, p. 67; *PR 3 John*, p. 290.
10. *Memoriale*, vol. II, p. 230.
11. *RLP*, p. 199b.
12. *Calendar of Patent Rolls, 1216–25* (London, 1901), p. 20.
13. *Memoriale*, vol. II, p. 232.
14. *EHD III*, no. 22.
15. *Histoire des ducs*, p. 182.
16. *Ann. Mon.*, vol. III, p. 49; *Memoriale*, vol. II, p. 237.
17. *HWM*, vol. II, pp. 314–15 (ll. 16,264–8).
18. Ibid., pp. 318–19 (ll. 16,335–40).
19. Ibid., pp. 326–7 (ll. 16,490–8).
20. Ibid., pp. 332–3 (ll. 16,617–22).
21. Ibid., pp. 326–7 (ll. 16,491–2).
22. *EHD III*, nos 23–4.
23. *Calendar of Patent Rolls, 1216–25*, pp. 200–1.

Epilogue

1. Gerald of Wales, *Opera*, vol. VIII, p. 312.
2. Gerald of Wales, *Expugnatio*, p. 224 (my translation).

Suggestions for Further Reading

The literature on this period is extensive and these suggestions only begin to scratch the surface of what is available. They are designed to give interested readers some idea where to go next, to fill in some of the many gaps I have left, and to address some of the many questions I have been unable to answer.

Prologue

The story of Mélusine was well known in the twelfth century and, like Mélusine herself, could take many forms. This particular version was told by Gerald of Wales in his work *On the Instruction of a Prince* (Gerald of Wales, *Opera*, vol. VIII, p. 301).

There are many sound, thorough overviews of this period in print. For Europe as a whole, Malcom Barber, *The Two Cities: Europe, 1050–1320* (2nd edn, London, 2004), is very useful, whilst Robert Bartlett, *The Making of Europe: Conquest, Colonisation and Cultural Change* (London, 1993), focuses on the expansion of Western Christendom. As for Britain, the best four general works, for different reasons, are the following: David Carpenter, *The Struggle for Mastery: Britain 1066–1284* (London, 2004); Robert Bartlett, *England under the Norman and Angevin Kings, 1075–1225* (Oxford, 2002); M.T. Clanchy, *England and its Rulers, 1066–1307* (4th edn, London, 2014); and, with its decidedly continental focus, John Gillingham, *The Angevin Empire* (2nd edn, London, 2000). For an illuminating French perspective, see Martin Aurell, *The Plantagenet Empire, 1154–1224*, trans. David Crouch (Harlow, 2007).

This period can also be looked at reign by reign, and there is more than one good modern biography of each of the post-conquest English kings. I would recommend David Bates, *William the Conqueror* (3rd edn, Stroud, 2004); Emma Mason, *King Rufus: The Life and Murder of William II of England* (Stroud, 2008); Judith Green, *Henry I* (Cambridge, 2006); David Crouch, *The Reign of King Stephen, 1135–1154* (Harlow, 2000); W.L. Warren, *Henry II* (London, 1977), as well as his *King John* (revised edn, London, 1997); and John Gillingham, *Richard I* (London, 2002).

The two classic accounts of Scottish history during the period covered by this book are A.A.M. Duncan, *Scotland: The Making of the Kingdom* (Edinburgh, 1975), and G.W.S. Barrow, *Kingship and Unity: Scotland 1000–1306* (London, 1981). The most recent is Richard Oram, *Domination and Lordship: Scotland 1070–1230* (Edinburgh, 2011). Welsh affairs, meanwhile, are magnificently dealt with in R.R. Davies, *The Age of Conquest: Wales, 1063–1415* (Oxford, 1987).

For Ireland, Sicily, Germany and France, see the suggestions for Chapters 4, 6 and 7 below.

All of the individuals whose tales this book tells, as well as just about anyone of any importance in British history during this period, are the subjects of entries in the *Oxford*

Dictionary of National Biography, ed. Colin Matthew, Brian Harrison, Lawrence Goldman and David Cannadine (Oxford, 1992–). This is an extraordinary and immensely helpful resource, both in its printed and its online form (http://www.oxforddnb.com/). Written by leading specialists, the essays are scholarly, informed and digestible.

Chapter 1 – William Atheling

There are several near contemporary accounts of the *White Ship* disaster. The fullest are Orderic Vitalis, *Ecclesiastical History*, vol. VI, pp. 296–306, and William of Malmesbury, *Gesta Regum*, pp. 758–63. Two detailed studies of the shipwreck provide some clarity and no little controversy: V. Chandler, 'The Wreck of the White Ship: A Mass Murder Revealed?', in *The Final Argument: The Imprint of Violence on Society in Medieval and Early Modern Europe*, ed. D.J. Kagay and L.J. Andrew Villalon (Woodbridge, 1998), pp. 179–84; and T. Brett Jones, 'The White Ship Disaster', *The Historian*, 64 (1999), pp. 23–6.

Other biographies cast extra light on the events of this chapter. For example, C. Warren Hollister, *Henry I* (London, 2003); Lois L. Huneycutt, *Matilda of Scotland: A Study in Medieval Queenship* (Woodbridge, 2003); and William M. Aird, *Robert 'Curthose', Duke of Normandy (c.1050–1134)* (Woodbridge, 2011).

Chapter 2 – Hugh Bigod

The scene at Henry I's deathbed was described by several contemporary chroniclers, none of whom witnessed any of the events in person. Amongst them are Orderic Vitalis, *Ecclesiastical History*, vol. VI, pp. 448–9; Henry of Huntingdon, *Historia Anglorum*, pp. 490–1; William of Malmesbury, *Historia Novella*, pp. 22–7; *Gesta Stephani*, pp. 10–13. Another important source, a letter from the abbot of Cluny, is included in R.H.C. Davis, *King Stephen* (3rd edn, London, 1990), pp. 12–13.

The only focused and detailed study of Hugh Bigod's life and career is Andrew Wareham, 'The Motives and Politics of the Bigod Family, c.1066–1177', *Anglo-Norman Studies*, 17 (1994), pp. 223–42. Another important article about the family is R.A. Brown, 'Framlingham Castle and Bigod, 1154–1216', *Proceedings of the Suffolk Institute of Natural History and Archaeology*, 25 (1950), pp. 127–48, repr. in idem, *Castles, Conquest and Charters: Collected Papers* (Woodbridge, 1989), pp. 187–208. For something related and more extensive, David Crouch, *The Beaumont Twins: The Roots and Branches of Power in the Twelfth Century* (Cambridge, 1986), is a revealing and expert study of the aristocratic experience in England and Normandy during this period.

More broadly, there are several excellent surveys of King Stephen's reign and of 'The Anarchy', in which Bigod regularly features. For a long time the starting point has rightly been R.H.C. Davis, *King Stephen*, but since that book was published many other studies have appeared. K.J. Stringer, *The Reign of King Stephen: Kingship, Warfare and Government in Twelfth-Century England* (London, 1993), provides a short and punchy reassessment of the reign whilst Edmund King, *King Stephen* (London, 2010), gives the most detailed coverage of all. Indispensable, however, is Marjorie Chibnall, *The Empress Matilda* (Oxford, 1991), a ground-breaking account of a remarkable life. The end of Stephen's reign and the beginning of Henry II's have been the subject of two important in-depth studies: Emilie M. Amt, *The Accession of Henry II in England: Royal Government Restored, 1149–1159* (Woodbridge, 1993), and Graeme J. White, *Restoration and Reform, 1153–1165: Recovery from Civil War in England* (Cambridge, 2000).

Chapter 3 – Herbert of Bosham

The meeting between Herbert of Bosham and Henry II at Angers in 1166 was described by William Fitz Stephen: *MTB*, vol. III, pp. 25–6; Staunton, *Lives*, pp. 142–4. William served as a clerk in Becket's household between 1162 and 1164, he was present at the Council of Northampton in 1164, and he witnessed Becket's murder in 1170. However, he did not go into exile with the archbishop, and, although he met Becket more than once thereafter, it is unlikely that he was at Angers himself to witness the events he later described in his *Life of St Thomas*. Of course, he may have been told what happened by John of Salisbury or by Herbert of Bosham himself.

The best modern introductions to the Becket Dispute are both by Anne Duggan. Her biography, *Thomas Becket* (London, 2004), and her essay 'Henry II, the English Church and the Papacy, 1154–76', in *Henry II: New Interpretations*, ed. Christopher Harper-Bill and Nicholas Vincent (Woodbridge, 2007), pp. 154–83, are both invaluable. Her edition of Becket's correspondence (*CTB*) is a work of outstanding scholarship. Two other good biographies are Frank Barlow, *Thomas Becket* (London, 1986), and John Guy, *Thomas Becket: Warrior, Priest, Rebel, Victim: A 900-Year-Old Story Retold* (London, 2012). Older, but nevertheless classic, studies of the quarrel include David Knowles, *The Episcopal Colleagues of Archbishop Thomas Becket* (Cambridge, 1951), and Beryl Smalley, *The Becket Dispute and the Schools* (Oxford, 1973).

There is a very helpful short overview on the subject of education during this period in Bartlett, *England under the Norman and Angevin Kings*, pp. 506–12. On the origins of the universities and the studies pursued there, David Knowles, *The Evolution of Medieval Thought* (London, 1962; 2nd edn ed. D.E. Luscombe and C.N.L. Brooke, Harlow, 1988), chs 13–14, is still useful, although much has been done to develop understanding in this area since this book was first published.

Both I.S. Robinson, *The Papacy, 1073–1198: Continuity and Innovation* (Cambridge, 1990), Part II, and Colin Morris, *The Papal Monarchy: The Western Church from 1050–1250* (Oxford, 1989), chs 4, 5, and 7, provide good introductions to Gregorian Reform, the Investiture Dispute and the development of canon law during this period, as does, from a more directly British perspective, Henry Mayr-Harting, *Religion, Politics and Society in Britain, 1066–1272* (Harlow, 2011), esp. ch. 2 (on Gregorian Reform). Ch. 4 (on the Becket Dispute itself) is also valuable.

Chapter 4 – Strongbow

The siege of Dublin in 1171 is described most fully in Gerald of Wales, *Expugnatio*, pp. 78–85, and *Song*, ll. 1,796–1,964. It is considered in Gerald of Wales, *Expugnatio*, pp. 306–8, nn. 115–26, and in *A New History of Ireland. Volume II: Medieval Ireland, 1169–1534*, ed. Art Cosgrove (Oxford, 1987), ch. 3 (by F.X. Martin), pp. 82–5.

Meanwhile, the best and most digestible modern introductions to Irish history during this period include Robin Frame, *Colonial Ireland* (Dublin, 1981), and Sean Duffy, *Ireland in the Middle Ages* (Basingstoke, 1997). The standard, and much more detailed, works have long been G.H. Orpen, *Ireland under the Normans*, 4 vols (Oxford, 1911–20), and A.J. Otway-Ruthven, *A History of Medieval Ireland* (London, 1968). But for the latest thorough treatments, see *A New History of Ireland: Volume II*, ed. Art Cosgrove, ch. 1 (by F.J. Byrne) and chs 2–4 (all by F.X. Martin), and Marie Therese Flanagan, *Irish Society, Anglo-Norman Settlers, Angevin Kingship: Interactions in Ireland in the Late 12th Century* (Oxford, 1989). The latter's 'Strongbow, Henry II and the Anglo-Norman Intervention in Ireland', in *War and Government in the Middle Ages: Essays in Honour of J.O. Prestwich*, ed. J. Gillingham and J.C. Holt (Woodbridge, 1984), pp. 62–77, is also a good place to start.

Chapter 5 – Henry, the Young King

Louis VII's plans for the succession, his son's illness, his trip to England and Philip's coronation were described by Roger of Howden (idem, *Gesta Henrici*, vol. I, pp. 240–3). Roger was the priest of Howden in the East Riding of Yorkshire, but from about 1174 until Henry II's death in 1189 his time was spent mainly as a clerk in royal service. He carried out various official duties, as diplomat and judge, for example, and he later went on the Third Crusade with Richard I. So Roger's sources for the events of 1179 were probably sound. He may even have participated in some of those events himself. The tournament at Lagny is described at length by William Marshal's biographer in *HWM*, vol. I, pp. 242–53 (ll. 4,750–4,970). Nothing is known about this writer apart from his name, John, and that he knew the Marshal well and travelled widely with him. It is certainly possible that his account of the tournament is a first-hand one.

The only extended account of the Young King's career remains O.H. Moore, *The Young King Henry Plantagenet, 1155–83, in History, Literature and Tradition* (Columbus OH, 1925). But this is very old and very difficult to find! Two important shorter studies have been published in recent years, however: Matthew Strickland, 'On the Instruction of a Prince: The Upbringing of Henry, the Young King', in *Henry II: New Interpretations*, ed. Harper-Bill and Vincent, pp. 184–214, and R.J. Smith, 'Henry II's Heir: The *Acta* and Seal of Henry the Young King, 1170–83', *EHR*, 116 (2001), pp. 297–326. Henry's coronation in 1170, and its relevance to the Becket Dispute, are also the subject of Anne Heslin (now Duggan), 'The Coronation of the Young King in 1170', *Studies in Church History*, vol. II, ed. G.J. Cuming (London, 1968), pp. 165–78.

The standard works on the medieval tournament are now David Crouch, *Tournament: A Chivalric Way of Life* (Hambledon, 2005), and Richard Barber and Juliet Barker, *Tournaments: Jousts, Chivalry and Pageants in the Middle Ages* (Woodbridge, 2013). There is also an excellent briefer introduction to the topic in Maurice Keen, *Chivalry* (New Haven CT and London, 1984), ch. 5. William Marshal, the greatest knight of his day, is the subject of David Crouch's exemplary biography, *William Marshal: Knighthood, War and Chivalry, 1147–1219* (2nd edn, London, 2002).

Chapter 6 – Joan of Sicily and Toulouse

The account of the negotiations surrounding the proposed marriage between Joan and al-Adil was written by an author usually known in English sources as Baha al-Din. He had been a noted scholar and teacher in Baghdad and Mosul before he met Saladin for the first time in 1184. From 1188, Baha al-Din was permanently employed in Saladin's service, and he was still carrying out official business for his successors two years before he died, at the age of eighty-nine, in 1234. It has been suggested most recently that his *Rare and Excellent History of Saladin* was written some time between 1198 and 1216 (ibid., pp. 6–7). Baha al-Din was told about the discussions between Richard and al-Adil by al-Adil himself, and he was the messenger who took news of the proposal to Saladin and brought back his reply (ibid., pp. 187–8). Baha al-Din was a trusted servant and there is no reason to doubt that the discussions did take place essentially as he describes them.

Eleanor of Aquitaine has been the subject of as much mythologising as proper historical assessment. An excellent starting point is Jane Martindale, 'Eleanor of Aquitaine', in *Richard Coeur de Lion in History and Myth*, ed. Janet L. Nelson (London, 1992). D.D.R. Owen, *Eleanor of Aquitaine: Queen and Legend* (Oxford, 1993; repr. 1996), is a good overview, whilst the most recent sensible study is Ralph V. Turner, *Eleanor of Aquitaine* (London, 2009). For a discussion of the possible links between Henry II's court and the development of Arthurian literature, see Martin Aurell's essay in *Henry II: New Interpretations*, ed. Harper-Bill and Vincent, pp. 362–94.

There is no study in English of the reign of William II of Sicily. But there is still plenty of good writing on the remarkable history of Sicily during this period. J.J. Norwich, *The Kingdom in the Sun, 1130–94* (London, 1970), remains a good introduction, whilst Donald Matthew, *The Norman Kingdom of Sicily* (Cambridge, 1992; repr. 1995), takes things further, as does E.M. Jamison, 'The Sicilian Kingdom in the Minds of Anglo-Norman Contemporaries', *Proceedings of the British Academy*, 24 (1938), pp. 237–85 (repr. in idem, *Studies on the History of Medieval Sicily and South Italy* [Aalen, 1992], pp. 159–207).

A helpful introduction to medieval Germany is Alfred Haverkamp, *Medieval Germany, 1056–1273*, trans. H. Braun and R. Mortimer (2nd edn, Oxford, 1992), whilst Peter Munz,

Frederick Barbarossa: A Study in Medieval Politics (London, 1969), continues to provide a sound overview of the reign.

All general histories of the crusades will give their own accounts of Richard I's expedition to the Holy Land. For one of the latest, see Thomas Asbridge, *The Crusades: The War for the Holy Land* (London, 2010), Part III. However, chs 7–13 of John Gillingham, *Richard I*, are essential.

Chapter 7 – Arthur of Brittany

The conversation between William Marshal and Hubert Walter about who should succeed Richard I, and the respective claims of Arthur and John, was recorded by the Marshal's biographer: *HWM*, vol. II, pp. 92–7 (ll. 11,833–908). The legal and political issues are discussed most fully in J.C. Holt, 'The Casus Regis: The Law and Politics of Succession in the Plantagenet Dominions, 1185–1247', in his *Colonial England, 1066–1216* (London, 1997), pp. 307–26.

The starting point for Breton history during this period is now J.A. Everard, *Brittany and the Angevins: Province and Empire, 1158–1203* (new edn, Cambridge, 2006). This can be reinforced over a longer period with Patrick Galliou and Michael Jones, *The Bretons* (Oxford, 1991). The rise of French royal power under Philip II, meanwhile, has been dealt with in great detail in John W. Baldwin, *The Government of Philip Augustus: Foundations of French Royal Power in the Middle Ages* (new edn, Los Angeles, 1992), whilst more immediately accessible introductions to French history during this period include J. Dunbabin, *France in the Making, 843–1180* (2nd edn, Oxford, 2000), Elizabeth M. Hallam, *Capetian France, 987–1328*, rev. Judith Everard (2nd edn, London, 2001), and Jim Bradbury, *Philip Augustus: King of France 1180–1223* (London, 1997).

The loss of John's continental lands continues to generate vigorous scholarly debate. The cornerstone of such discussions remains F.M. Powicke, *The Loss of Normandy, 1189–1204: Studies in the History of the Angevin Empire* (2nd edn, Manchester, 1961; repr. 1963). However, in more recent decades other great historians have locked horns over the issues. The works of J.C. Holt remain essential. Amongst the most important of these are 'The End of the Anglo-Norman Realm', *Proceedings of the British Academy*, 61 (1975), pp. 3–45, reprinted as ch. 2 of his collected essays, *Magna Carta and Medieval Government* (London, 1985), and 'The Loss of Normandy and Royal Finance', in *War and Government in the Middle Ages*, ed. Gillingham and Holt, pp. 92–105. John Gillingham, in *The Angevin Empire*, holds to the view that the catastrophe of John's reign was down to his own incompetence, whilst others have focused on wider issues such as the relative financial strength of the two sides and the deeper long-term political strains within Normandy. The works of Daniel Power, Nick Barratt and Vincent Moss have been ground-breaking in these areas. See their essays in *King John: New Interpretations*, ed. S.D. Church (Woodbridge, 1999), namely Power, 'King John and the Norman Aristocracy', at pp. 117–36, Barratt, 'The Revenues of King John and Philip Augustus Revisited', at pp. 75–99, and Moss, 'The Norman Exchequer Rolls of King John', at pp. 101–16. For the more ambitious reader, Power's monumental *The Norman Frontier in the Twelfth and Early Thirteenth Centuries* (Cambridge, 2004) leaves few stones unturned.

Chapter 8 – William de Briouze

The story of Matilda de Briouze's defiance in the face of John's envoys appears in an entry for the year 1208 in one of the works of the St Albans monk, Roger of Wendover (d.1236): *Flores*, vol. II, pp. 48–9. It was copied in the great chronicle of Roger's successor as historian at St Albans, Matthew Paris (d.1259): *Chronica Majora*, vol. II, pp. 523–4. Where the story ultimately comes from is unclear. It is quite possible, although we will never know for sure, that Roger simply made it up. If he did, it is at least clear evidence of what he thought Matilda de Briouze was like.

There is no full-scale study of the Briouze family, although Brock Holden, 'King John, the Braoses and the Celtic Fringe, 1207–1216', *Albion: A Quarterly Journal Concerned with British Studies*, 33 (2001), pp. 1–23, is a good, short reassessment of William's relationship with King John; and Colin Veach, 'King John and Royal Control in Ireland: Why William de Briouze had to be Destroyed', *EHR*, 129 (2014), pp. 1,051–78, appeared just in time to be considered here. Other work has done much to reassess the context within which these events were played out. Nick Barratt, 'The Revenues of King John', *EHR*, 111 (1996), pp. 835–55, has shed wholly new light on the intensity of John's financial exploitation of England between 1207 and 1214. And Sean Duffy's analyses have altered perceptions of John's policies towards Ireland: see his 'King John's Expedition to Ireland, 1210: The Evidence Reconsidered', *Irish Historical Studies*, 30 (1996–7), pp. 1–24, and his 'John and Ireland: The Origins of England's Irish Problems', in *King John: New Interpretations*, ed. Church, pp. 221–45.

Chapter 9 – Stephen Langton

The meetings at St Paul's and Bury St Edmund's in 1214 were first described by Roger of Wendover (*Flores*, vol. II, pp. 83–7, 111–2) and then repeated by Matthew Paris (*Chronica Majora*, vol. II, pp. 552–4, 582–3). *Ann. Mon.*, vol. II, p. 277, has details of Langton's sermon at St Paul's. There is much doubt about the credibility of the St Albans accounts. The evidence is reviewed and Wendover's version dismissed in J.C. Holt, *Magna Carta* (2nd edn, Cambridge, 1992), pp. 224–6. A recent attempt to give the story more credence has also been questioned: J.W. Baldwin, 'Master Stephen Langton, Future Archbishop of Canterbury: The Paris Schools and Magna Carta', *EHR*, 123 (2008), pp. 811–46, at pp. 827–32; David A. Carpenter, 'Archbishop Langton and Magna Carta: His Contribution, his Doubts and his Hypocrisy', *EHR*, 126 (2011), pp. 1,041–65, at pp. 1,047–50.

The starting point for discussions of Langton's career remains F.M. Powicke, *Stephen Langton* (Oxford, 1928). For the importance of his sermons, see Phyllis B. Roberts, *Stephanus de lingua-tonante: Studies in the Sermons of Stephen Langton* (Toronto, 1968), and for some of the texts themselves her *Selected Sermons of Stephen Langton* (Toronto, 1980). But Langton has also been the subject of several much more recent studies. Whilst differing considerably in their emphases and their conclusions, they complement each other well and give fresh impetus to this neglected area. In order of publication, they are D. D'Avray, 'Magna Carta: Its Background in Stephen Langton's Biblical Exegesis and its Episcopal Reception', *Studi Medievalii*, 3rd series, 38 (1997), pp. 425–38; Baldwin, 'Master Stephen Langton, Future Archbishop of Canterbury'; N. Vincent, 'Stephen Langton, Archbishop of Canterbury', in *Étienne Langton: Prédicateur, Bibliste, Théologien*, ed. L.-J. Bataillon, N. Bériou, G. Dahan and R. Quinto (Turnhout, 2010), pp. 51–123; Carpenter, 'Archbishop Langton and Magna Carta'. Langton's problems with Rochester Castle are dealt with in I.W. Rowlands, 'King John, Stephen Langton and Rochester Castle, 1213–15', *Studies in Medieval History Presented to R. Allen Brown*, ed. C. Harper-Bill, C.J. Holdsworth and J.L. Nelson (Woodbridge, 1989), pp. 267–80.

Quite understandably, the origins, creation and subsequent history of Magna Carta have generated a huge amount of scholarly analysis. Indispensable, however, remain the works of J.C. Holt, the two most important of which are *The Northerners: A Study in the Reign of King John* (Oxford, 1961; repr. 1992) and *Magna Carta*. On a different scale altogether, but invaluable in its own way, is Nicholas Vincent, *Magna Carta: A Very Short Introduction* (Oxford, 2012). All other introductions to the charter have now been surpassed, however, by *Magna Carta, with a New Commentary* by David Carpenter (London, 2015). This book does indeed contain a new translation of the charter and a new commentary on it. But it also contains so much more than that and amounts to a wholesale reassessment of John's reign in particular and of the Angevin period more generally.

Chapter 10 – Nicola de la Haye

The story of Nicola's meeting with John in 1216 (*Rotuli Hundredorum*, vol. I, p. 309) is a rare survival. Its preservation on some level for sixty years before it was permanently recorded suggests Nicola's standing amongst those who remembered it and its likely integrity.

Nicola's life and career are the subject of a short but consummate modern case study: Louise J. Wilkinson, *Women in Thirteenth-Century Lincolnshire* (Woodbridge, 2007), pp. 13–26. D.A. Carpenter, *The Minority of Henry III* (Los Angeles, 1990), chs 1–2, gives the best introduction to this brief but decisively important moment in English history, whilst Sean McGlynn, *Blood Cries Afar: The Forgotten Invasion of England, 1216* (Stroud, 2013), is a welcome extended account of the events. The siege and battle of Lincoln in 1216 are also fully described in J.W.F. Hill, *Medieval Lincoln* (Cambridge, 1948), pp. 200–5.

Epilogue

Gerald of Wales describes his dream about the fate of Henry II's corpse in *On the Instruction of a Prince* (Gerald of Wales, *Opera*, vol. VIII, p. 312). My views are heavily reliant on Robert Bartlett, *Gerald of Wales: A Voice of the Middle Ages* (Oxford, 1982; repr. Stroud, 2006), ch. 3. He considers the dream at pp. 78–9 and Gerald's attitude towards the Capetians at pp. 79–86. But the whole chapter is concerned with Gerald's views about the Angevins.

Index